HUGH GLASS

SOUTH
DAKOTA
BIOGRAPHY
SERIES

Laura Ingalls Wilder
by Pamela Smith Hill

Wild Bill Hickok and Calamity Jane
by James D. McLaird

Seth Bullock
by David A. Wolff

Red Cloud
by John D. McDermott

Hugh Glass
by James D. McLaird

HUGH GLASS

GRIZZLY SURVIVOR

JAMES D. MCLAIRD

South Dakota
Historical Society
Press *Pierre*

Hugh Glass is Volume 5 in the South Dakota Biography Series.

 This publication is funded, in part, by the Deadwood
Publications Fund provided by the City of Deadwood
and the Deadwood Historic Preservation Commission.

Library of Congress Cataloging-in-Publication Data
Names: McLaird, James D., author.
Title: Hugh Glass : grizzly survivor / James D. McLaird.
Description: Pierre : South Dakota Historical Society Press,
[2016] | Series: South Dakota biography series ; volume 5 |
Includes bibliographical references and index.
Identifiers: LCCN 2016013151 | ISBN 9780985290535 (alk. paper)
Subjects: LCSH: Glass, Hugh, approximately 1780–approximately
1833. | Frontier and pioneer life—West (U.S.) | Trappers—West
(U.S.)—Biography. | Fur traders—West (U.S.)—Biography. |
Bear attacks—South Dakota. | Grizzly bear—History.
Classification: LCC F592.G55 M35 2016 | DDC 978/.02092—dc23
LC record available at http://lccn.loc.gov/2016013151

Printed in the United States of America

The paper in this book meets the guidelines for permanence
and durability of the Committee on Production Guidelines for
Book Longevity of the Council on Library Resources.

Please visit our website at sdhspress.com

20 18 17 16   1 2 3 4 5

Cover and frontispiece: Denver Public Library

Designed and set in Arnhem type by Rich Hendel

TO BRIAN AND DONNA DIPPIE,

friends and companions on the trails of the West

Contents

Acknowledgments

This biographical exploration of Hugh Glass originated in the office of Nancy Tystad Koupal, director of the South Dakota Historical Society Press, and thus it is appropriate to begin by acknowledging her role in its creation. I vividly recall the day we were chatting about the South Dakota Biography Series, and she asked if I had any suggestions for future subjects. Since I had already written *Wild Bill Hickok and Calamity Jane: Deadwood Legends* (2008), I assumed she meant possible topics for other authors to consider. I barely got the name "Hugh Glass" out of my mouth when she responded, "I'll take it." That remark resulted in a couple of years of research, writing, and editing. I will be more cautious in the future! However, it has been a fascinating subject, and I want to express my appreciation to Nancy for her enthusiasm as well as for her patience and support.

I soon learned that most accounts of Hugh Glass were published in an era when romanticized biographies of larger-than-life heroes were popular. I also discovered that the documentary evidence needed for a biography was limited. It became clear that a book-length study would have to blaze a different trail. Within a few months, I made an outline that included not only Glass's life story, but the growth of his legend and a reexamination of the relationships between trappers and American Indians and trappers and the environment, especially grizzly bears. All of which meant, of course, additional research.

Finding the resources required professional help, and I want to acknowledge my appreciation to Kevin Kenkel, Director of Learning Resources at the McGovern Library, Dakota Wesleyan University, who tracked down important documentary material and ordered innumerable books and articles via interlibrary loan. Likewise, University Archivist

Laurie Langland located obscure articles that otherwise would have not found their way into this work. Those unnamed librarians who responded to their requests for materials also warrant acknowledgment, although I cannot begin to list them. I especially want to express my appreciation to the staff of the William Robertson Coe Library, Yale University, for providing a copy of the Rowland Willard manuscript that only came to my attention toward the end of my research.

It would be a severe omission not to mention the support provided by Brian Dippie. We have chatted regularly about this book and issues surrounding heroic Western figures. Every once in a while, he mentioned an item I had forgotten, such as Charles M. Russell's illustration of Hugh Glass fighting the bear. My wife and I have been friends with Brian and his wife Donna since our graduate-school days at the University of Wyoming, and we treasure our memories of our meetings with them at historical conferences throughout the American West. I would also be remiss if I did not mention my wife's patience while I closeted myself with documents and manuscript.

Finally, I want thank the editorial staff at the South Dakota Historical Society Press who worked to improve this story. Any errors or omissions, of course, are the fault of the author and not those who worked so hard to improve the manuscript. I hope readers will enjoy it, and not wish I had kept my mouth shut when I proposed Hugh Glass as a subject for this series.

HUGH GLASS

The West of Hugh Glass

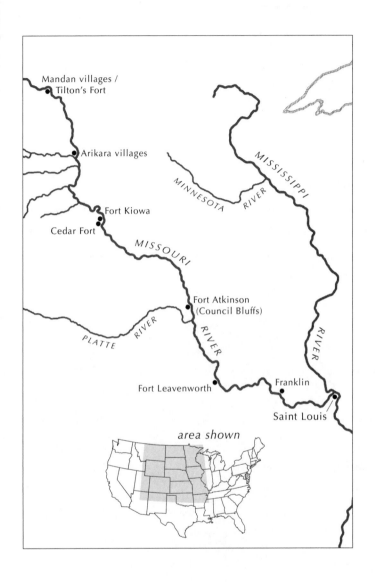

Mandan villages /
Tilton's Fort

Arikara villages

Fort Kiowa

Cedar Fort

MISSOURI

MINNESOTA RIVER

MISSISSIPPI RIVER

Fort Atkinson
(Council Bluffs)

PLATTE RIVER

RIVER

RIVER

Fort Leavenworth

Franklin

Saint Louis

area shown

Introduction

Had it not been for a chance encounter with a grizzly bear along the Grand River in what is now northwestern South Dakota in 1823, Hugh Glass would barely warrant a passing note in fur-trade history. Unlike more important contemporaries, he made no notable discoveries and never became a significant leader. Glass appears to have been an ordinary trapper, perhaps with an independent streak and a bit inclined to disobedience. Several of his associates maintained that Glass encountered the bear only because he wandered off against orders to gather berries from the bushes along the river. Yet, this incident won him a lasting place in history.

Indeed, according to literary scholar John R. Milton, many writers consider Glass's story to be "the greatest of western tales."[1] Historian and geographer David J. Wishart asserts that the story "seems to be true, and no other piece of fur trade lore has been so durable."[2] Almost two centuries after surviving the bear's attack, Glass remains among the best known of the fur trappers. He has been featured in histories, biographies, school texts, children's books, popular magazines, poetry, fiction, and film.

But there is more behind Glass's lasting fame. After all, other men survived attacks by grizzly bears. Yet, in the Glass legend, the mauling is only the beginning. Because his trapping party had to continue its trek westward to reach winter quarters, its leader, Andrew Henry, asked for volunteers to remain with Glass until he either recovered or died. According to early storytellers, the two men who agreed to care for Glass betrayed their trust and deserted him. Worse, they took his rifle and other equipment with them. Nevertheless, Glass managed to survive, crawling about two hundred miles to the nearest trading post. After regaining his strength, he immediately set out to take revenge on the men who had abandoned him. On the way, he miraculously escaped two hostile Indian attacks. Then, when he finally found his deserters, Glass forgave them. As one historian noted, "this was the stuff of legend."[3]

Despite the story's wide circulation, however, few contemporary documents mention Hugh Glass. It is impossible to determine when and where he was born, and more importantly, no eyewitnesses left records describing the mauling, desertion, survival, and forgiveness. Descriptions of these events are second- and thirdhand, and most did not appear until years or even decades after the mauling. These reports disagree about significant details, and their authors clearly molded events to support their particular interpretations.

The paucity and inconsistency of the evidence caused historian Jon T. Coleman to introduce his recent work on Glass as "more a missing-person report than a biography."[4] Some researchers have even suspected that the mauling might never have actually occurred. James Bridger biographer J. Cecil Alter, for example, decided that most of the Hugh Glass story was fiction. "I would not eliminate this biggest of all 'bar' stories entirely from the books," he concluded, "maybe just from those that pretend to be historical!"[5] Writer Robert M. McClung found that preparing an accurate Glass biography for young readers was a formidable task. After discovering that "contemporary accounts of Hugh's adventures, although in broad agreement concerning the main events, differed so much in detail that it was impossible to know exactly what had happened to him in each incident," McClung decided to write a novel instead.[6] No wonder then that professor Don D. Walker, after noting that only one letter by Glass is known to exist, remarked: "historians, in their wishful moments, must still dream of a diary beginning, 'Today damn near killed by a big she bitch of a grizzly. If I live, I'll somehow make it back.'"[7]

Although the lack of reliable source material makes Glass a perplexing subject for biographers, it has provided fruitful ground for novelists, poets, and writers of popular history. For these storytellers, secondhand information became definitive, and mere hints in documents were expanded into paragraphs and chapters. Imagination filled in the remaining gaps. Indeed, creative writers have promoted Glass into a figure of heroic proportions. The earliest published account, emphasizing his ability to endure hardship and survive apart from civilized society, compared him to Robinson Crusoe. A later biographer claimed that Glass's accomplishments surpassed those of the famous frontiersman Daniel Boone. Still others compared him to epic figures in the classics, such as Achilles and Sinbad. In contrast, the fragmentary historical evidence suggests that Glass was probably more ordinary than heroic. In fact, little evidence outside the storytelling tradition suggests that he was a superior hunter or trapper, or even that his physical prowess surpassed that of his companions.[8]

Under these circumstances, writing a traditional biography of Hugh Glass would seem to be an insurmountable challenge. Nevertheless, a serious study of his career is long overdue, and if approached carefully, sufficient evidence exists to piece together a sketch—or sketches—of his life and adventures. Unfortunately, major gaps in the documentary record remain, and Glass's experiences before 1823 are especially problematic. The prospective biographer must therefore weigh the merits of conflicting and sometimes speculative accounts. One acquaintance claimed that Glass had been a mariner who narrowly escaped execution at the hands of Lafitte's pirates. Captured again by Pawnee Indians who planned to burn him at the stake, Glass had a second miraculous escape before finally making his way to Saint Louis and joining a trapping expedition. A completely different version of Glass's origins, based on a newspaper advertisement, suggests that he may have been an apprentice gunsmith who ran away and escaped nothing more than a difficult master.

Whatever his background, in 1823 Glass enlisted with the expedition that William Ashley and Andrew Henry organized in Saint Louis to ascend the Missouri River to trap furs. After suffering a long hiatus, the fur trade was then entering a boom period, and Ashley and Henry developed innovative strategies that forever changed the business. Thus, Glass's departure from Saint Louis with their expedition occurred at a pivotal moment in fur-trade history and brought him into association with a remarkable cast of mountain men, including Jedediah Smith, James Clyman, Daniel Potts, Edward Rose, and Jim Bridger.

As they made their way up the Missouri to the rich beaver locations in the Rocky Mountain region, Ashley's party suffered a deadly attack by the Arikara Indians. Thirteen men were killed and another eleven wounded, including Glass. Afterward, Glass wrote a compassionate letter to the parents of one of those killed; it is the only known example of his writing. As a result of the confrontation, an army expedition from Fort Atkinson joined the trappers in a campaign against the Arikaras, resulting in the first military engagement between the United States Army and Indians west of the Mississippi River. This August 1823 fight, which also involved Glass and his companions, is especially significant in view of changing perspectives about the relationship between American Indians and European Americans; it demands careful reexamination of traditional accounts portraying the Arikaras as treacherous savages and condemning Colonel Henry Leavenworth for a lackluster campaign.

Shortly after the battle with the Arikaras, Glass encountered the grizzly bear that made him famous. Reexamining contemporary documents to determine how much of this story is accurate is a daunting but necessary task. No less important is the rest of Glass's life: eventually he left the company on the upper Missouri to join trapping expeditions in the Southwest. A decade later, he returned to the upper Missouri region, only to be killed by Arikara Indians. As his adventures draw to a close, it is worth asking why men like Glass became trappers and how well they fared.

A study of Hugh Glass would be incomplete, however, if it stopped there. He is now, after all, a larger-than-life character who occupies a place in American lore. Besides relating the facts of Hugh Glass's life, the serious biographer must tell the history of his story, as well. Each of the early writers who wrote accounts of Glass introduced different information and framed it with unique themes. Indeed, there are as many Hugh Glass stories as there were writers to tell them. These writers laid the groundwork for a legend that has now become a staple in American popular culture. During the twentieth century, John G. Neihardt made Glass an epic hero in his poetry, and Frederick Manfred enhanced Glass's popularity even further in his novel *Lord Grizzly*, which became a national bestseller. Historical monuments commemorate Glass's achievements, and his story has appeared in a wide spectrum of popular publications, including newsstand magazines, comic books, and even sheet music. New images of Glass have emerged over time, and his legend has waxed and waned with changes in American society. Today it is waxing, as Leonardo DiCaprio plays Hugh Glass in a new film, *The Revenant*, and an annual "Hugh Glass Rendezvous" has been inaugurated at Lemmon, South Dakota.

And what about the bear? Given our contemporary awareness of the environment, the grizzly bear deserves some attention, as well. Most writers of the Glass story have demonized grizzly bears and depicted their behavior inaccurately. Indeed, like Glass himself, the bear has been the subject of conflicting stories; for example, some writers claim the grizzly was a mother that attacked Glass to protect or feed her cubs, while others suggest it was a rogue bear that charged without provocation. Because nineteenth-century Americans typically shot at grizzly bears on sight, causing them to attack, it is possible that Glass unnecessarily provoked the bear. Perhaps the key to understanding what really happened to Hugh Glass lies in examining what trappers knew, or thought they knew, about bears and how to interact with them.

In short, with so many diverse topics to consider, there is more than enough material for a biography of Glass. The added perspectives make him more than a mere archetype of the heroic frontiersman; he embodied both good and bad qualities and worked in a fragile and complicated environment. Viewed through the lenses of biography, western history, popular culture, and ecology, Hugh Glass remains larger than life.

A NOTE TO THE READER

Because our understanding of Hugh Glass arises only through those who have shaped his legend, this biography will present the words of these storytellers and other important sources exactly as they first appeared. Nonstandard spellings and sentence structures have been altered with brackets only when they would cause confusion to the reader. Some of these writers expressed their limited worldview in words that we find offensive, such as "savage" and "squaw," but these terms, too, have been retained, to remind us of the culture of the day. Finally, emphasis has been neither added to nor subtracted from quoted material; words are italicized or underlined exactly as they appeared in the original sources.

1

The Witnesses
and the Testimony

"One man was . . . tore nearly all to peaces by a White Bear," wrote trapper Daniel T. Potts to a friend on 7 July 1824, "and was left by the way without any gun," but he "afterwards recovered."[1] Although this vague account does not even mention Hugh Glass by name, it is the first written report of Glass's encounter with a grizzly bear; in the early nineteenth century, these creatures were often called "white bears" because of the white or gray fur along their faces and upper backs. Potts did not write this letter until almost a year after the event, but it contains most of the significant features in the Hugh Glass saga, including his mauling by a bear, his abandonment, and his survival. However, Potts learned of the event secondhand. In the spring of 1822, he had accompanied Major Andrew Henry's fur-trapping expedition up the Missouri River from Saint Louis to the mouth of the Yellowstone, where they built a trading post. Glass's ordeal occurred in the fall of 1823, as he traveled toward the Yellowstone along the Grand River, a lower tributary of the Missouri, with another party led by Henry. Potts, who had remained at the Yellowstone fort during this period, could only have learned about the incident later.[2]

Trapper James Clyman, who enlisted with Henry and General William H. Ashley in 1823, also learned about the mauling secondhand. At this time, Clyman was with a party led by Jedediah Smith. While Henry's party followed the Grand River, Smith's group crossed present-day South Dakota farther south, following the White River and traveling through the Black Hills en route to the Rocky Mountains. At some point, Clyman learned the details from his former companions. his observations are valuable because he had been with Glass earlier that summer and knew him personally. Clyman's description of Glass is hardly flattering: "amongst this party was a Mr Hugh Glass who could not be rstrand and kept under Subordination[.] he went off of the line of march one afternoon and met with a large grissly Bear which he shot at and wounded." The grizzly bear immediately chased Glass, who "attemptd to climb a tree but the bear caught him . . . tearing and lacerating his body in fearful rate." Although several members of the party hurried to his aid, they "could not shoot for fear of hitting Glass." Finally, when the bear "appea[r]ed to be satisfied and turned to leave," some of the men fired. Instead of alleviating the situation, however, their shots caused the bear to attack again, giving Glass "a second mutilation." Again, the bear moved away from Glass, and again the men fired their guns, causing the bear to pounce on the downed man for a third time. Finally, however, the shots proved fatal, and the bear "fell dead over his body."[3]

Had these brief accounts by Potts and Clyman been the only documents describing Glass's encounter with the grizzly bear, he would never have become a prominent figure in American folklore. However, several aspiring authors, hearing the story from other men who claimed to have personal knowledge, or possibly even from Glass himself, later published lengthy accounts of the incident. All of them regarded it as a great story of survival, but each writer provided unique details and new interpretations. Indeed, it is fair to say there are several Hugh Glass stories rather than one. Among the most significant contributions these authors made to the story were Glass's vow of vengeance against the men who deserted him, his heroic return alone while injured, and his subsequent act of mercy. These themes of human endurance, vengeance, and forgiveness elevated the Hugh Glass story into one of the epic tales of the American West.

The first detailed account of Glass's encounter with the grizzly bear appeared in March 1825 in the *Port Folio*, a journal published in Philadelphia, and was soon reprinted in newspapers throughout the West. The article, "The Missouri Trapper," was unsigned, and several scholars later attributed authorship to Alphonso Wetmore. However, later research revealed that the true author was James Hall, a judge in Shawneetown, Illinois, and the brother of *Port Folio* publishers John Elihu Hall and Harrison Hall. Hall's article is noteworthy, not only because it was the earliest lengthy account, but also because Hall claimed that the information for his story came, albeit indirectly, from Hugh Glass himself.[4]

James Hall (1793–1868) was born in Philadelphia. His formal schooling was limited to brief attendance at an academy; his later advocacy of educational reforms, such as banning spankings by schoolmasters, may suggest why he disliked the experience. Nevertheless, he received a reasonably good education from his mother. During the War of 1812, Hall enlisted in the Washington Guards organized to defend Philadelphia, and he remained in military service until 1818. Meanwhile, he studied law, and in 1820 moved to Shawneetown, where he became a prosecuting attorney and later a circuit judge. From 1828 to 1833, he also served as the state treasurer of Illinois before moving to Cincinnati, Ohio, where he lived the remainder of his life.

Hall became a significant literary figure in early nineteenth-century America, advocating western development in numerous newspaper and magazine articles. Indeed, one of his biographers called him the "spokesman of the new West." Eventually, Hall established the *Illinois Western Monthly*, featuring articles by western writers, and published a number of books on western subjects. Although Hall's primary intention in his publications was to promote the region's development, he also hoped to convince readers in both England and New England that the people of the

West were their cultural equals. Thus, as a writer and editor, he sought uniquely American stories.[5]

Western frontiersmen especially intrigued him. During Hall's youth, he found the sight of a Kentucky backwoodsman walking down the streets of Philadelphia fascinating. "I thought I could see in that man, one of the progenitors of an unconquerable race," he said. "He had the will to dare, and the power to execute; there was a something in his look which bespoke a disdain of controul, and an absence of constraint in all his movements, indicating an habitual independence of thought and action."[6] Thus, when he heard the story of Hugh Glass's encounter with a grizzly bear, Hall naturally penned an account for the *Port Folio*, then one of the leading journals in the nation. For Hall, the perseverance and survival of Hugh Glass revealed the strength of the American character.

Hall gained his information about Glass from an informant who had visited Fort Atkinson, a military post on the Missouri River in present-day Nebraska, in June 1824. "An old man arrived . . . from the upper Missouri," the man reported, and several officers recognized him as Hugh Glass. They were surprised to see him alive because they had heard rumors that he had been "devoured by a white bear," and more recently, a couple of trappers who visited the post had claimed that Arikara Indians had killed him. After resting briefly, Glass explained to the crowd what had transpired during "the last ten months of his perilous career."[7]

The ordeal began as Glass was traveling from the Missouri to the Yellowstone River with Andrew Henry's party, which he had joined as a trapper. "It is usual for one or two hunters to precede the party in search of game, that the whole may not be forced, at night, to lie down supperless," Hall explained. "The rifle of Hugh Glass being esteemed as among the most unerring," Glass was one of two men sent ahead to hunt. While a "short distance in advance of the party," Hall reported, Glass entered a thicket where he encountered a "white bear" that had "imbedded herself in the sand" only three yards in front of him. Before he "could 'set his triggers,' or turn to retreat, he was seized by the throat, and raised from the ground." The bear then dropped him and "tore out a mouthful of the cannibal food which had excited her appetite, and retired to submit the sample to her yearling cubs, which were near at hand." Glass tried to escape in this brief respite, but the bear returned "and seized him again at the shoulder," ripping into his left arm and inflicting "a severe wound on the back of his head." Glass's companion hurried to help and probably prevented the cubs from joining in the attack, although one of them chased him into the river. Standing in the water, the second trapper shot the cub, or as he put it, "burst the varment." Soon, the other trappers arrived and fired seven or eight shots, killing the mother grizzly, who was still standing "over her victim."[8]

Examining Glass, the party concluded that his wounds were probably mortal. "His whole body was bruised and mangled, and he lay weltering in his blood, in exquisite torment," wrote Hall. Moving Glass would be difficult, but remaining with him would place the entire party in a perilous situation; there were "hostile Indians" in the area, and the party's safety "depended on the celerity of their movements." Yet, "to remove the lacerated and helpless Glass, seemed certain death to him."[9]

Since the trappers would not consider leaving Glass entirely alone, Henry offered "an extravagant reward" and thus "induced two of his party to remain with the wounded man" until he either died or recovered sufficiently to be moved to a trading post. Despite their promise, Hall said, the two men "cruelly abandoned him" after five days, "taking with them his rifle, shot-pouch, &c. and leaving him no means of either making fire or procuring food." Hall did not mince words, calling them "unprincipled wretches." The men hurried to catch up with the rest of the party, reporting "that Glass had died of his wounds, and that they had interred him in the best manner possible." To confirm their assertions, they produced Glass's equipment and thus "readily obtained credence."[10]

Unbeknownst to them, Glass had survived. Regaining consciousness, he crawled "with great difficulty" to a nearby spring and rested for ten days, eating wild cherries for sustenance. After regaining some of his strength, he began crawling southeast toward Fort Kiowa, "about three hundred and fifty miles distant." Either Hall, his informant, or Glass himself stretched this distance considerably; the fort was about two hundred miles from the probable site of the mauling. Regardless, it was a long and difficult journey. "It required no ordinary portion of fortitude to crawl . . . through the hostile country, without fire-arms, with scarcely strength to drag one limb after another, and with almost no other subsistence than wild berries," Hall wrote. Luckily, at one point Glass enjoyed a feast, driving some wolves from the carcass of a buffalo calf they had killed. Having no means to make a fire, however, he had to eat the meat raw.[11]

After reaching Fort Kiowa on the Missouri River, Glass immediately joined five trappers departing for the Yellowstone. "The primary object of this voyage was declared to be the recovery of his arms, and vengeance on the recreant who had robbed and abandoned him in his hour of peril," wrote Hall. Here, for unknown reasons, Hall changed a significant detail in his story. Earlier in his article, he had said that two men had deserted Glass, but now he wrote that Glass sought vengeance against only one "recreant."[12]

While ascending the Missouri River, Glass experienced another close call. As the party neared an old Mandan village, he left the boat to hike toward the village "by a nearer route than that of the river." Shortly after he departed, Arikara Indians attacked his recent companions, killing all of them. Although Glass was out of sight when the attack occurred, two Arikara women spotted him and alerted the men, who immediately began pursuit. "Suffering still under the severity of his recent wounds, the poor fugitive made but a feeble essay at flight," said Hall, and the warriors soon came within rifle shot. Just in the nick of time, however, two friendly Mandan warriors appeared, bringing him a "fleet horse" and escorting him to Tilton's Fort, located at their nearby village.[13]

Despite the presence of hostile warriors in the vicinity, Glass "crept out of the fort" as soon as night fell and began a thirty-eight-day trip alone to Henry's camp, now located at the confluence of the Bighorn and Yellowstone rivers. Hall's description of this journey is sketchy, and he does not describe the reaction among Henry's men when Glass, whom they presumed to be dead, arrived at the post. He does, however, mention Glass's frustration upon learning that the deserter he sought had left for Fort Atkinson. It is not surprising that when Henry asked for volunteers to carry a message there a few weeks later, Glass stepped forward. According to Hall, Glass began the long journey on 28 February 1824 with four other men, traveling overland to the Powder River, then crossing to the Platte River and building "skin boats" to float downriver to the Missouri.[14]

While boating down the Platte, Glass would miraculously escape death for a third time when the trappers again encountered Arikaras. Worse, it was the party previously led by Gray Eyes, who had died the previous summer in a battle against an American force that included Glass and the Ashley and Henry men. Despite their recent animosity, the new chief, Elk Tongue, welcomed Glass "with the cordiality of an old friend." Indeed, said Hall, Glass knew Elk Tongue well, having previously "resided with this tawny old politician during a long winter," hunting with him, smoking his pipe, and cracking "many a bottle by the genial fire of his wigwam." Despite his profession of friendship, however, Elk Tongue had hostile intentions. Too late, Glass saw the women of the tribe "bearing off the arms and other effects of his party." Realizing their danger, Glass and his companions fled. Assailants soon overtook and killed two of them, "one of them within a few yards of Glass," but Glass, "versed in all the arts of border warfare," was able to "baffle his bloodthirsty enemies." Hiding among some rocks, he sneaked away that night. Although he had lost his rifle, this time Glass "felt quite rich" because he still had his knife, flint, and steel. "These little fixens," he said, "make a man feel righ[t] *peart*, when he is three or four hundred miles *from any body or any place*—all alone among the *painters* [Indians] and wild *varments*."[15]

Fifteen days later, Glass arrived at Fort Kiowa. He then descended the Missouri to Fort Atkinson, where he finally located "his old traitorous acquaintance." However, the man was now wearing "the garb of a private soldier," shielding "the delinquent from chastisement." Although no longer able to exact revenge, Glass told his story to the gathered crowd, "astounding, with his wonderful narration, the gaping rank and file of the garrison." After hearing his tribulations, the commanding officer ordered the deserter to return Glass's rifle, and the men at the post provided other "*fixens*, as he would term them, as put him in plight again to take the field." According to Hall, "this appeased the wrath of Hugh Glass."[16]

In Hall's rendition of Glass's adventures, there is no act of forgiveness. The deserter is protected because he became a soldier, and Glass must be content with the restoration of his property. Instead, Hall focuses on Glass's physical endurance and miraculous survival. "Glass became a symbol of the unique qualities of physical stamina and will that have ever since been recognized as the necessary traits of the frontiersman," noted scholar Edgeley Todd.[17] Indeed, Hall compared the adventures of Hugh Glass to those of Robinson Crusoe, the hero of Daniel Defoe's recent novel, who showed what people could do when separated from civilized society.

It is, of course, impossible to determine how much of Hall's narrative is true. If Glass truly narrated this tale to an audience, he may have exaggerated certain aspects to appear more heroic. Fur trappers were notorious storytellers, increasing distances traveled and magnifying encounters with Indians and animals. In addition, Hall or his informant may have added new twists to the story. Nevertheless, because Hall's article was the first detailed account of the story to be published, it played a significant role in establishing Glass's legend and has served as a primary source for biographers ever since. Although he thus created a framework for future writers, Hall's account is flawed in several aspects. During the course of his narrative, one of the two deserters simply vanishes. In addition, Glass drops his vendetta merely because the object of his wrath is now a soldier and his stolen belongings have been restored. Whatever the historical truth of the encounter at Fort Atkinson may have been, as a storyteller, Hall settled for a weak ending.

Another writer, however, would step in to refine the tale. In 1857, Lieutenant Philip St. George Cooke included an account of Hugh Glass in *Scenes and Adventures in the Army*, detailing Glass's quest for vengeance and his confrontation with the younger deserter. For many years, however, historians wondered where Cooke obtained the unique information not found in Hall's account. The discovery of Friedrich Wilhelm von Wrede's *Pictures of Life from the United States of North America and Texas* (1844), published in Germany, seemed to answer the question. Von Wrede's book "is factual and well-written," declared fur-trade historian Aubrey Haines, "with a frankness which makes it difficult to disbelieve him." The Hugh Glass story, for example, "is entirely without the romanticism and inept usages of contemporary accounts." After comparing the accounts by von Wrede and Cooke, Haines concluded that Cooke's version was simply a translation: "The sentence structure is quite often German in its complexity, there are errors which materially alter the meaning of entire passages, and constant use of alternative wording and phrasing in an attempt to avoid a close similarity." Cooke, he noted, "had a flair for languages and a penchant for translating—in a day when the unacknowledged use of a foreign work was more likely to be thought of as research than plagiarism."[18]

Von Wrede, born in Westphalia about 1790, became a soldier for the Kingdom of Hanover. In 1825, he retired from military service and later decided to emigrate to Texas. When he arrived in New Orleans in 1836, however, Texas was in rebellion against Mexico, and von Wrede decided to settle temporarily in the United States. While traveling by steamboat up the Mississippi River, said von Wrede, he noticed an unusual man boarding the boat at Hopefield, Arkansas. He had a "powerful stature and possession of the spirit of a certain wild boldness, which was emphasized by a pair of flashing eyes." It was Hugh Glass, who, Von Wrede said, "belonged to that class of men who find their life's pleasure in hunting the Blackfeet Indians, ferocious bears and buffalo of the Rocky Mountains."[19] Von Wrede learned that Glass had entered the fur trade at age fourteen and had only left the wilderness now to attend his brother's funeral. Unfortunately for von Wrede, at the time of their purported meeting, Glass had been dead for three years.[20]

Subsequent research revealed that the Hugh Glass story that Cooke included in *Scenes and Adventures in the Army* was actually a reprint of a long-forgotten newspaper article that he had originally published in the *St. Louis Beacon* on 2 and 9 December 1830. In fact, it was von Wrede who had plagiarized from Cooke! The newspaper had identified the author only as "The Borderer," and von Wrede had somehow located a copy of that early article and translated it into German, carelessly mistranslating phrases and omitting sections of Cooke's story. In addition, he evidently invented the encounter with Hugh Glass on a steamboat to convince readers of the authenticity of his tale.[21]

Cooke (1809–1895) entered West Point at age fourteen. His first post was at Jefferson Barracks, Missouri, and in 1833, the army assigned him to the newly formed dragoons. Cooke had a strong sense of honor, was sincerely religious, and believed in stern discipline. He saw action in the war with Mexico and later commanded troops in Texas and Kansas, fought against the Sioux at the Battle of Ash Hollow, and commanded the cavalry in the Utah War. During the Civil War, he served as a Union cavalry general, and his *Cavalry Tactics* (1861) was adopted as a training manual. Cooke retired a brevet major general after forty-seven years in military service.[22]

It is not clear precisely when and where Cooke first heard the Hugh Glass story. Upon his arrival in Saint Louis in 1827, he encountered "a floating population of trappers, traders, boatmen, and Indians." These well-armed men, he said, exhibited "the independence, confidence, and recklessness of their wild and lawless way of life," and he may have learned about Glass's adventures from some of them. However, it seems more likely that he learned the details of the Glass saga a few years later when stationed at Fort Leavenworth on the Missouri River. Although the post was relatively isolated, there were numerous visitors, including "members of the Fur Company, fresh from natural scenes, and full of racy anecdote of adventure." According to Cooke, they provided "an enlivening addition to our small society."[23]

Although Cooke's account of Glass is generally similar to Hall's, it includes significant new material. He names the older deserter, for example, and includes Glass's confrontation and forgiveness of the younger one. Most likely, Cooke learned these details from visiting fur trappers during storytelling sessions, tapping into an emerging oral tradition. Some of the storytellers may have been Glass's former companions.

For Cooke, Glass served as an example of those heroic "self-exiled wanderers and hunters, whose restless or savage natures, lead them to sever every tie of kindred and country, and to prefer the privations and dangers of barbarism, among even hostile Indians, to the comforts and most exciting pursuits of their kind." More significantly, however, Cooke hoped to disprove the notion that men succeed only because of "fortune or good luck." Instead, he asserted that success really comes from "superiority in qualities." Thus, although superficial examination might make one conclude that Hugh Glass endured because of "*fortunate* escapes" or "*lucky* accidents," said Cooke, his survival was actually the "natural result of physical strength, cool intrepidity, and untiring patience."[24]

Like Hall, Cooke began his story as Major Henry's 1823 party trekked across the prairie along the Grand River from the Missouri to the mouth of the Yellowstone. A battle with the Arikaras had delayed their journey, so the party of eighty men traveled rapidly, hoping to make a fall hunt for beaver. On the fifth day of their trip, Hugh Glass, hunting with two companions in advance of the party, killed some buffalo. As they waited for the rest of the trappers, Glass wandered down to a nearby stream, "intending to drink of its waters." Suddenly, a grizzly bear emerged from the opposite bank near Glass, whose companions were "overcome by their fears" and ran.[25]

Glass's survival "depended upon the success of his first and only shot," said Cooke, and "with an aim, cool and deliberate, but quick, . . . he fired his rifle." The shot was accurate and ultimately fatal, but its immediate result was to make the animal even more ferocious. Glass ran, but the bear was faster, its "claws literally baring of flesh the bones of the shoulder and thigh." Then it pursued Glass's two companions. Fortunately, the bear had now lost so much blood that it became too weak and slow to catch them. "The sacrifice of a deserted comrade had saved their lives," Cooke declared. Hurrying back to camp, the two men described their miraculous escape and informed the party that Glass was dead. Henry immediately dispatched several men to the site, where they found the dying bear and finished it off. However, they discovered that Glass was still alive. Although his wounds were considered mortal, the men carried him back to camp and bandaged him "as well as their circumstances would admit."[26]

Henry saw that Glass could not be transported to the Yellowstone in his present condition. Therefore, said Cooke, he asked for two volunteers to "await his death, and then overtake the party." After being offered eighty dollars for their service, a man named Fitzgerald and an unnamed seventeen-year-old agreed to stay. For two days these men "faithfully administered" to Glass's wants, but "their inactive stay became very irksome," and "from innate depravity," Cooke asserted, "they conceived the horrid idea of deserting him." Finally, "these most heartless of wretches, taking advantage of his first sleep," took his rifle, knife, and other equipment. All they left him was "a small kettle containing water," a "wallet on which his head rested," and a razor.[27]

Upon regaining consciousness, Glass confronted his situation. "Helpless from painful wounds, he lay in the midst of a desert," Cooke wrote. "His prospect was starvation and death." However, he had a strong motive to survive: revenge. "He swore, as if on his grave for an altar, his endless hatred, and if spared, his vengeance on the actors in so foul a deed." Here, Cooke also introduced his theme that Glass survived not merely because of luck, but because of his superior qualities. "Few are aware, until tried, of their capacity for endurance," wrote Cooke. "Glass did not despair; he had found he could crawl." Inching to a nearby stream for water, he rested for several days. Then, although he managed only two miles a day, he edged himself toward the Missouri River, living for more than forty days primarily "upon roots and buffalo berries." Once, he drove wolves away from the carcass of a buffalo calf, feasted, and made hide patches to cover his raw knees and elbows. Later, Glass tamed a stray dog in a deserted Arikara village along the Missouri River, then killed it with his razor and feasted once again.[28]

Although some of Glass's wounds began to heal, he was still unable to walk, and the lacerations on his back remained "in a dreadful condition." Fortunately, several Sioux Indians discovered him, and acting "the part of a good Samaritan," washed the worm-filled wound on his back, applying "an astringent vegetable liquid" to heal it. They then took him to a small trading post eighty miles downriver, and there, for two months, he rested.[29]

Glass had been "a mere skeleton" when he reached the post, said Cooke, but because he had "a vigorous frame and strong constitution, inured to constant exercise and rough labors," he quickly recovered. He suffered psychologically, however, experiencing "feverish dreams." One nightmare featured a grizzly bear: "the horrid, the threatening grin of its features; now its resistless paw was suspended over his head, with nought to avert the death-inflicting blow—and now its bloody teeth mangled his vitals." In another dream, he saw the deserters: "goblin-like they danced before him; retreated, advanced, in mockery of the impotence of their intended victim."[30]

After hearing his story, the men at the trading post supplied Glass with a rifle, knife, clothing, and other necessary equipment. He then joined a party of six men under a trader named Longevan who were ascending the Missouri to trade with the Mandan Indians. Glass intended to continue past the Mandan villages to the mouth of the Yellowstone; his "great object, it may be readily conjectured, was to meet the two wretches he was so much indebted to." Longevan's party spent nearly the entire month of October struggling upriver against the strong current, and Glass frequently went ashore to hunt for the party.[31]

Unfortunately, the Arikaras were now living in a previously abandoned village below the Mandans. Having fought a combined army of soldiers and traders that summer, said Cooke, the Arikaras' "immemorial hostility to whites was but aggravated to fresh deeds of outrage." When the traders were about twenty miles short of their destination, Longevan once again sent Glass ashore to hunt; he was barely out of sight when the Arikaras attacked the party. "On the instant rose the shrill cry of war from a hundred mouths," wrote Cooke, and every man was killed, whereupon the Arikaras, "with horrid grimaces and convulsive action . . . hewed into fragments the dumb, lifeless bodies" and then "returned to their camp a moving group of dusky demons, exulting in revenge, besmeared with blood, bearing aloft each a mangled portion of the dead—trophies of brutal success."[32]

Glass, "his lucky star still prevailing," had been out of sight when the attack began. However, just when he "thought himself nearly safe," he encountered an Arikara scout. Simultaneously, Glass fired his rifle and the Indian threw his tomahawk, and the two men then "rushed into each other's grasp, either endeavoring to crush his adversary by the shock of the onset."[33] Although Glass had wounded his opponent, the Indian still had the advantage because Glass had not fully recovered from his mauling. Just as the Arikara sensed victory, however, he died from his wound. Still, Glass remained in danger as more Arikaras rushed toward the scene. Luckily, a Mandan Indian rode to his rescue and frustrated their efforts to capture him, taking him safely to his village.[34]

Glass impressed his hosts with his "recital of his escapes, which nought but the greatest prowess could have accomplished," said Cooke, "and nothing is better calculated effectually to engage the interest and admiration of Indians." Glass remained with the Mandans "a few days" before setting out for Henry's post. Although alone and afoot, he felt secure, having "a rifle, small axe, and the ever necessary knife; his dress, a blanket capote, perhaps a flannel shirt, leather leggins and moccasins and a fur cap: he was, in addition, equipped with a blanket, spare moccasins, and a small kettle, composing a bundle suspended on his back." Although he was entering the territory of the Blackfoot Indians, who, according to Cooke, were being "incited by British traders," Glass safely reached the Yellowstone two weeks later, "having met neither white man or Indian."[35]

Still, Glass had "more than three hundred miles" to travel before reaching Henry's post. He was tired, and "it had set in very cold." He considered retracing his steps to winter with friendly Indians, but he persevered, and "one morning in December," he met one of Henry's hunting parties. They could not believe it was Hugh Glass, for two witnesses had described his death. After questioning him thoroughly, however, the men concluded that these witnesses were guilty of "black treachery." In turn, Glass learned that Henry's fort was only a few miles away, and although Fitzgerald had left the region, the younger deserter was still with the company.[36]

Glass raced to the post, where he immediately met the young man. "All attempt must fail to describe the effect of his appearance upon the youth," said Cooke. He "stood without power of any motion; his eyes rolled wildly in their sockets; his teeth chattered, and a clammy sweat rose upon his ashy features." The scene caused Glass to reconsider his vow of vengeance. "The more guilty object of his revenge had escaped," he decided, and "the pitiful being before him was perhaps but the unwilling and over-persuaded accomplice of his much elder companion." Consequently, Glass decided to spare the young man's life, although he admonished him for his action: "Young man, it is Glass that is before you; the same that . . . you robbed, helpless as he was, of his rifle, his knife, of all with which he could hope to defend, or save himself from famishing in the desert." However, he added, "I cannot take your life; I see you repent; you have nothing to fear from me; go—you are free—for your youth I forgive you." The young man, his conscience bothering him immensely, stood speechless.[37]

Although Glass still hoped to meet the older deserter, said Cooke, he postponed this act "to a more convenient season."[38] With this decision, Cooke abruptly ended his narrative, omitting Glass's subsequent trip to Fort Atkinson, his escape from the Arikara Indians along the Platte River, and his confrontation with Fitzgerald. Although Cooke does not always succeed in his intention of convincing readers that Glass survived because of his strength and courage, rather than luck, his description of Glass's vow of vengeance and subsequent act of forgiveness seems more satisfying than Hall's conclusion.

Less than a decade after Cooke first published his story, Edmund Flagg, a writer, journalist, and lawyer, contributed another account of Glass's encounter with the grizzly bear. His "Adventures at the Head Waters of the Missouri" appeared in 1839 in the *Louisville Literary News-Letter*, a periodical that he helped publish with George D. Prentice. Born in Maine in 1815, Flagg graduated from Bowdoin College before moving to Louisville, Kentucky, where he began a career in journalism. In 1836, he moved to Saint Louis to study law. He also published *The Far West* (1838), an account of a summer he spent on the prairies of Illinois and Missouri. In subsequent years, he worked as a journalist, publisher, editor, lawyer, diplomat, and public servant, as well as pursuing a writing career. He died in Virginia in 1890.[39]

Although Flagg may have learned about Glass's adventures from trappers visiting Saint Louis, his primary source was "the rough notes of a very intelligent man" who "could have had no object in an untrue recital." Despite Flagg's optimism, it is clear that his source did not have firsthand knowledge about the mauling. For example, Flagg claimed that Glass encountered the bear on the Cheyenne rather than the Grand River and asserted that Glass was "thousands of miles from all surgical succour" when he was mauled.[40]

Nonetheless, Flagg's informant may have gained his information from Glass or his acquaintances. Indeed, there are clues within Flagg's account that help identify the author of the "rough notes." Flagg is the first writer to describe Glass's adventures after he left Fort Atkinson, including his life in the Southwest and his death on the upper Missouri. It is likely that Flagg's informant also talked with other trappers, for some of his information depicts Glass unfavorably.

Although it is impossible to identify Flagg's informant with absolute certainty, a "very intelligent man" who had known Glass on the upper Missouri happened to be living in Saint Louis at the same time as Flagg. Apparently Englishman James A. Hamilton, bookkeeper for Kenneth McKenzie at Fort Union, had met Glass during the winter of 1832–1833, shortly before the trapper's death. "Glass had told Hamilton the story of his whole life," Prince Maximilian of Wied reported after visiting the fort in 1833. "For many years this old man [Glass] led the dangerous lifestyle of a beaver trapper. He had numerous wounds [that] he owed to Indians."[41] Maximilian added that Hamilton had drafted a biography of Glass.

Artist George Catlin, who met Hamilton during his voyage up the Missouri River in 1832, said that Hamilton's "intellectual and polished society has added not a little to my pleasure and amusement since I arrived here." Hamilton's mind, he added, seemed to be "a complete store-house of ancient and modern literature and art," and he had "the stamp of a gentleman, who has had the curiosity to bring the embellishments of the enlightened world, to contrast with the rude and the wild of these remote regions."[42] Prince Maximilian also found Hamilton to be pleasing company, and he and his companions "visited Mr. Hamilton regularly every evening to talk with him. He usually served us some kind of whisky punch with sugar and hot water while we smoked our pipes."[43]

Hamilton was a unique figure on the upper Missouri, dressing in London's latest fashions, with "ruffled shirt-fronts" and a gold chain hanging from his neck.[44] Trader Charles Larpenteur remembered that Hamilton "habitually lived high, in consequence of which he had the gout. This brought him to the two extremes of being either very pleasant or very crabbed, but, upon the whole, kept him crabbed; so he was not liked, though much respected."[45] Similarly, army surgeon and ethnologist Washington Matthews learned that Hamilton was "an object of wonder and gossip" to the people on the upper Missouri. Some French Canadians told Matthews, "in tones of awe," that Hamilton "took a bath and put on a clean shirt every day." Hamilton also disliked Indians, and he once burned "a beautiful colored silk handkerchief" because "an admiring Indian had picked it up to examine it."[46]

Hamilton left the upper Missouri in the mid to late 1830s and was living in Saint Louis at the time Flagg was there. It would have been natural for the writer and the English intellectual to meet, and it is possible that Hamilton provided Flagg with a copy of his notes. By that time, Hamilton may have decided he would never publish his biography of Glass. He died in 1840.[47]

Flagg begins his account of Glass in a familiar manner, with Henry and his trappers marching westward toward the Yellowstone River. Because there were "roving tribes" in the area, Henry gave "strict orders" that "the party should move on compactly and in order, and that none of the hunters should on any account separate from the main body." Despite these orders, Glass and George Harris wandered away in search of "wild fruit," and Glass encountered the grizzly bear during their foraging expedition. The rest of the party only learned that something was amiss when they heard "a fearful shriek." Assuming that Indians were attacking, they "seized their weapons," but instead they saw Harris rushing out of the trees on the other side of the river, pursued by a grizzly bear. As Harris turned and fired, the men joined in the shooting, killing the bear. It was "a young female with a cub," Flagg observed, "which accounted for its more than ordinary ferocity." Still, the screaming continued, and the party crossed the river to find Glass "lying at the foot of a tree, most terribly torn and mangled by the bear." He had at least fifteen wounds, said Flagg, "any one of which would under ordinary circumstances have been considered mortal."[48]

Even though they were certain that Glass could not survive his wounds, the men carried him back to their camp, dressed his wounds, built a litter, and for three days carried him with them on their march. Finally, at a spring with "a fine grove some distance from the route of any of the wandering tribes," they held a "consultation" and decided that two men should remain with Glass while the remainder of the party continued to their destination. According to Flagg, "Fitzgerald and Bridges" volunteered to remain with Glass "until he recovered sufficiently to follow the expedition, or, as was hourly apprehended, should expire of his wounds." The rest of the men donated three hundred dollars as a reward and then departed.[49]

Although Flagg blamed Glass for disobeying orders, he condemned Fitzgerald and Bridges for subsequently deserting him. Despite having "kindly intentions," these men were "lawless," and it was in their best interest that Glass should "as soon as possible, cease to live." Finally, they left him to die alone, and when they caught up with the rest of the party, they said that Glass had died on the sixth day after they had left. Glass's rifle was then "disposed of to the highest bidder." As Fitzgerald expressed "a wish to return to St. Louis," he was issued a draft against General Ashley for his share of the reward and departed, never to appear again in Flagg's narrative.[50]

"Early one fine frosty morning," wrote Flagg, "to the utter astonishment of the whole company, who should appear at the Fort, but the identical individual, who, four months before, had been left on the banks of the Chian [Cheyenne] River, as a dead man!" They "gazed upon his ghostly features and skeleton" with dread, and Bridges "could with difficulty be persuaded to enter his presence." Instead of confronting Bridges, however, Glass narrated his experiences to the party.[51]

Flagg's account of Glass's survival is similar to the prior ones, differing only in numbers and details, and without mention of revenge, confrontation, and forgiveness, it seems comparatively bland. Indeed, Flagg's major purpose in telling Glass's story was not to dramatize it, but to contrast the easy life of his own times with the primitive conditions of the earlier West. Although hunters still faced the "cruelty of the savage," as well as grizzly bears, famine, and drought, "what must have been these hardships and dangers twenty years ago," Flagg mused, "when but few, if any of his present facilities were afforded the adventurer."[52]

The most significant and controversial new information in Flagg's narrative is his identification of Glass's young deserter as "Bridges." Western historians have concluded that he meant James Bridger, who was part of the expedition and later one of the West's most respected trappers and explorers. This identification adds an entirely new dimension to the story: if young Bridger was guilty of desertion, historians had to reconcile this disreputable action with his later greatness.

J. Cecil Alter, the leading biographer of Jim Bridger, insisted that Flagg's identification was tentative at best and argued that much of the Hugh Glass saga was probably a tall tale. Glass simply experienced too many miraculous escapes for his story to be believable. "No matter how difficult the situation, our hero, Hugh Glass, always got out of it," he wrote. "Too bad Ned Buntline missed him!" Furthermore, said Alter, if one traces the stories back in time, the original source always seems to be Glass himself, and he "never names an individual nor identifies a place or an episode in such a manner as to admit of proof or refutation. There are no other firsthand witnesses to any part of the bear story; and 'Fitzgerald' is a nobody in western literature."[53]

Even if the young deserter had been Bridger, said Alter, he would have had justifiable reasons for deserting Glass and taking his rifle. Indians had killed two men in Henry's party on the same day that Glass was mauled, and because the attackers probably remained in the area, it would have been foolish for Fitzgerald and Bridger to remain with Glass for an extended time. It also "would have been imprudent," Alter wrote, "to leave a good gun and other trappers' equipment beside the body of a dead man."[54]

The last significant historical account of the Hugh Glass story came from trapper George Yount, who was born in 1774 in North Carolina. His family later moved to a farm in Missouri, and while he never attended school or learned to read or write, he married and began farming on his own. After losing his savings, perhaps due to a neighbor's corruption, he took a job as a teamster with a caravan going to Santa Fe, perhaps the same one taken by the runaway apprentice Kit Carson. Arriving in Santa Fe in the fall of 1826, he joined Ewing Young's party and trapped the headwaters of the Gila and Salt rivers. The next year, Yount himself organized a trapping expedition of twenty-four men, including Hiram Allen and possibly Hugh Glass. Finally able to pay his debts, he left with a party for the Green River, wintering in the Bear Valley in 1828–1829. It was one of the worst winters on record, and Yount froze his feet. After learning that divorce papers had been served against him, Yount joined William Wolfskill's expedition to California. There, he settled on a large tract of land and became a well-known local figure. Many notable individuals visited his estate, and

Yount entertained these visitors with tales of the West, including the Hugh Glass story.[55]

Unfortunately, Yount only become acquainted with Glass several years after the mauling and did not relate his memoirs until 1855. Worse, despite a reputation for a good memory, Yount sometimes exaggerated and even invented tales. Charles L. Camp, who later edited Yount's narrative, noted that he "often doubles the number of Indians and the sizes of objects—grizzlies weighing 1,500 pounds, 12-foot rattlesnakes," and so forth. "Perhaps some of this was unconscious," wrote Camp, "but I suspect it was for the delectation of himself and his audiences. . . . He was not allergic to 'fish stories.'"[56]

Because Yount himself was illiterate, Orange Clark, an Episcopal priest, recorded his reminiscences for him, including his rendition of the Glass story. Clark sometimes added a religious tone to the account; nevertheless, he insisted that the information was accurate. "Glass," he said, "told to Yount all which we have here written & Allen confirmed the truth of it all."[57] Clark was referring to Hiram Allen, who was also with Henry's party in 1823. In addition, another of Glass's companions, Lewis Dutton, told Yount about Glass's adventures following his departure from Henry's camp on the Yellowstone to seek vengeance against one of the deserters. Consequently, Yount's account is a mixture of things he heard from Allen, Dutton, and Glass himself, with Clark's commentary.[58]

Clearly, Allen was the primary source for Yount's account of the mauling, in which Glass is held to be at fault. Just as in Flagg's account, Henry ordered his men not to wander away from the main party as they marched toward the Yellowstone River because Arikara Indians were in the area. Two "distinguished hunters" provided food for the men, but Glass was not one of them. Instead, Allen and an unnamed individual were chosen. Despite Henry's command, however, Glass, "as was usual, could not be kept, in obedience to orders," and he meandered "alone through the bushes & chapparel." Allen eventually noticed Glass "dodging along in the forest alone; & said to his companion,"—with phenomenal foresight—"there look at that fellow, Glass; see him foolishly exposing his life—I wish some Grizzly Bear would pounce upon him & teach him a lesson of obedience to orders, & to keep in his place—He is ever off, scouting in the bushes & exposing his life & himself to dangers."[59]

About half an hour later, the two hunters heard screams. Hastening to the source of the noise, they found a "huge Grizy Bear, with two Cubs" near Glass's body. According to Allen, "the monster had seized him, torn the flesh from the lower part of the body, & from the lower limbs—He also had his neck shockingly torn, even to the degree that an aperture appeared to have been made into the windpipe, & his breath to exude at the side of his neck." Despite Allen's graphic description of Glass's wounds, Yount did not believe that Glass's windpipe had been punctured. Moreover, he added, Glass's arms and hands were uninjured and no bones were broken.[60]

When the remainder of Henry's party arrived, they killed the bears and dressed Glass's wounds. For six days, they carried him with them in a litter. "He retained all his faculties but those of speech & locomotion," said Yount; "too feeble to walk, or help himself at all, his comrads every moment waited his death." Finally, deciding that the delay might cause them to miss the trapping season, the party left two men, one only a boy, to care for him. Yount did not identify either of these individuals, who soon deserted Glass even though they had been promised four hundred dollars to remain with him. Perhaps Reverend Clark supplied the religious flourish with which Yount condemned their conduct: "Quite discouraged & impatient for his death, as there remained no hope of his recovery, the two resolved to leave him there to die alone in the wilderness—They took from him his knife, camp kettle & Rifle, laid him smoothely on his blankets, & left him thus to die a lingering death, or be torn in pieces by the ferocious wild beasts & to be seen no more till they should meet him at the dread tribunal of eternal judgment."[61]

According to Yount, Glass was conscious when his companions abandoned him. He "could hear their every word, but could not speak nor move his body." However, he retained the use of his arms and "stretched them out imploringly, but in vain—They departed & silence reigned around him." After they left, Glass "became delirious," but "visions of benevolent beings" assured him that "all would be well at last." Thus, after regaining consciousness, he was optimistic about his chances of survival. He drank water from the nearby stream, ate some berries, and killed a rattlesnake lying beside him for meat. After a few weeks, he gained sufficient strength to crawl, each day increasing the distance. Eventually, he reached Fort Kiowa, where he spent the entire winter recovering.[62]

The following spring, Glass decided to rejoin Henry and his men. Despite the danger, including the escape from the Arikaras recorded in previous accounts, Yount described this trip as "no more than a season of pastime & pleasure" compared to "the scenes of the previous Summer & Autumn." Indeed, according to Yount, Glass "knew no fatigue but after a day's travel, could leap and frolic, like the young fawn."[63]

Meanwhile, "the man & boy, false to their trust," had reported to Henry "that Glass had died & they had decently buried his remains." In confirmation, they presented his gun and other belongings and received "the promised reward for their fidelity." Only the younger deserter was still with Henry when Glass finally arrived and disproved their story, but instead of threatening him, Glass told him that he would have to live with his conscience. "Go, my boy," Glass said. "I leave you to the punishment of your own conscience & your God—If they forgive you, then be happy." Similarly, when he later met the older deserter, Glass said harshly, "You was well paid to have remained with me until I should be able to walk . . . or to wait my death and decently bury my remains—I heard the bargain. . . . Settle the matter with your own conscience & your God. Give me my favorite Rifle."[64]

Besides adding religious tones to Yount's narrative, Clark probably provided the moral of the story. Trappers, he asserted, were "the noblest specimins of humanity," and from them "the young men of our country may learn lessons of enterprize, & even of goodness & right living." These heroic westerners stood in stark contrast to the undeserving examples surrounding the younger generation in his time. These "too often self[-]inflated, proud & dishonest merchants of our cities, availing themselves of every bankrupt-law, or secreting their property, will flee from their creditors, & their just debts into the new settlements opened by these honest & hardy backwoodsmen." Unlike these merchants, the early trappers "would gather the fruits of their exposures & return thousands of miles, to repay all they had ever promised; to meet their every obligation; & they would rather die than compromise their honor."[65]

The idea that trappers might serve as models for young people is surprising, given the portrayal of Glass and his companions. Glass was disobedient, and the two deserters left him alone to die. Their behavior hardly bears out the writer's conclusion that "among those rude & rough trappers of the wilderness, fellow feeling & devotion to each others wants is a remarkable & universal feature or characteristic" and is "worthy [of] the imitation of even the highest grade of civilized men."[66] If Clark penned these words, perhaps he was thinking of George Yount himself rather than the others.

While they disagreed on distances traveled, reasons for the bear's attack, the extent and nature of Glass's wounds, and Glass's pursuit of revenge, Hall, Cooke, Flagg, and Yount all agreed that Glass's survival was an epic tale revealing the strength of the American character. Future storytell-ers expanded on this theme, picking and choosing details from these early accounts to fit their particular inclinations.

Interestingly, only one of these early writers provided an account of Glass's life before his enlistment with Henry's party in 1823, and only two related events after he tracked down his deserters. None of these storytellers described Glass's role in the war with the Arikara Indians just before his encounter with the grizzly bear, even though Glass was wounded in the fight. For the full context of the ordeal that made Glass famous, historians must consider these topics, beginning with the one most shrouded in uncertainty—his origins.

2

Hugh Glass
before 1823

On 23 April 1795, Pittsburgh gunsmith Henry Wolf offered a reward of six pence for the return of runaway apprentice Hugh Cook Glass. According to Wolf's advertisement in the *Pittsburgh Gazette*, Glass was approximately twenty years old, "about 5 feet 6 or 7 inches high, marked with small pox, short black hair, darkish complexion." In addition to skipping out on his work obligations, Glass stole a "continental rifle." Wolf thought Glass might be "going down the river" and would attempt to "pass for a gunsmith."[1] As Wolf realized, escaping to the West via the Ohio River would be an obvious route for a runaway.

There is no evidence that Wolf's apprentice ever returned, and it is impossible to determine whether this Hugh Cook Glass of Pittsburgh is the same individual as the famous fur trapper. Nevertheless, this advertisement is significant, being the only known contemporary reference to an individual named Hugh Glass prior to the well-known trapper's days in the fur trade. Researcher Don Baird accepts that this document correctly identifies the famous frontiersman and suggests that Hugh Cook Glass may have been the son of Pittsburgh gunsmith John Glass; it was not uncommon for gunsmiths to apprentice their sons to professional associates. However, without substantiating evidence, this identification remains tentative. If this Hugh Cook Glass was the same person later mauled by the grizzly bear, he would have been about forty-eight years old in 1823. Since most individuals enlisting with the Ashley-Henry expedition that year were young men, this age differential might explain why Glass was sometimes called "Old Glass."[2]

It was not unusual for apprentices to flee their work obligations. In the eighteenth century, apprenticeships typically lasted about seven years. In this legally binding relationship, the master agreed to teach the apprentice his trade in return for the apprentice's labor. After the apprentice satisfied his obligations, the master gave him tools and a suit of clothing; these were important gifts, for these young men had little opportunity to accumulate the resources necessary to open their own businesses. Initially, masters typically assigned their apprentices menial jobs "such as cleaning the shop, sharpening tools, starting the forge fire, pumping the bellows, or polishing gun parts."[3] If masters continued to give them nothing but boring chores or treated them roughly, youngsters sometimes fled. Henry Wolf, a leading gunsmith in Pittsburgh for twenty years, may have been a difficult master; several of his apprentices ran away. In 1808, for example, Wolf offered six dollars for the return of eighteen-year-old Joshua Bennet, and two dollars for fourteen-year-old James Mahaffy.[4]

Hugh Glass would not have been the only trapper who began his career training to be a craftsman. Kit Carson, for example, was once an apprentice saddler. His master, David Workman of Franklin, Missouri, advertised for his return in the *Missouri Intelligencer* on 6 October 1826. Christopher Carson, he said, was "a boy about 16 years old, small of his age, but thick-set," who had "light hair." Workman warned people "not to harbor, support, or assist said boy under the penalty of the law." However, he offered only a "one cent reward" for Carson's return.[5] Probably unaware that young Carson had run away, merchant Charles Bent hired him to haul goods from Saint Louis to Santa Fe, thus providing him with the means to go west. Jim Bridger also began his career as an apprentice. Although there is no evidence that he ran away before completing his obligations, Bridger left Saint Louis to enter the potentially more profitable and exciting fur trade after working for blacksmith Phil Creamer for five years.[6]

Prior to the discovery of the newspaper item advertising for the return of a runaway apprentice, there had been few clues about Glass's origins. Writer James Hall thought that Glass might have been Irish or a Pennsylvanian of Scotch-Irish descent. Rowland Willard, who met Glass near Santa Fe in 1825, claimed that Glass was Scottish and wore kilts asserting his nativity. Only George Yount provided a thorough account of Glass's early years, and his rendition reads like a dime novel. Yount probably heard the story from others, or he made it up to impress listeners as he regaled them with the tale of Glass and the grizzly.[7]

According to Yount, Glass began life not as a gunsmith, but as a sailor. On one of his voyages out of Philadelphia, his ship was "captured by the desperate band of Pirates under the notorious [Jean] Lafitte," a smuggler, pirate, and privateer who operated in the Gulf of Mexico. The members of the crew were given a choice: join the pirates or be executed. Glass and one companion "instantly decided to become Pirates; & were hailed as good fellows." They took the "oath of allegiance," which, said Yount, "was an awful one, & too horid to be written here."[8] By implication, the rest of Glass's shipmates refused and were put to death.

After spending an entire season with the pirates, Glass and his companion concluded they could no longer participate in the tortures and murders demanded of them. "As they shuddered from their inmost souls & shrunk from those deeds," said Yount, "it was impossible for them to conceil from their despotic lord the emotions of their hearts." Because of their reluctance, the two men were "deemed unfit for the work of pirates" and faced execution. That night, while the ship was anchored off the coast of Texas, Glass and his friend "swam from the ship to the land & fled for life." Having no knowledge of the region, they simply traveled "far back into the trackless wilderness, they knew not whither nor wherefore." Finally, far to the north, they encountered a band of Pawnee Indians who captured them.[9]

They soon discovered that they were no better off with the Pawnees than they had been with the pirates; once again both men faced death. Glass had to watch his companion's execution. "An awful scene it surely was," Yount said. Orange Clark, who recorded Yount's narrative, undoubtedly added interpretative commentary to the episode. The captive's entire body was "stuck thick with splinters of pitch-pine," and when these were lit "in the darkness of midnight, his spirit ascended in flames to Him who had given it being." Now it was Glass's turn. As the chief approached to put the first splinter into his skin, which was "deemed the royal privilege," Glass reached into his pocket for some vermilion, "an article which the savages value above all price." Handing it to "the proud & haughty Brave, with an air of respect & affection," Glass "bowed his final farewell." The gift saved his life. The chief untied him, took him to his "wigwam," and treated him "paternally." However, after spending only a few months in their village, Glass escaped while traveling with the Pawnees to Saint Louis.[10]

No documents verify Yount's account of Glass's life among the pirates and Pawnees. Nevertheless, lacking alternative versions, most biographers accepted this story. Author John Myers Myers, for example, titled his 1963 biography of Glass *Pirate, Pawnee, and Mountain Man*. Even though the tale may be spurious, it is possible that Glass or one of his companions told it to Yount. Trappers could easily have heard about pirates while residing in the Saint Louis area. Jean Lafitte had become a national hero when he aided Andrew Jackson against the British in the Battle of New Orleans. He returned to piracy after the battle, headquartering at Galveston Island in 1817, and from information in Yount's narrative, Myers concluded that Lafitte captured Glass around this time. Glass and his associates could also have learned about pirate life from acquaintances in the fur trade. For example, Edward Rose, one of Glass's trapping companions, was rumored to have been a river pirate.

According to author Washington Irving, Rose was "a designing, treacherous scoundrel" who "had formerly belonged to one of the gangs of pirates who infested the islands of the Mississippi, plundering boats as they went up and down the river."[11]

It is doubtful, however, that Glass ever participated in piracy. Author Richard Henry Dana heard Yount relate the tale of Hugh Glass during a visit in 1859 and jotted down the key elements in his journal. Dana had described his own adventures as a sailor in *Two Years before the Mast* (1840), and he should have found Glass's maritime experiences especially fascinating. However, while his outline of Glass's life in his journal is otherwise similar to Yount's account as recorded by Clark, Dana does not mention Glass's encounters with pirates or Pawnee Indians. Yount may have simply forgotten to mention these adventures, or perhaps Dana did not think them credible enough to record. Either way, Dana's notes raise suspicion about the origins of the tale.[12]

Additional factors cast doubt on Glass's Pawnee captivity, as well. First, it is difficult to believe that Glass and his companion wandered from the Gulf Coast to the Great Plains without first encountering other Indians. Even supposing that earlier encounters were not recorded, several aspects of the captivity story are suspect. Myers asserted that the Pawnees lived far from white settlements, where Glass "could not expect to encounter any of his own kind." Consequently, "he lived as a savage for several years."[13] However, in his history of the Pawnee Indians, George E. Hyde describes numerous visits by traders, trappers, dignitaries, and government officials to the Pawnee Indians during the time while Glass supposedly was with them, and Myers himself speculated that Glass escaped during a Pawnee visit to sign a treaty in Saint Louis. Pawnee chiefs did indeed visit the city to negotiate treaties, including a set of three agreements concluded on 18–20 June 1818. However, it is unlikely that the newspapers would have failed to notice Glass's escape, for they covered Indian visits extensively. The story of human sacrifice also seems unlikely. The Skidi Pawnees did occasionally sacrifice a captive to the Morning Star, but such events became rarer when they began to interfere seriously with the tribe's relations with European Americans. Stories about such incidents were widely publicized in Saint Louis newspapers, and from such accounts, Glass or another of Yount's informants might easily have incorporated a distorted version of a Pawnee sacrifice into his life story.[14]

Having accepted Yount's version of Glass's life as recorded by Clark, Myers speculated further. Pondering why Glass did not return to Pennsylvania after he escaped from the Pawnees, Myers decided that he might have been married before his misadventures, and might have suspected or learned that his wife had remarried during his long absence. Wanting to avoid a painful reunion, Glass remained in the West. Similarly, Myers suggested that Glass did not return to his life as a mariner because he feared that someone might recognize him as a former pirate. Adding to these rather fanciful assertions, Myers stated that Glass acquired his rifle during his captivity with the Pawnees. However, nothing is known about the origin of Glass's rifle, unless it was the one he stole from his master gunsmith when he ran away. Moreover, there are no documents to indicate a marriage and little reason to believe that Glass would have faced serious consequences for having been a pirate captive.[15]

On the other hand, it is possible that Glass was in either Pawnee or Arikara country prior to 1823. According to James Hall, Glass had met the Arikara chief Elk Tongue prior to their hostile encounter along the Platte River in 1824. Glass spent a winter as a guest of the chief, said Hall, and they became good friends after hunting, drinking, and smoking together. If Hall's statement is true, it implies that Glass traveled up the Missouri River to the Arikara villages prior to 1823, or that Glass and Elk Tongue met in Pawnee country. Yount mentions no such visit, stating only, "with these

Pawnees Glass roamed the wilderness in security many months."[16]

The only certainty is that Glass was in Saint Louis by 1823, when he enlisted as a trapper and proceeded up the Missouri River with the Ashley and Henry expedition. If he was a runaway apprentice, he may have lived in the area for some time. The Ohio River leads directly to the Mississippi, and from their confluence it is only a short distance to Saint Louis. Once he was in that city, the fur trade would have naturally beckoned.

"One thing only had made St. Louis the largest and most thriving town on the frontier," asserted historian Daniel Morgan, and that was "the fur trade of the Far West." Although it had "made fortunes for some and ruined others," few people in the city "did not in some way depend on what was happening up the great rivers." The "imposing residences" of Auguste and Pierre Chouteau, both giants in the fur trade, stood on the heights overlooking the river. In contrast to these mansions, the buildings and streets along the waterfront were "narrow and crowded," with warehouses and stores dominating the area.[17]

With a population of fifty-five hundred in 1821, Saint Louis was the largest city in the West. That year, John A. Paxton enumerated the city's establishments in his *St. Louis Directory and Register*, which provides a glimpse into the bustling life of the city. Already, there were three weekly newspapers: the *St. Louis Enquirer*, *Missouri Gazette*, and *St. Louis Register*. In addition, the city contained three "large Inns, together with a number of smaller Taverns & boarding houses," six livery stables, fifty-seven grocers and bottlers, twenty-seven attorneys, thirteen physicians, three druggists, and three midwives. There were tanneries, soap and candle factories, brickyards, stonecutters, carpenters, blacksmiths, gunsmiths, watchmakers, cabinet makers, saddle and harness manufacturers, hatters, tailors, boot and shoe manufacturers, hairdressers and perfumers, coopers, bakers, and a "Bell-man." Saint Louis also boasted a bookstore and a portrait painter "who would do credit to any country," as well as a brewery that manufactured beer, ale, and porter "of a quality equal to any in the western country." Five billiard tables paid "an annual tax of $100 each, to the state, and the same sum to the corporation." Professional musicians played at balls, "which are very frequent and well attended by the inhabitants, more particularly the French, who, in general, are remarkably graceful performers, and much attached to so rational, healthy and improving, an amusement." The city also boasted a new cathedral for its Catholic residents; the Baptists and Episcopalians also had churches, while the Methodists and Presbyterians held services in the city's public buildings. The pride of the city, however, was a new theater.[18]

Despite these accomplishments, Paxton was defensive about the city's reputation. He protested "against the many calumnies circulated abroad to the prejudice of St. Louis, respecting the manners, and the disposition of the inhabitants." The people comprising "the respectable part of the community" were, he asserted, "hospitable, polite, and well informed" and did not participate in the activities "which have so far so much injured the town."[19] He may have been referring to several highly publicized duels fought at Bloody Island, making the city "infamous the country over."[20]

This reputation also stemmed from Saint Louis's earlier history. After the Louisiana Purchase, Americans had rushed into the region, and according to a 1941 guidebook, "the town was overrun with adventurers, gamblers, and freethinkers who boasted that 'God would never cross the Mississippi.'" Along the levee, "street brawls were almost nightly occurrences." Disreputable behavior was not isolated to the lower classes. Some of those representing "wealth and culture" also participated, and "many a gentleman lost a fortune on the turn of a card, or won one by the correct appraisal of a fighting cock."[21]

Indeed, the city's image was so bad that its first mayor, William Carr Lane, felt obliged to defend it. "Our town is changing its physical and moral character for a better one daily," he said in 1824. "There is as little crime here as in any town of equal population and commerce in the Union, and the people are as sober, as obedient to laws, as orderly and as decent in their deportment, particularly in their public assemblies, as anywhere." Although Lane admitted that in the past, "disease, vice and violence have been associated with the very name of St. Louis," he emphasized the recent improvement: "the town is very healthy three-fourths of the year," and "riot, broils and wounds are . . . rare."[22]

No matter how or when he arrived in Saint Louis, Hugh Glass now found himself in the middle of sweeping changes to both the city itself and the business that had built it, and in 1823, he made the fateful choice to join the fur trade.

3

The Fur Trade

Glass chose an opportune moment to become a trapper. After a decade of decline, the fur trade on the upper Missouri River was experiencing a resurgence, and Glass signed on with a company that led the field through innovation, boldness, and good hiring practices. The remarkable people that William Ashley and Andrew Henry hired, men such as the legendary Jedediah Smith, tell us much of what we know about the life that trappers like Hugh Glass lived in this era.

Before the Louisiana Purchase, French, Spanish, and British traders had ascended the Missouri River from Saint Louis or traveled westward from Lake Winnipeg and the Great Lakes region. Indeed, the British were actively trading with the Mandan Indians before Lewis and Clark ascended the river. However, traders from Saint Louis mostly worked in a limited area. Although parties reached the Mandans in the 1790s and traders built a post called Cedar Fort near present-day Chamberlain, South Dakota, in 1802, few traders had traveled up the Missouri River beyond Council Bluffs.[1]

The Louisiana Purchase brought dramatic changes. Indeed, one of the goals of the expedition led by Meriwether Lewis and William Clark in 1804–1806 was to foster the fur trade. President Thomas Jefferson had instructed the captains to determine the abundance and location of fur-bearing animals, as well as to assert American authority over the newly-acquired territory. Traders immediately took advantage of the change in sovereignty; in 1806, as Lewis and Clark returned from the Pacific coast, they encountered American fur traders ascending the Missouri.[2]

The most notable fur trader operating on the upper Missouri in the years immediately after the Lewis and Clark expedition was Manuel Lisa. His first expedition departed from Saint Louis in the spring following the captains' return from the Pacific. Lisa's party of about sixty men built a fort at the confluence of the Yellowstone and Bighorn rivers, where they traded with the Crow Indians and trapped the region's rivers. He returned to Saint Louis in the summer of 1808 with a profitable load of furs.[3]

Lisa's success led to the formation of the Missouri Fur Company; among his partners were Pierre and Auguste Chouteau, Reuben Lewis (brother of Meriwether Lewis), William Clark, and Andrew Henry, who would later figure prominently in Hugh Glass's story. In the spring of 1809, Lisa's second party of one hundred sixty men left Saint Louis. Its primary objective was to send trapping parties from the post already established at the junction of the Yellowstone and Bighorn rivers. Andrew Henry was in command. However, the Blackfoot Indians, who had had unpleasant experiences with the Lewis and Clark expedition and various other trappers, refused to accept this intrusion into their territory. In fact, Blackfoot attacks became so severe that it was difficult for the trappers to leave the post except in large groups, and their failure to bring back sufficient furs led the company to abandon its fort on the upper Missouri River. The company's future looked bleak, and although it was reorganized several times in the next few years, its trade occurred primarily in the area below the Mandan villages.[4]

In addition, the company faced increasing competition. In 1810, the Pacific Fur Company, a subsidiary of John Jacob Astor's American Fur Company, launched a major enterprise to trap furs in the Pacific Northwest. The company intended to supply its trappers by sea at Astoria, its post on the Columbia River, and ship its furs directly to the flourishing market in China. However, the company also hoped to establish a viable land route to the Pacific, and in 1811, an overland party led by Wilson Price Hunt followed part of a route discovered by three of Henry's former employees who accompanied the expedition. Although they eventually reached Astoria, their route was unsatisfactory, and the War of 1812 thwarted Astor's plans when the British assumed control of the fort. The British navy also closed shipping routes between New Orleans and the east coast, causing a decline in the upper Missouri trade, as well. An economic recession followed, and it was difficult for fur companies to make profits as beaver prices declined from four dollars to two and a half dollars per pelt.[5]

American fur companies also blamed governmental policies for their problems. Wanting to encourage American Indians to become agriculturalists, the government had developed the "factory system" in 1796, establishing government posts where Indians could exchange furs for "tools, blankets, seeds, and the like."[6] Private fur companies, however, did not want Indians to become farmers, preferring them to trap and hunt to provide hides and pelts in exchange for manufactured goods that the companies' own traders supplied. In addition, private traders complained that the government failed to protect them from hostile Indians. The government was caught between two competing philosophies. Some influential policymakers wanted to stop private trading, believing that these traders caused conflict with the Indians by cheating them and intruding on their lands. Conversely, other officials wanted to end the factory system and to encourage and protect private traders with military force.[7]

Finally, in 1822, Astor's American Fur Company used its strong political influence to get the factory system abolished. Even earlier, the government had announced that it would provide protection for its citizens in Indian country. In 1819, it sent an expedition up the Missouri River, intending to build forts at Council Bluffs, the Mandan villages, and the mouth of the Yellowstone River. In the end, the government only built a post at Council Bluffs, which was later abandoned; nevertheless, these policy changes, coupled with the return of peace with Great Britain and the end of the recession, led to a major revival of the fur trade.[8]

"Since the abolition of the United States' factories, a great activity has prevailed in the operation of this trade," the *St. Louis Enquirer* reported in September 1822. "Those formerly engaged in it have increased their capital and extended their enterprize, many new firms have engaged in it, and others are preparing to do so." The newspaper estimated that a thousand men, mostly from the Saint Louis area, were already employed on the Missouri, about five hundred of them on the upper reaches of the river. The Missouri Fur Company alone had more than three hundred men headed for the mountains, the *Enquirer* claimed, and the company intended to trap in the Columbia River country as well. "Others have the same destination," it concluded, "so that the rich furs of that region will soon cease to be the exclusive property of the Hudson Bay Company."[9]

In 1821, the Missouri Fur Company, with dynamic new leaders including Joshua Pilcher, Andrew Drips, and Robert Jones, established a post at the mouth of the Bighorn. Another organization, Berthold, Pratte, and Chouteau, known as the French Fur Company, built Fort Kiowa near Cedar Fort in the autumn of 1822. The Columbia Fur Company, composed of men set adrift after the merger of the North West and Hudson's Bay companies, planned to trade with the Mandan Indians via the headwaters of the Mississippi and Minnesota rivers. However, it was the company organized by William Ashley and Andrew Henry that would gain the most attention in fur-trade history.[10]

Ashley and Henry announced their entrance into the trade dramatically. An advertisement in the Saint Louis *Missouri Gazette & Public Advertiser* on 13 February 1822 proclaimed: "To Enterprising Young Men. The subscriber wishes to engage ONE HUNDRED MEN, to ascend the river Missouri to its source, there to be employed for one, two or three years." Interested men were directed to Major Andrew Henry, "near the Lead Mines, in the County of Washington, (who will ascend with, and command the party)." They could also enlist with the subscriber, William H. Ashley, in Saint Louis. Hugh Glass did not join Ashley and Henry's company that year. Why he was not among the first to enlist is unknown. Perhaps he was not in the Saint Louis area at that time or was otherwise employed. Perhaps he did respond to the advertisement but was not selected because of his age or other considerations. Nevertheless, the 1822 expedition forms the background for Glass's experiences the next year.[11]

William Henry Ashley, born in Virginia in 1778 or shortly thereafter, migrated to Missouri in 1802. He was the best man at his neighbor Andrew Henry's wedding in 1805. Although he was undoubtedly familiar with Manual Lisa's fur-trading activities, Ashley, unlike Henry, did not participate in Lisa's enterprise. In 1811, he moved to Potosi, Missouri, and after discovering deposits of potassium nitrate nearby, constructed plants to extract commercial saltpeter and manufacture gunpowder. A decline in the demand for gunpowder after the end of the War of 1812, combined with several explosions at the plant, caused Ashley to quit this business. By 1819, he had moved to Saint Louis, where he was involved in land speculation and became an important public figure. He advanced in rank in the territorial militia from captain to brigadier general and became lieutenant governor of the newly created state of Missouri in 1821. His political connections and prestige ensured favorable responses when loans and goods were needed for the new fur company.[12]

Andrew Henry, born in Pennsylvania at about the time of the American Revolution, reportedly "was fond of reading and could play the violin well."[13] He moved to Missouri before 1803 and invested in lead mining near Potosi with his friend Ashley. A strong demand for lead shot kept "Henry's Diggings" operating profitably for several years. Henry was also active in the fur trade, becoming one of Lisa's partners in the Missouri Fur Company and commanding one of the trapping parties to the mountains in 1809. After his party suffered repeated attacks by the Blackfeet, he and his men crossed the continental divide and built the first fur post west of the Rocky Mountains. Henry returned to Saint Louis in 1811. He retained some financial interest in the Missouri Fur Company, but he decided to take a less active role in the company's field operations.[14]

With improved economic conditions after the War of 1812 and the repeal of the factory system, Ashley and Henry determined to invest in the fur trade. Taking advantage of his previous experience, Henry would be the primary figure in the field, while Ashley would manage financial operations in Saint Louis, gathering needed equipment, men, and supplies. According to the 29 October 1822 issue of the *Missouri Intelligencer*, the potential for profit was high. That fall, the newspaper noted, Captain Perkins of the Missouri Fur Company had arrived from the Yellowstone country with furs valued at fourteen thousand dollars, and shortly afterward, a second boat arrived with furs worth ten thousand dollars more.[15]

Ashley and Henry intended to employ their men to trap beaver themselves instead of trading with Indians for furs. This strategy was controversial because government policy only allowed fur companies to build trading posts where Indians could bring peltries to exchange. However, many Indians were not interested in trapping. In addition, as the number of fur-bearing animals in the vicinity of the posts declined, trading had become less profitable. Rather than relying on the Indians for furs, Ashley and Henry intended to send trappers to the rich beaver sites of the Rocky Mountains.[16]

Like other men in the fur business, Ashley and Henry obtained a federal trading license, even though they actually intended to trap more than trade. Benjamin O'Fallon, United States Indian agent for the upper Missouri region, immediately expressed his concerns to Secretary of War John C. Calhoun. "I understand that License has been granted to Messrs Ashley & Henry to trade, trap, and hunt, on the upper Missouri," he said. "I have not seen it, but am in hopes that limits have been prescribed to their hunting and traping on Indian Lands, as nothing is better Calculated to alarm and disturb the harmony so happily existing between us and the Indians in the vicinity of the Council Bluffs." Despite these concerns, O'Fallon interpreted the law broadly, freeing Ashley and Henry from restrictive regulations. "I think there is no impropriety in allowing hunting and traping above the Mandans, on the lands of Indians who are unfriendly to us, and under foreign influence," he said, "but, as soon as we have an opportunity of counteracting that influence, and producing a good understanding between us and those Indians, then, hunting and traping should be prohibited and our traders confined alone to a fair and equitable trade with them."[17]

Besides their emphasis on trapping rather than trading, historians have credited Ashley and Henry with other important innovations, such as paying their men for each fur they trapped instead of giving them a salary. In fact, these practices had antecedents; Manuel Lisa's men had both trapped and traded for furs more than a decade earlier, and Wilson Price Hunt had paid his trappers by the number and quality of the furs each man gathered. Nevertheless, Ashley and Henry were the first to adopt these practices on a systematic basis, reasoning that the incentives would cause trappers to work harder and collect more peltries.[18]

Ashley and Henry's new approach concerned their competitors. On 3 April 1822, Thomas Hempstead of the Missouri Fur Company wrote to his partner Joshua Pilcher,

"Genl Ashley's company starts this day with one boat and one hundred & fifty men by land and water[.] they ascend the Missouri river to the Yellow Stone where they build a Fort." Their recruits, he noted, were "all generally speaking untried" and comprised "evry description and nation." However, he was mostly concerned about their terms of employment. Although Ashley and Henry engaged their boat hands and clerks on the same terms as the Missouri Fur Company, their hunters and trappers were "to have one half of the furs &c they make[.] the Company furnish them with Gun Powder Lead &c &c, they only are to help to build the fort & defend it in case of necessity." Hempstead believed this would cause a lack of discipline. "Regularity, subordination, system which is highly necessary to have on that river should be the first object of any company," he noted. With the terms given by Ashley and Henry, "Should the hunters wish after they get above to leave them in a mass in what way will they prevent them, this kind of buisness of making hunters will take some time and much trouble."[19]

Ashley and Henry would later introduce the rendezvous system to the fur trade, as well. The discovery of South Pass, allowing wagon travel through the Rocky Mountains, provided Ashley the opportunity to haul goods overland after hostile Arikara and Blackfoot Indians blocked the river route to the upper Missouri. Each year, Ashley met the trappers at a convenient site in the mountains to purchase their furs and sell them supplies. The first rendezvous occurred in 1825, and it eventually became an annual festival as well as a place for business transactions.[20]

Besides introducing innovative strategies, Ashley and Henry recruited many of the most colorful and talented personnel in fur-trade history. Besides Glass, Ashley and Henry engaged Jim Beckwourth, Jim Bridger, James Clyman, Mike Fink, Thomas Fitzpatrick, David E. Jackson, Daniel T. Potts, Edward Rose, Jedediah Smith, William L. Sublette, and Louis Vasquez. These men left their mark throughout the

West, trapping and exploring from the Missouri River to the Pacific coast.

This cast of characters is all the more remarkable because finding qualified young men in 1822 was difficult. On 5 May, Hempstead wrote that he had never seen "such great demand for men, as there is at this time."[21] Boats were also difficult to secure. One month earlier, he had written, "there was not a boat at this place less than our boat when I got home. Ashley has purchased the only two boats that might have answered us." Likewise, there was a shortage of supplies and trading goods. "I have purchased some Knives which perhaps will do at all events they are the only ones in town as Genl Ashleys Company has taken all they get," Hempstead wrote.[22]

Ashley and Henry divided their enterprise into two groups. Henry left for the headwaters of the Missouri with the first party on 3 April 1822. Noting his departure, the *St. Louis Enquirer* optimistically reported that the Three Forks of the Missouri possessed "a wealth in *Furs*, not surpassed by the mines of Peru," and that if this location did not meet expectations, Henry might continue westward to the mouth of the Columbia. One hundred eighty young men composed the party, "many of whom have relinquished the most respectable employments and circles of society, for the arduous but truly meritorious undertaking."[23]

There had been "numerous applicants" for the expedition, and Ashley, with "his thorough knowledge of character," selected the best. "The animation created in St. Louis in the preparations for this great mountain expedition, will be long remembered by our citizens who were dwellers here at that period," the editor of the Saint Louis *Missouri Saturday News* later reminisced. "Armed and equipped fitly for desperate encounters with the red man, or his genial spirit the grizzly bear, these men paraded the streets while putting the last finish to desperate preparations. Like the reckless crew of a man of war about to cruise against an enemy's squadron, they indulged deeply in the luxuries they might never again realize."[24]

Daniel T. Potts was among these men, and his later correspondence to family and friends describes the party's subsequent difficulties. Instead of hauling provisions up the river, Potts explained, Henry intended to obtain his food by hunting. Unfortunately, game was scarce. "We . . . arived at Cedar fort about the middle of July when we where reduced to the sad necessity of eating any thing we could catch as our provision where exhausted," wrote Potts. Now "five hundred miles above the fronteers, we were glad to get a Dog to eat and I have seen some geather the skins of Dogs up through the Camp sing[e] and roast them and eat hearty." The destitution was so great that Potts and eight other men deserted. Somehow, Potts became separated from the other deserters, and "without gun amunition provition or even cloths to my back," he had to eat "young Birds, frogs, and Snakes," which he consumed raw because he did not have the means to start a fire. Fortunately, he encountered friendly Indians who treated him "with great humanity." Nevertheless, by the time he returned to a trading post, he was so hungry that he ate too much too quickly, resulting in "a severe spell of sickness which all but took my life."[25]

While Henry's party, less its deserters, worked its way up the Missouri, Ashley remained in Saint Louis outfitting the second keelboat, the *Enterprize*. Hempstead reported that Ashley had to delay its departure while "awaiting for Some guns for his expedition."[26] Ashley and Henry's second party, commanded by Daniel S. D. Moore, finally left Saint Louis on 8 May 1822. Their competitors from the Missouri Fur Company followed five days later, with Louis Bompart in charge.[27]

Jedediah Smith described the daily activities of Ashley and Henry's second party in his personal journal. "I had passed the summer and fall of 1821 in the northern part of Illinois," he said, and in 1822, "I came down to St. Louis and

hearing of an expedition that was fiting out for the prose-
cution of the fur trade on the head of the Missouri, by Genl
Wm H. Ashley and Major Henry, I called on Genl Ashley to
make an engagement to go with him as a hunter. I found
no difficulty in making a bargain on as good terms as I had
reason to expect."[28]

Although progress was "slow, Laborious and dangerous,"
wrote Smith, they ascended the river "without any material
occurrence for the first three hundred miles." Then, as they
passed "a point full of sawyers [trees]," the mast caught on
"a tree that hung over the water," and the *Enterprize* capsized in the powerful current.[29] Both ship and cargo were
lost. Daniel Moore left immediately for Saint Louis to deliver the bad news to Ashley while his men waited in a temporary camp. Not far behind, Louis Bompart of the Missouri
Fur Company "found among a mass of floating logs a box
of mirrors which came from the lost boat belonging to Mr.
Ashley."[30] Despite the fierce competition between the companies, he rescued the items for his rivals. According to the
Saint Louis *Missouri Republican*, the property lost was valued at ten thousand dollars, and "it was with difficulty that
the hands were saved."[31] Undeterred, Ashley had another
boat and forty-six men ready to leave Saint Louis within
eighteen days. This time, Ashley took charge of the expedition personally. When he reached the site of the accident, he
picked up the men awaiting him at their temporary camp.[32]

Unlike most traders on the Missouri, remarked Jedediah
Smith, Ashley "had laid in a plentiful supply of provision,
consisting of sea Bread and Bacon, so that we were not de-
pendant on the precarious supply derived from hunting."
Still, Ashley sent hunters out regularly, and Smith, who
was one of them, reported "Black Bear, Deer, Elk, Raccoon
and Turkeys in abundance." In addition, "the Country was
well stocked with Bees," providing "a plentiful supply of
honey."[33] Thus, unlike Potts and his companions in Henry's
party, Ashley's men were well fed. They met Potts as they

ascended the river, and surprisingly, Ashley talked him into rejoining the expedition.[34]

"In the progress of the Journey we passed the mouth of the river Platte," wrote Smith.[35] The Platte was considered a dividing point between the lower and upper Missouri. Often, travelers ascending the river for the first time endured an initiation ceremony there, although Smith does not mention one. Next, they reached Council Bluffs, where about five hundred soldiers were stationed at Fort Atkinson under the command of Lieutenant Colonel Henry Leavenworth. The party also began to encounter Indians, including the Omahas and Poncas, who lived in "stationary villages" and raised corn, as well as "some bands of the Sioux," who, Smith noted, "had no permanent residence, but moved about wherever the game was most abundant." Ashley "held council with them and smoked the pipe of Peace."[36]

Smith found the Sioux villages especially pleasing, with tipis "clustered together with their yellow sides and pointed tops," children playing, and "men going out or coming in from hunting." A large number of horses grazed on the prairie outside the village, and he saw numerous dogs sleeping and playing in the vicinity. He especially enjoyed seeing the Sioux women "at their several Labors and the boys at their several Sports." Indeed, Smith concluded, the sight "would almost persuade a man to renounce the world, take the lodge and live the careless, Lazy life of an indian." The landscape was also changing dramatically. Instead of woodlands, Smith now saw "one extensive prairae interrupted only by the narrow fringes of timber along the rivers." This land, "gently undulating and covered with grass," supported "immense herds of Buffalo" and "antelope in abundance," as well as bear, deer, and elk.[37]

On 8 September 1822, Ashley's party reached two Arikara villages located about three hundred yards from the river in present-day north-central South Dakota. These Indians were "not roving bands like the Sioux," said Smith, and therefore they built their lodges "in a more permanent manner." The houses were "circular in form," and the roofs constructed "to sustain a considerable weight," being "covered to a considerable debth with earth." Inside, there was "a narrow scaffold" along the side of the building where the inhabitants slept. Many lodges also had covered entranceways about four feet high and ten feet long.[38]

Because it was late in the season, Ashley decided to purchase horses from the Arikaras and travel overland with some of his men to the mouth of the Yellowstone while the remainder continued up the Missouri in the much slower boat. Ashley took personal command of the overland party. We "moved with great care," said Smith, because Ashley was "somewhat apprehensive of danger" from the Arikaras. They experienced no difficulties, however, and even stopped along the way to visit the Mandan villages to the north of the Arikaras, once again smoking the "pipe of peace" with the principal chiefs.[39]

Before they reached the Mandan villages, Smith spotted huge herds of buffalo. Indeed, he said, it appeared "that all the buffalo in the world were running in those plains, for far as the eye could see the plains and hills appeared a moving body of life. . . . They moved in deep, dense and dark bodies resembling the idea I have formed of the heavy columns of a great army." When the buffalo became aware of the men, "they ran, making the ground tremble with the moving weight of animal life."[40]

Meanwhile, Henry's party was located only a hundred miles farther northwest. He had traveled the entire way by boat, while some of his men drove between forty and fifty horses along the river. Unfortunately, Assiniboine Indians stole much of their livestock. Nevertheless, Henry's party reached the mouth of the Yellowstone in early September and immediately began building Fort Henry, meant to serve as the company's operational center while the men trapped furs.[41]

On 1 October, Ashley's overland party joined Henry at the site of their new headquarters. A couple of weeks later, Ashley's boat also arrived, and the party was now together. Potts, who evidently arrived on the boat, described the Yellowstone location as "one of the most beautiful situations I ever saw."[42] Ashley and Henry immediately "commenced arrangements for business," said Smith, and provided supplies to the parties that would trap beaver along the Yellowstone and Missouri rivers. Then Ashley left for Saint Louis in a large pirogue, taking with him several "Packs of Beaver" already secured by Henry's men.[43] He would organize another expedition to join the men at the post the next spring.

Henry divided his trappers into two parties. Henry himself led one party of twenty-one men up the Missouri to the Milk River. The other group, probably under the leadership of John H. Weber, a former Danish sea captain who had known Ashley and Henry since their earliest days in Missouri, went up the Yellowstone to the mouth of the Powder River. Meanwhile, the Missouri Fur Company's expedition, forty-three men now led by Michael Immell and Robert Jones, stopped briefly to visit. They planned to winter at the mouth of the Bighorn, competing directly with the Ashley and Henry men for the furs of the upper Missouri.[44]

Jedediah Smith, already recognized for his leadership skills, was placed in charge of procuring meat for the post on the Yellowstone. Shooting sufficient game to supply the fort did not take long, and Smith and his hunters soon followed Henry up the Missouri. Before traveling far, they met Henry and eight men already returning to the fort. Henry told Smith that the trappers he was to join would be wintering at the mouth of the Musselshell River, and Smith reached the site on about 1 November. Already, "the River was fast filling with ice and we were admonished to prepare for the approaching winter," said Smith, "which in that latitude must of course be much colder than the winters of the country from which most of us came."[45]

Assuming that the buffalo "had abandoned the country for the winter," Smith worried about finding sufficient meat to sustain the Musselshell camp. Immediately, the best hunters began shooting "all the small game of the vicinity, particularly antelope and deer," while the others hurried to finish building their cabins. When finally "well prepared for the increasing cold," they were surprised to see buffalo arriving from the north by the thousands, proving their fears unfounded. They also had sufficient food for their horses; the bark of the cottonwood trees along the river served as fodder. "Forced to eat this bark from necessity," wrote Smith, the "horses soon become verry fond of it and require little other assistance than the felling of the trees."[46]

Smith found life at the Musselshell enjoyable. "In our little encampment, shut out from those enjoyments most valued by the world, we were as happy as we could be made by leisure and opportunity for unlimited indulgence in the pleasure of the Buffalo hunt and the several kinds of sport which the severity of the winter could not debar us from."[47] Potts, on the other hand, found life at the Musselshell camp less pleasing. He felt lucky to retain his scalp, he said, "as two larg parteys of Indians winterd within twenty miles of us." Some were Blackfeet, notorious for their hostility to American trappers. Moreover, the winter was severely cold, and "the River froze to the emmence thickness of four feet and did not brake up until the fourth of April."[48]

Neither Potts nor Smith mentioned the most memorable event of the season. Mike Fink, the famous boatman, had also accompanied Henry's party, possibly as the commander of one of the keelboats. "The great frontiers of American history have usually produced their real or mythical heroes in the style of Daniel Boone as forest pioneer, Paul Bunyan of the loggers, and Pecos Bill of the Southwestern cowboys," wrote historian Richard Maxwell Brown. "Representing the keelboat era is the legendary Mike Fink."[49] Born between 1770 and 1780 in the Pittsburgh area, Fink became the most famous keelboat man on the Ohio and Mississippi rivers. It is not clear why he joined Ashley's 1822 expedition to the upper Missouri; perhaps he relocated because steamboats were replacing keelboats on the larger rivers or simply because a new opportunity beckoned. In any event, Fink and his friends Bill Carpenter and Levi Talbot wintered at the Musselshell, returning to Fort Henry the next spring.

Fink and Carpenter purportedly quarreled, perhaps over a woman. Nevertheless, they continued their ritual of shooting cups of whiskey off of each other's heads when drinking. "By a letter received in town from one of Gen. Ashley's expedition," reported the Saint Louis *Missouri Republican* on 16 July 1823, "we are informed that a man by the name of *Mike Fink* well known in this quarter as a great marksman with the rifle . . . was engaged in his favorite amusement of shooting a tin-cup from off the head of another man, when aiming too low or from some other cause shot his companion in the forehead and killed him." After Fink killed Carpenter, Talbot "remonstrated against Fink's conduct, to which he, Fink replied, that he would kill him likewise, upon which the other drew a pistol and shot Fink dead upon the spot."[50]

Carpenter and Fink were not the only casualties. After the ice had finally broken up on 4 April, ending the winter, the trappers broke into smaller groups, some heading upstream and others down the river. On 11 April, Potts was "severely wounded by a wiping stick [a gun-cleaning tool] being shot through both knees which," he said, "brought me to the ground[.] this disabled me for the springs hunt and allmost for ever."[51] Badly wounded, he was taken to Henry's post, possibly by Jedediah Smith. Then, on 4 May, at the mouth of the Smith River just above the Great Falls, the Blackfeet attacked one of Henry's parties, killing four men. "The rest," noted historian Robert M. Utley, "burying 172 steel traps and abandoning 30 more set in the river, fled the country . . . precipitately."[52]

Immell and Jones of the Missouri Fur Company were also concerned about Blackfoot hostility and decided to move toward the safer territory of the Crow Indians. On 31 May, however, the Blackfeet ambushed their party of twenty-nine men as it made its way along a "Buffaloe trace" on the "side of a steep hill" along the Yellowstone River. According to survivor William Gordon, the trappers were unable to defend themselves effectively because they were scattered over a "considerable distance." Seven men were killed, including Immell and Jones. The remainder escaped "by making a raft and crossing the Yellow Stone."[53] Besides the men, the company lost its horses, furs, traps, and equipment, all worth more than twelve thousand dollars.

These disasters forced the fur companies to change strategies. Although the headwaters of the Missouri were rich with beaver, they could not be trapped successfully because of the Blackfeet. The Missouri Fur Company soon decided to withdraw completely from the upper Missouri region, and henceforth traded only from posts below the Mandan villages. Ashley and Henry eventually found a different route to the mountains that bypassed the Blackfeet. These changes, however, occurred later. Because of the lag in communication, company leaders in Saint Louis did not learn about the disasters on the upper Missouri for many weeks.

Thus, for the moment, Ashley and Henry continued planning for their upcoming season. Henry intended to proceed with his trapping ventures and sent word to Ashley that he needed more horses. Ashley, now in Saint Louis, continued preparing the next spring's expedition, and this time Hugh Glass would be among the new recruits.[54]

4

The Arikara War
1823

On 15 January 1823, William Ashley posted another advertisement in the *Missouri Republican* calling for "One Hundred MEN, to ascend the Missouri river to the *Rocky Mountains*, there to be employed as Hunters." Instead of sharing profits from the sales of furs, as in the previous expedition, this time each man would receive an annual salary of two hundred dollars, and the party would leave Saint Louis by 1 March. Hugh Glass joined this ill-fated expedition, which would find itself at the center of the Arikara War of 1823. Although he appears to have played a minor role in the conflict, this episode marks the beginning of the historical record of the man who survived the grizzly attack, and it provided the occasion for the only known letter from his pen.[1]

Trapper James Clyman, who related the expedition's day-to-day adventures, helped to recruit many of these men. Born on a farm in Virginia in 1792, he first ventured westward to Ohio, then to Indiana, where he learned surveying from a son of Alexander Hamilton. Traveling to Saint Louis in February 1823 to collect his pay, he heard about Ashley's advertisement. Ashley gave him glowing reports of the Yellowstone River region, with its "immence Quantities of Beaver whose skins ware verry valuable selling from $5 to 8$ per pound at that time." Still, Clyman hesitated, but he must have impressed Ashley, for later, when they met on a city street, Ashley asked him to assist in recruiting men for his expedition. That evening, Ashley gave Clyman instructions "as to whare I would most probably find men willing to engage which [were to be] found in grog Shops and other sinks of degredation." Ashley rented a house for the recruits and furnished it with provisions, including bread and pork, "which the men had to cook for themselves."[2]

Ashley had to delay the expedition's departure because a supplier did not arrive with the needed goods on time. Still, he and his party of about a hundred men managed to leave by 10 March, sailing in two keelboats, the *Rocky Mountains* and the *Yellow Stone Packet*. As they departed, Clyman recalled, they "fired a swivel which was answered by a Shout [from] the shore which we returned with a will and porceed up stream under sail." He did not mince words about the men he helped recruit: "A discription of our crew I cannt give but Fallstafs Battallion was genteel in comparison."[3]

As in the previous year, the party experienced several accidents. One man fell overboard and drowned on the first day of travel. About a week later, a man smoking a pipe ignited some gunpowder as it was being hauled to the boats. "The explosion was tremendous," reported the *St. Louis Enquirer*, and three men "were blown into the air to the height of several hundred feet."[4] At Franklin, Missouri, however, an impromptu ball held in Ashley's honor may have helped to lighten the mood. "Notwithstanding the shortness of the notice," reported the local newspaper, "the assembly in the evening was attended by most of the respectable gentlemen of the place . . . and by the greatest portion of the female beauty and accomplishment with which our social circle is, for a spot so remote, so eminently furnished."[5] It is doubtful that the trappers and boatmen were invited.

The trip was less eventful after the expedition left Franklin. "We proceeded slowly up the Misourie River under sail wen winds ware favourable and [by] towline when not," said Clyman. Using a towline, also called a cordelle, was tedious work; the men walked along the shore and pulled the boat upstream with a long rope. Still, an occasional moment of hilarity enlivened the journey. Clyman recalled that several men left the boats one night and returned with eggs, turkeys, and other livestock. The next morning, settlers from the neighborhood searched the boats for their missing animals, but they found nothing. Once again the boats began working their way upstream, and encountering a "sailing breeze," the men unfurled the sails. "Out droped pigs and poultry in abundance," Clyman recalled.[6]

Some men quit as they ascended the river; fortunately "a few new men of a much better appearance than those we lost" replaced them, Clyman wrote. At Fort Atkinson, for example, located near Council Bluffs, between eight and ten of Ashley's men enlisted in the army, while two or three soldiers whose terms of enlistment were expiring joined the trappers. In addition, the officers at the fort "furnished us with a Quantity of vegetables," said Clyman, and the expedition now left "the last appearance of civilization."[7]

Their next scheduled stop was the Arikara villages, located north of the Grand River. Ashley had received an express from Henry asking him "to purchase all the horses I could on my way," and he planned to buy some from the Arikaras.[8] However, he was apprehensive about the meeting. During the winter, Missouri Fur Company traders had had a confrontation with the Arikaras at Cedar Fort. Evidently, the Arikaras had taken several Sioux women captive, and one of them escaped and made for the fort. Her captors gave chase, but as they neared the post, some of the traders fired and killed two of them, including the son of chief Grey Eyes. The Arikaras now "considered war was fully declared between them and the whites," said Clyman. Ashley hoped somehow to convince the Arikaras that his men "were not respo[n]sable for Injuries done by the Missourie fur company."[9]

Ashley's party arrived at the Arikara villages on 30 May. "For feare of a difficulty, the boats ware kept at anchor in the streame, and the skiffs were used for communications [between] the boats and the shore," said Clyman.[10] Ashley reported that he and two of his men met with "the principal chiefs who . . . expressed a wish that I should trade with them." Nevertheless, he proceeded cautiously. "I consented to send some goods on shore to exchange for horses, but proposed that the chiefs of the two towns would meet me on the sand beach, where a perfect understanding should take place before the barter commenced." There, Ashley explained to the chiefs that he was aware of the incident at Cedar Fort, then made them "a small present" of powder and muskets, "which appeared to please them very much." In return, they explained that the "affray alluded to, had caused angry feelings among them, but that those feelings had vanished."[11]

Trading began, and by the evening of 31 May, Ashley's men had acquired about twenty horses. Ashley intended to leave the following morning, but a severe wind forced him to remain in camp for another day. Late in the afternoon of 1 June, "the principal chief of one of the towns" invited Ashley to visit him. Although hesitant, Ashley decided to go, "as I did not wish them to know that I apprehended the least danger from them." Edward Rose, who had lived with the Arikaras for a few years, accompanied him as interpreter. Ashley said that he "was treated with every appearance of friendship."[12]

Ashley and about fifty others spent the night of 1 June in the boats, about ninety feet off shore. However, approximately forty men were ashore with the horses and vulnerable to attack. Hugh Glass and James Clyman were among them. "Several of our men without permition went and remained in the village," Clyman recalled later, and about midnight, Rose "informed us that one of our men was killed in the village and war was declared in earnest."[13] Ashley, learning the same news "just before day light," was told that the Indians "in all probility would attack the boats in a few minutes."[14]

At daylight, "the Indians commenced a heavy and well directed fire from a line extending along the picketing of one [of] their towns and some broken ground adjoining," said Ashley. When he saw that some of the horses and two or three men had been killed, he ordered the men to move the horses to a sand bar located mid-river. Before they could accomplish anything, however, "the fire became very destructive."[15] According to Clyman, "we had little else to do than to Stand on a bear sand barr and be shot at, at long range[.] Their being seven or Eigh hundred guns in village and we having the day previously furnished them with abundance of Powder and Ball."[16]

In an effort to rescue the men, Ashley ordered the boatmen to move the keelboats toward the shore. However, they "were so panic struck," said Ashley, that he could not get them to obey.[17] Despite "many calls for the boats to come ashore and take us on board," Clyman recalled, "no prayers or threats had the [slightest effect] the Boats men being completely Parylized." Finally, two skiffs made the attempt. When the first skiff finally arrived, too many men jumped in, Clyman said, "and came near sinking it but it went the boat full of men and water[.] the shot still coming thicker and the aim better we [made] a brest work of our horses . . . they nerly all being killed." Later, one of the skiffs went adrift when "the men clambering on [board]," in their "eagerness to conceal themselves from the rapid fire of the enemy," failed to steer it.[18]

Glass was probably among those who escaped in the skiffs. By this time, so many in the shore party had been killed or wounded that they could no longer effectively defend themselves. As one of the men with Ashley vividly recalled, "finding all lost, those on the beach attempted to swim to the boats; some who could not, fell alive into the hands of the Indians; many who attempted to swim, were, by the violence of the current, driven below the boats and drowned."[19] Clyman remembered eleven bodies being "left on the sand bar and their Scalps taken for the squaws to sing and dance over."[20]

Clyman finally left his "hiding place behind a dead hors, ran up stream a short distance to get the advantage of the current and concieving myself to be a tolerable strong swimer," jumped in. "Not having made sufficien calculation for the strong currant," he was quickly swept downstream. Thomas Eddie saw him from one of the boats, but the shooting was so intense that he could not get a pole within Clyman's reach. Still wearing his clothing and carrying his rifle, Clyman now dumped all these "encumbrances," including his hunting shirt, "which was buckskin and held an immence weight of water." He almost drowned when the lock on his rifle caught on his belt, but when he finally surfaced, he "heard the voice of encoragemnt" from Reed Gibson, who had "caught the skiff the men had let go afloat." Gibson hauled the exhausted Clyman into the skiff, but then cried out, "oh, god I am shot." Clyman managed to land the boat on the eastern shore, where he told his wounded companion to wait while he checked out their situation.[21]

According to Ashley, "it was about fifteen minutes from the time the firing commenced until the surviving part of the men had embarked."[22] With most of the men aboard, the keelboats began drifting downstream. Clyman and Gibson, meanwhile, spotted several Arikaras swimming toward their spot on the eastern shore. Gibson told Clyman to save himself because, he said, "I am a dead man and they can get nothing of me but my Scalp." While Gibson hid in some brush, Clyman "steered directly for the open Prarie and looking Back," saw three Indians headed in his direction. Having a head start of twenty or thirty rods, he ran "an even race for about one hour," then began to suffer heart palpitations. Finding a hole about three feet long and two feet deep, "with weeds and grass perhaps one foot high surrounding it," Clyman clambered down and hid. Once the three warriors had passed and were far enough away, he stood, "made them a low bow," and thanked God for his "present Safety and diliveranc."[23]

Being unarmed and far from the nearest post, Clyman noted that his "pro[s]pects ware still verry slim." Soon, however, he spotted "the boats floating down the stream the [men] watcing the shores saw me about as soon as I saw them the boat was laid in and I got aboard." Clyman learned that they had also picked up Gibson, but he was "in the agonies of Death the shot having passed through his bowels." Clyman wept "over him who lost his lifee but saved mine."[24]

According to Clyman, the party "fell down a few miles and lay by several day to wait and [see] if any more men had escaped the but[c]hery." Sure enough, Jack Larrison, assumed to be dead, "came to us naked as when he was born and the skin peeling off of him from the effects of the sun[.] he was wounded a ball passing through the fleshy part of one thigh." Larrison had hidden between two dead horses and escaped by swimming down the river after the boats left. Within a few days, Clyman reported, "he was hobbling around."[25]

Ashley's losses were thirteen killed and eleven wounded. Hugh Glass received a leg wound, but it was not considered serious, and he soon recovered.[26] John S. Gardner was not so lucky, and before he died, he asked Glass to notify his parents. The letter that Glass penned to Gardner's family is the only known example of his writing and warrants a complete transcription:

Dr Sir,
    My painfull duty it is to tell you of the deth of yr
Son wh befell at the hands of the indians 2nd June in
the early morning. He lived a little while after he was
shot and asked me to inform you of his sad fate[.] We
brought him to the ship where he soon died. Mr Smith
a young man of our company made a powerful prayr wh
moved us all greatly and I am persuaded John died in

peace. His body we buried with others near this camp and marked the grave with a log. His things we will send to you. The savages are greatly treacherous. we traded with them as friends but after a great storm of rain and thunder they came at us before light and many were hurt. I myself was hit in the leg. Master Ashley is bound to stay in these parts till the traitors are rightly punished.

Yr Obt Svt

Hugh Glass[27]

In this letter, Glass displays compassion toward his dying companion, some religious convictions, and negative attitudes toward American Indians. His reference to Jedediah Smith's "powerful prayr" has been commemorated with a historical monument referring to it as the "first act of Christian worship in South Dakota."[28]

Meanwhile, Ashley tried to restore order and discipline. "To describe my feelings at seeing these men destroyed, is out of my power," he wrote. He thought that few of his men would have died if the boatmen had followed orders, and they continued to thwart his wishes. Ashley still hoped to join Henry at the mouth of the Yellowstone, and after floating downstream to a more defensible location, he discussed his plans with his men. "To my great mortification and surprise," he said, "they positively refused to make another attempt to pass the towns, without a considerable reinforcement." Even after he "made known to them the manner in which I proposed fixing the boats and passing the Indian villages," they defied him. He then asked them to remain at least "until I should hear from Maj. Henry, to whom I would send an express immediately, and request that he would descend with all the aid he could spare from his fort at the mouth of the Yellow Stone.—Thirty only have volunteered, among whom are but few boatmen."[29] Glass evidently was one of those who agreed to stay with Ashley.

Even the reliable James Clyman had misgivings. "Before meeting with this defeat," he wrote, "I think few men had Stronger Ideas of their bravery and disregard of fear than I had but standing on a bear and open sand barr to be shot at from bihind a picketed Indian village was more than I had contacted for and some what cooled my courage." Lacking support for his plan to get past the Arikara villages, Ashley relocated below the Moreau River, twenty-five miles downstream. From there, he sent two men, Jedediah Smith and an unidentified French Canadian, to Henry. Next, said Clyman, "one boat containing the wounded and discouraged was sent down to Council bluffs with orders to continue to St. Louis[.] This being the fore part of June[.] here we lay for Six weeks or two months living on Scant and frquentle no rations allthough game was plenty on the main Shore."[30]

The *Yellow Stone Packet* reached Fort Atkinson on 18 June, carrying forty-three men, including five wounded. It also carried Ashley's letter to Indian agent Benjamin O'Fallon describing the attack. Ashley wrote that he "thought proper to communicate this affair to you . . . believeing that you would feel disposed to make those people account to the government for the outrage committed." Optimistically, he added that "you will oblige me much If you will send me an express (at my expense if one can be procured) that I may meet and cooperate with you." A "six pounder" would be necessary for an eventual confrontation, he noted. During the interlude, he planned to "remain between this place & the Ricaree Towns not remaing any length of time in one place as my force is small[,] not more than twenty three effective men."[31]

In another letter, published in the *Missouri Republican*, Ashley commended the men who had been on shore during the fight: "Never did men in my opinion act with more coolness and bravery than the most of those exposed on the sand beach." He also explained that because of the location of their villages, the Arikaras were a "formadable enemy to traders." They had about six hundred warriors, and "I think about three fourths of them are armed with London Fuzils that carry a ball with great accuracy, and force, and which they use with as much expertness as any men I ever saw handle arms."[32] If the government did not send troops "as high as the mouth of the Yellow Stone, or above that place," he said, "the Americans must abandon the trade in this country."[33]

Meanwhile, Henry hurried downriver upon learning the news, leaving only about twenty men at the Yellowstone post. According to Samuel M. Smith, who accompanied Henry downstream, "the Ricaras came down on the beach" as the boats passed their villages "and invited them, in a friendly manner by signs with Buffaloe Robes to land— Majr Henry knowing the deception they were attempting to practise upon him for the purpose of getting him into their power, proceeded down the river."[34]

At Fort Atkinson, O'Fallon consulted with Colonel Henry Leavenworth, commander of the Sixth Regiment, about an appropriate response to the attack. O'Fallon had reacted emotionally to Ashley's news. "It appears to have been the most shocking outrage to the feelings of humanity ever witnessed by Civilized men—unexampled in the annals of the world," he wrote. Not surprisingly, he believed that immediate military action was necessary to "assist in collecting and burying the broken bones of fourteen, and appeasing the spirits of fifty of our murdered, mangled, and still insulted Countrymen."[35]

Because it would take too long to obtain official orders from Brigadier General Henry Atkinson in Saint Louis, Leavenworth decided to take action on his own initiative. He based the guiding principles of his campaign on orders he had received in 1820 while stationed at Fort Snelling. At that time, Secretary of War John C. Calhoun had asserted that the objects of the government were twofold: to enlarge and protect the fur trade and to secure peace on the frontier. In order to "prevent hostility on the part of the Indians they ought to be fully impressed with our capacity to avenge any injury which they may offer us," Calhoun had said, but "they should be equally impressed with our justice and humanity."[36]

O'Fallon immediately sent word to Ashley that Leavenworth would march upriver with two hundred and thirty officers and men, augmented by forty to fifty men of the Missouri Fur Company under Joshua Pilcher. In contrast to Leavenworth's humanitarian principles, O'Fallon wanted decisive action. "A mere exhibition of soldiers—a mere military display will not be enough—The blood of *A'rickarars* must run from many vital veins or the laudable enterprise of American Citizens is at once arrested."[37]

Before the troops departed, O'Fallon tried to shame the forty-three men who had deserted Ashley into joining the expedition. He asked them how they would explain their actions to others: "Will you tell them that you have left the A'rickaras mangling the bodies and decorating themselves with the reeking sculps of 14 of your Comrads[?]" Leavenworth's soldiers had "but little experience in navigation," O'Fallon said, and he needed skilled boatmen. By volunteering, these men could redeem their "Character, which should be dearer to you than your lives."[38] Despite his emotional plea, only a handful of men rejoined.

The Sixth Regiment left Fort Atkinson on 22 June. Most of the troops marched by land, while Ashley's *Yellow Stone Packet* and two other keelboats hauled their supplies and two six-pounder cannons up the river. Pilcher started later but caught up with Leavenworth by 27 June, bringing Leavenworth's five-and-a-half-inch howitzer and sixty employees of the Missouri Fur Company on two boats. O'Fallon had appointed Pilcher as a subagent, and Pilcher hoped to persuade the Sioux to join the expedition against the Arikaras, their frequent enemies.[39]

Not long after Leavenworth left Fort Atkinson, another express arrived from the upper Missouri, finally delivering the news that on 31 May, Blackfoot Indians had killed Michael Immell, Robert Jones, and five of their men near the Yellowstone River. Other Blackfeet had killed four of Henry's men. The messengers intimated that British traders were "exciting the Indians Against us."[40] A decisive victory against the Arikaras now seemed more necessary than ever.

Not everything was running smoothly for Leavenworth, however. On 3 July, about one hundred fifty miles above Fort Atkinson, one of his boats capsized, drowning a sergeant and six soldiers and spilling muskets, bayonets, and salt pork into the river. Later, a storm damaged another boat. Nevertheless, Leavenworth remained optimistic. "After so many disasters I am happy to inform you that we are yet efficient," he wrote O'Fallon. "Our powder was miraculously preserved. . . . I have borrowed 10 Rifles of Mr. Pilcher and can have 23 more of General Ashley, but 8 only are necessary to complete." Leavenworth stopped for three days at Cedar Fort to refit. Here Pilcher's plan to recruit the Sioux began to pay off, and a band of Yanktons joined the expedition. The force continued upriver toward Ashley's camp on 23 July, and about two hundred Lakotas swelled its numbers a few days later.[41]

At first unaware that Leavenworth had already initiated a campaign against the Arikaras, Ashley and Henry had been making contingency plans. Guessing that there would be no military action before the end of the summer, they descended to the Bad River to buy horses for an overland expedition. They needed to trap that fall if possible, for the number of "furs & peltries" that Henry had brought from the Yellowstone country was small. However, suddenly learning that Leavenworth was approaching, the partners worked to "have thing[s] in readiness to Join him with 80 men." Ashley estimated that Leavenworth might have a total of eight hundred men at his disposal, including the Sioux. These numbers, he thought, would be "sufficient to destroy the greater part of the Aricaras in a verry short time."[42] If they could be defeated quickly enough, he and Henry might still be able to send trapping parties out that fall.

Leavenworth's command reached the trappers' camp near the mouth of the Bad River at the end of July, and the leaders paused to organize the combined "Missouri Legion." Ashley's men formed two companies under the command of captains Jedediah Smith and Hiram Scott. Other men also received positions of leadership, but Hugh Glass was not among them. Pilcher's employees also formed a company, and Pilcher himself served as the major in command of the Sioux auxiliaries. According to Clyman, "after 2 days talk a feast and an Indian dance," the whole force proceeded upstream, and finally they "came near the arrickaree villages[.] again a halt was made arms examined amunition distributed and badges given to our friends the Sioux which consisted of a strip of white muslin bound around the head to distinguish friends from foes."[43]

On 9 August, the Missouri Legion began its final advance on the villages. Leavenworth's primary concern was that the Arikaras might escape before his force could engage them, but when "2 or three miles from the villages," Clyman reported, "the Sioux made a breake[.] being generally mounted they out went us although we ware put to the double Quick." The Arikaras met the Sioux half of a mile outside their villages, and by the time the army arrived, Clyman said, "the plain was covered with Indians which looked more like a swarm [of] bees than a battle field." The Arikaras withdrew into their towns as soon as they spotted the soldiers, but already, there were "quite a number of dead Indians streued over the plain." One Sioux chief approached the body of a fallen opponent and "brought one of his wives up with a war club who struck the corps a number of blow with [the] club he tantalizeing the Rees all the time for the cowardice" in allowing his wife to strike their men within gunshot of the village. Another Sioux, who "blonged to the grizzle Bear medicine" approached "the body of a dead Ree in the attitude of a grizzly Bear snorting and [mimicking] the bear in all his most vicious attitudes and with this teeth tore out mouth fulls of flesh from the breast of the dead body of the Ree."[44]

Preparing to attack, Leavenworth placed Ashley and his two companies against the river on the extreme right, a company of army riflemen under Captain Bennet Riley on the extreme left, and his five companies of the Sixth Regiment plus a light infantry company in the middle. Leavenworth advanced within three or four hundred yards of the villages and halted to await the artillery. Unfortunately, the boats, struggling against adverse winds, arrived with the cannons too late to launch an attack that day, and Leavenworth postponed the assault until morning.[45]

On the morning of 10 August, the artillery opened fire. The first shot killed the "celebrated and mischievous Chief called Grey Eyes," reported Leavenworth, "and the second cut away the staff of their Medicine flag." However, much of the cannonading seemed ineffectual. Leavenworth next marched the infantry to within three hundred yards of the village and fired a volley. Wanting to test the Indian positions before ordering a full assault, he asked Ashley to engage the lower, smaller village. Finding a ravine close to that village, Ashley's men "maintained a spirited action . . . well calculated to assist us in our design upon the upper town, by making a diversion in our favor."[46]

Several factors prevented Leavenworth from launching an immediate full-scale attack. In particular, he was uncertain of the cooperation of his Sioux allies, as they seemed mostly interested in looting the cornfields. He also heard rumors that some of them had been negotiating with the Arikaras. Thus, he decided to "make arrangements to prevent the enemy from escaping during the night and the next day to gain possession of the towns."[47] Leavenworth notified the Sioux before he withdrew temporarily from his positions near the upper village because he reasoned that the Arikaras might kill any stragglers remaining in the cornfields.

In the meantime, Leavenworth observed a Sioux and an Arikara parleying in front of the villages, and he went to join them. In their conversation, the Indian told him "that we had killed the man who had done all the mischief. . . . He wished we would permit the Chiefs to come out and speak to us and make peace . . . for we had killed a great many of their people and of their horses." Leavenworth sent word to the Arikaras "that if they were sincerely disposed for peace, I should expect to see the Chiefs come out immediately."[48]

Soon, about a dozen Arikaras arrived, and negotiations began. "I told them that they must make up the losses of Genl. Ashley and behave well in future," said Leavenworth, "and to make me certain that they would do so, they must give me five of their principal men as security or hostages." The Arikaras "replied that they would restore every thing they could." However, lowering expectations, they said that the Sioux had taken many of their horses and that others had been killed in the fight. They would, however, "return all the guns they could find and the articles of property which they received from Genl. Ashley. Even to the hats."[49]

Leavenworth agreed to this limited restoration of Ashley's property. "I thought proper to accept the terms," he said, after "considering my small force—the strange and unaccountable conduct of the Sioux and even the great probability of their joining the Aricaras against us. And also considering the importance of saving to our Country the expense and trouble of a long Indian war fare." Most of the fur men in the expedition disagreed. Indeed, when the pipe was passed for each participant to smoke, Joshua Pilcher declined and "walked back and forth with much agitation."[50] When the negotiations ended, Leavenworth's party, including the five Arikara hostages, started walking back to camp. However, Pilcher's attitude alarmed the hostages, who had been told that he was the most important figure among the whites, and they refused to continue. As the agreement unraveled, Pilcher told John Gale, an army surgeon, that the Arikaras might "seize the Colonel and drag him away," and Gale and two Missouri Fur Company men fired their weapons.[51] Fortunately, no one was hurt in the ensuing exchange, and the Arikaras returned safely to their villages.

In an effort to decrease tensions the next day, Leavenworth and the Arikara chief Little Soldier decided that a couple of officers should visit the village. Doctor Gale and Lieutenant William W. Morris volunteered; they reported being treated "with much hospitality" and said that the warriors "appeared very melancholy," having "just finished burying their dead."[52] Later, Major Abram R. Woolley also visited the villages, and he likewise concluded that the Arikaras "were acting with good faith," having been "severely flogged and humbled."[53]

Leavenworth decided to draft a treaty and asked Pilcher to assist him; Pilcher refused. Leavenworth then asked Henry, who had also been appointed a special subagent by O'Fallon, but Henry "politely replied that it was a matter in which he felt himself wholly incompetent to act as his powers were for a special purpose." As a result, Leavenworth wrote the treaty himself. His terms were the same ones he had presented the previous day; the Arikaras were to "restore to General Ashley as far as possible the articles of property taken and not in future obstruct the navigation of the river but treat the Americans as friends wherever they might meet them."[54]

Leavenworth, Ashley, and five military officers signed the treaty on behalf of the United States, and Little Soldier and nine other chiefs signed for the Arikaras. Although Pilcher complained that none of the principal chiefs signed, Leavenworth affirmed that every chief or principal man had signed the treaty "except one who had always been considered as the first soldier of the late Chief Grey Eyes and who was now considered no better than a dog in their villages."[55] He was referring to Elk Tongue, who would later play a prominent role in another encounter with Hugh Glass.

The moment now arrived for the Arikaras to restore Ashley's goods, but they brought only "three rifles, one horse and sixteen buffaloe robes and said that it was all they could do for him." Leavenworth declared that "it was not enough" and said that if they did not "remunerate Genl. Ashley" sufficiently, "we should again attack them."[56] He was certain that their failure to comply stemmed from Pilcher's threatening behavior. The Arikaras feared that they would need their horses to escape and their guns to fight if the soldiers attacked again. Indeed, Edward Rose, the interpreter, informed Leavenworth that "their women were packing up evidently for the purpose of going off."[57]

Once again, Little Soldier visited Leavenworth and was so "agitated and exhausted," Leavenworth wrote, that he "fainted almost as soon as he entered my cabin." After Doctor Gale "restored him," Little Soldier told the colonel that it was not possible to do anything more, for "the Sioux had carried away many of their horses and the rest we had killed." Moreover, the people of the upper village blamed those of the lower village for the conflict, and they were unwilling to "give up their horses to pay for the mischief which the Chief Grey Eyes of the lower village had done."[58]

Most of the officers and men favored an immediate attack, putting Leavenworth in a disagreeable situation. "It appeared to me that my reputation and the honor and brilliancy of the expedition required that I should gratify my troops and make a charge," he said, "but I also thought that sound policy and the interest of my Country required that I should not." He had too few soldiers and was short of provisions and artillery shot. "If we succeeded in our charge, all that we could expect was to drive the Indians from their villages and perhaps kill a few more of them," he observed. Worse, those not killed would be left "in a confirmed state of hostility to every white man." Leavenworth was convinced that the Arikaras "would behave well in future, if we left them undisturbed in their villages" and that Ashley could now "proceed without molestation, to the mouth of the Yellow Stone." For Leavenworth, the key question was whether the Indians had been "sufficiently humbled and taught to fear and respect us. On me lay the responsibility of decision."[59] He finally ordered the troops dismissed. The Sioux allies had already departed, taking six government mules and six or seven of Ashley's horses with them.

"The night was Quiet," recalled Clyman, very different from "the two previous" when they had heard the wailing of women and children and "the Screams and yelling of men the fireing of guns the awful howling of dogs the neighing and braying of hosses and mules . . . all intermingled with the stench of dead men and horses." Clyman soon learned why it was now less noisy, "the Rees having dserted thair village early in the night."[60] Leavenworth hurriedly sent Toussaint Charbonneau with a message asking the Arikaras to return: "your Villages are in my possession. Come back and take them in peace and you will find evry thing as you left them, you shall not be hurt if you do not obstruct the road or molest the Traders—If you do not come back there are some bad men and bad Indians who will burn your Villages."[61] Unfortunately, Charbonneau was unable to overtake them.

The campaign against the Arikaras was over, and four days later, Leavenworth and his command began their return to Fort Atkinson. The campaign had pitted about eleven hundred troops, trappers, and auxiliary Sioux warriors against six to eight hundred Arikara warriors. Two soldiers had been slightly wounded, and the campaign cost about two thousand dollars. Estimates on the number of Arikaras killed vary between thirty and fifty. Both the army and the traders probably underestimated the damage that they had inflicted; in addition to these casualties, the Arikaras lost much of their corn and many of their horses, and it would take years for them to recover.[62]

According to Clyman, the Missouri Legion remained "one night more in our stinking disagreeable camp when we loosed cable and droped down stream." Four men were left behind, "and in an hour after we left a great smoke arose and the acursd village was known to be on fire." Because Leavenworth "had given special orders that the village be left unmolested," he stopped the boats and conducted a roll call "to assertain who if any ware missing[.] the sargent called over the roles rapidly and reported all present[.] then [the inference was that] it must be Souix."[63]

Actually, two Missouri Fur Company officers, Angus Mac-Donald and William Gordon, were responsible. Not surprisingly, Leavenworth blamed Pilcher, who had openly opposed his decisions. "It is impossible for me to suppose that those men took that measure without consulting their Agent and obtaining his approbation and consent," Leavenworth wrote.[64] When he dismissed the Missouri Legion, Leavenworth gave Pilcher and other Missouri Fur Company officers dishonorable discharges, and he condemned Pilcher's behavior in his official report. Pilcher, on the other hand, blamed Leavenworth for poor decision-making and went on the attack after they returned. "You came to restore peace and tranquility to the country, & leave an impression which would insure its continuance," he wrote. However, "your operations have been such as to produce the contrary effect, and to impress the Indian tribes, with the greatest possible contempt for the American character." Thus, Pilcher concluded, "you have by the imbecility of your conduct and operations, created and left impassible barriers."[65]

Most fur-trade historians have sided with Pilcher. Hiram Martin Chittenden, for example, concluded that Leavenworth was "vacillating and ineffectual, and apparently governed by such an undue estimate of the obstacles in his way, and such a dread of incurring any loss, that he disgusted the

Indian allies . . . and excited the contempt and amazement of the trappers and mountaineers." Chittenden believed that an assault on the villages would have been successful and that Leavenworth should have attempted it. "Why had he come this great distance," Chittenden asked, "if it was not to inflict summary punishment upon these people?"[66]

South Dakota historian Doane Robinson, on the other hand, asserted that Leavenworth "accomplished everything which the expedition set out to accomplish." In Robinson's view, Leavenworth's greatest mistake "was his failure to visit upon Pilcher the highest and most exemplary punishment within his military power."[67] Will G. Robinson, who succeeded his father as state historian, later proposed a historical marker at the site of the Leavenworth battle with the words, "Here on August 10th, 1823 Col. Henry Leavenworth after a 637 mile battle with a flooded river, killed Grey Eyes, broke the power of the Aricara and humanely minimized bloodshed."[68]

Paul Wilhelm, Duke of Württemberg, who traveled up the Missouri River in 1823 on a scientific enterprise, agreed with the Robinsons. Having met both Pilcher and Leavenworth, and carefully weighing their arguments, he concluded that Leavenworth "could have caused a great carnage among the Arikaras," in which "many women and children would have perished, or would have been the prey to the cruelty of the auxiliary Indian tribes." He condemned fur traders in general for their unpardonable behavior. From his experience, "most of the aborigines deport themselves with more poise and decency in their social life than the descendants of many white Europeans, who live near the Indians, and whose crudeness often exceeds the bounds of decorum. Yet, in their self-satisfaction and conceit these whites apply the name of barbarian to their more sensible and unspoiled Indian neighbors."[69]

Indeed, the duke may have exposed the crux of the problem between the traders and the Arikaras. To a large degree, their conflict was rooted in cultural misunderstandings. Some earlier travelers found the Arikaras to be among the friendliest nations along the Missouri. Jean-Baptiste Truteau, a trader who spent the winter of 1794–1795 with them, concluded that among "the Indian nations living East and West of the Mississippi as well as those living on the Lower Missouri, I have found none who approach these in gentleness and kindness towards us." Although some traders claimed that the Arikaras were "thieves, slanderers, liars, cheats, and capable of all sorts of wickedness," Truteau asserted that these same traders were materialistic, selfish, and deceitful and that their "bad conduct" was the source of the conflict.[70]

One difficulty was that the Arikaras did not understand or accept capitalism. "It is a principle with them," wrote the French trader Pierre-Antoine Tabeau, "that he who has divides with him who has not." Thus, when he displayed his trade goods at their village, one Arikara told him: "You are foolish. . . . Why do you wish to make all this powder and these balls since you do not hunt? Of what use are all these knives to you? Is not one enough with which to cut the meat? It is only your wicked heart that prevents you from giving them to us. Do you not see that the village has none?" Had Tabeau needed a robe, the Indian added, he would have given him one, but he obviously had more robes than he needed. "All the logic and all the rhetoric in the world are thrown away against these arguments," Tabeau concluded.[71]

Lewis and Clark stopped at the Arikara villages in October 1804, and Clark described the people as "tall Stout men corsily featured, their womin Small & industerous. . . . They are Dirty, Kind, pore, & extravegent; possessing natural pride, no begers, rcive what is given them with pleasure." Clark was surprised at the great number of muskets the Arikaras owned, evidence of significant trading, and was impressed by their dislike of alcohol. However, a clash of values soon became apparent. The captains decided that one of their men, John Newman, deserved flogging for "re-peated expressions of a highly criminal and mutinous na-ture." This action "allarmd the Indian Chief verry much," said Clark, and "he Cried aloud." After the captains ex-plained the reason for the punishment, the chief responded that "he thought examples were also necessary, & he him-self had made them by Death, [but] his nation never whiped even their Children, from their burth."[72]

Considerable misunderstanding also resulted from sex-ual practices. "The Ricaras, have a custom Similar to the Sioux in maney instances," Clark observed; "they think they cannot Show a Sufficient acknowledgement without [giving] to their guest handsom Squars [women] and think they are despised if they are not recved."[73] The same behav-ior had bothered the otherwise sympathetic trader Truteau, who thought that Arikara men were "indifferent as to their women" because "husbands, fathers and brothers, are im-portunate with the white men who visit them, to make free with their wives, daughters and sisters." As a result, both girls and married women "are so loose in their conduct, that they seem to be a sort of common stock; and are so easy and accessible that there are few among them whose favours cannot be bought with a little vermillion or blue ribbon."[74]

Although European Americans repeatedly decried this custom, they seldom condemned their men for accepting sexual favors or pondered how their own behavior might appear to the Arikaras. Indeed, Henry M. Brackenridge, who visited the Arikaras in 1811, was surprised when an Indian asked him "whether you white people have any women amongst you." He assured him that they did. "Then why is it," the Indian asked, "that your people are so fond of our women, one might suppose they had never seen any before?"[75]

Tabeau considered Arikara men to be "idle barbarians" who exploited their wives. Arikara women, he said, were "re-duced to the most humiliating slavery by tyrants, who enjoy all the fruits of [their] labors." These women were "loaded with all the work," including the farming, "without which the men would probably not be able to live; because of their sloth and laziness."[76] Tabeau did not appreciate the division of labor in Arikara society, in which women farmed, handled food, and maintained the lodges, while the men were in charge of warfare and hunting. Because traders like Tabeau resided in the villages, they only observed certain aspects of Arikara life.[77]

Indeed, the lifestyle of the Arikaras was far more complex than European American visitors assumed. A Caddoan-speaking people, the Arikaras were closely related to the Pawnees in Nebraska. Agriculture was central to their life. They raised corn, beans, squash, and sunflowers in fields adjacent to rivers. Of these crops, corn, or maize, was most important. Most of it was dried and stored in large caches, or storage pits, in the ground. Usually, there was more than enough to meet the needs of the people, and the Arikaras traded the surplus to other tribes. However, about half their diet was meat, and hunting, especially of bison, was important. The Arikaras also fished, building traps with willow.[78]

Because of their dependence on agriculture, the Arikaras lived in semi-permanent villages of earth lodges near their fields, rather than leading a completely nomadic life like the Sioux. These lodges were thirty to sixty feet in diameter, built with posts and a sod overlay with a smoke hole located above the central fireplace. The Arikaras were not alone in this lifestyle; the Mandans, Hidatsas, Omahas, and Poncas, for example, also lived in earth lodges along the Missouri River.[79]

Despite living in adjoining villages, the Arikaras never developed a centralized political structure. Indeed, European Americans found their diffuse leadership confusing, as the experience of the Leavenworth expedition had shown. Arikara warfare customs also differed markedly from those practiced by whites. Instead of massive armies of warriors striving for a decisive victory against another tribe, small war parties raided neighboring peoples, hoping to kill unsuspecting enemies with little or no loss of life on their own side. Indeed, a warrior who lost too many men might never rise to a leadership position.[80]

Most visiting trappers also failed to notice the Arikaras' deeply spiritual way of life. A medicine lodge stood prominently in each village. Mother Corn was central to their religious culture, and the most important religious ceremony was a three-day vernal festival blessing the corn crop. Indeed, the Arikaras believed that they had brought the knowledge of corn to the Great Plains. Despite this, visitors such as Tabeau considered the Arikaras to be "incapable of reasoning, too limited to formulate principles and to draw inferences from them so as to develop a belief," and to "have no religion that is fixed or established." Although they spoke of a "master of life," the concept was "so vague," Tabeau claimed, that in his opinion, their gods were essentially "the sun, the moon, Venus, and the thunder."[81]

The traders' biased observations obscure the Arikaras' important role in the economic history of the region. Like their neighbors the Mandans and Hidatsas, the Arikaras were pivotal players in trade on the Northern Great Plains and beyond. Archaeological excavations of the village sites of these peoples have yielded obsidian from the Yellowstone region, shells from the Gulf of Mexico, and copper from the Great Lakes. Indeed, their role in regional commerce gave these tribes a strong incentive to prevent fur companies from trading with other tribes farther up the river. When the Arikaras and their neighbors obtained goods from traders, they could swap them for merchandise from those more remote tribes. If European American merchants traded directly with those peoples, on the other hand, then the Arikaras and their neighbors would lose their strategic economic role. Moreover, if the tribes upriver obtained guns, they could become a military threat to the Arikaras.[82]

There were other causes for tension with traders. The Arikaras recognized that their entire way of life was changing; long before Ashley arrived at their villages, they felt the impact of European American culture. Horses from Spanish domains and guns from English and French sources had been traded from tribe to tribe, transforming life on the plains. Later, iron hoes replaced buffalo scapula hoes, metal pots displaced homemade earthenware, and iron arrow points ended the use of flint. Slowly, the Arikaras realized that they were becoming dependent on goods provided by traders.[83]

Worse, new diseases arrived, and because of their long isolation from other continents, the Indians had little resistance to them. The deadliest was smallpox. According to Tabeau, the Arikaras had once occupied thirty-two villages, but by the time he arrived, smallpox had reduced their numbers so severely that only two villages remained. Epidemics appear to have struck the Arikaras, Mandans, and Hidatsas in approximately eighteen- to twenty-year cycles. One scholar concluded that the first epidemic probably occurred in the 1740s, shortly after the visit of Verendrye, and that others struck in the 1760s and early 1780s.[84]

This severe reduction in numbers made it difficult for the Arikaras to defend themselves. The Sioux, who had adopted an almost completely nomadic style of life thanks to the horse and the gun, were beginning to dominate the region. According to Truteau, "the Sioux nations are feared and dreaded . . . on account of the fire arms with which they are always well provided; their very name causes terror, they having so often ravaged and carried off the wives and children of the Ricaras."[85] Tabeau claimed that the Sioux considered the Arikaras as a "kind of serf, who cultivates for them and who, as they say, takes, for them, the place of women."[86] Still, in 1823, the Arikaras were a formidable foe for a small party of trappers.

Before Ashley and Henry arrived in 1822 and 1823, other incidents had led traders to believe that the Arikaras were more bellicose than their neighbors. Lewis and Clark had encouraged American Indian leaders to visit Washington, and an Arikara chief agreed to go. He died during the trip, raising suspicions among his people. A Mandan chief named Big White, on the other hand, completed the trip, but when it was time for him to return to his village, the Arikaras and Mandans were at war, and the Arikaras forcibly prevented Ensign Nathaniel Pryor and his small force from escorting him home. Another incident was the encounter recounted by Clyman, in which traders killed two Arikaras who were pursuing an escaped Sioux captive. This incident may have precipitated the Arikara attack on Ashley's party.[87]

Similarly, the conflict of 1823 reinforced the perception of Arikara hostility for years to come. A decade later, trader Francis Chardon still referred to the Arikaras as "the Horrid Tribe."[88] As the steamboat carrying Prince Maximilian of Wied neared the Arikara villages in 1833, the travelers loaded their weapons because they expected trouble. Fortunately, Maximilian reported, the villages had been temporarily abandoned.[89]

In the long run, however, the Arikaras' reputation for being troublesome was overinflated. According to historian Roy Meyer, "the events of the summer of 1823 are important . . . because, except for the Arikara attack on Ensign Pryor in 1807, this was the only time in history that any of the Three Tribes [Mandan, Hidatsa, and Arikara] fought in open warfare against the United States. The Mandans and Hidatsas were pretty consistently friendly to the whites, and the Arikaras, though they continued to enjoy an unsavory reputation for some years, never again demonstrated their hostility in such vigorous form."[90] Although the Arikaras eventually rebuilt their villages and were involved in minor skirmishes with trappers, the 1823 conflict was the only time they seriously interfered with river traffic. In fact, in ensuing decades, Arikara warriors served as scouts with the United States Army in its wars against the Sioux.

In 1823, however, trappers like Hugh Glass considered the Arikaras to be treacherous savages. It is unlikely that he or his companions reflected on their own ethnocentrism, as Truteau had in 1795: "Certain it is that if these people whom we call barbarians and savages knew the disposition of the White Men," especially "their lack of charity for one another; . . . the vile and contemptible deeds done by them for the sake of money, the worries and torments of body and mind imposed upon them by the sword, the gown and the counting house; if they knew . . . the frauds, the crimes . . . which [whites] practice . . . in order to satisfy their ambition and to accumulate riches, they might justly apply to us the designation of savages and barbarians which we have given to them."[91] Within a year, Hugh Glass would encounter the Arikaras again with no greater humility and with similarly mixed results.

James Hall wrote the first published account of Hugh Glass's life, drawing on an informant who claimed to have heard the story from Glass himself. University of Minnesota Press

Philip St. George Cooke argued that superior qualities, and not merely good luck, enabled Glass to survive. Harper's Weekly, 12 June 1858

The "Jim Bridges" that writer Edmund Flagg identified as one of Glass's deserters was likely James Bridger, who later became a renowned frontiersman in his own right. Denver Public Library

Of the four most significant early chroniclers of Glass's life,
only George Yount claimed to have met his subject personally.
University of South Carolina Digital Library

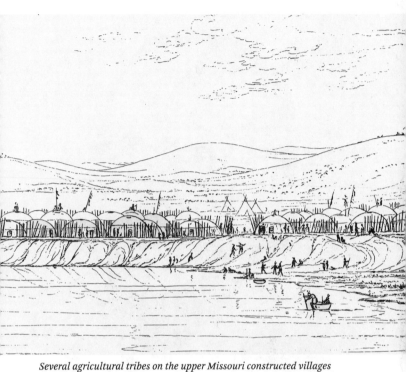

Several agricultural tribes on the upper Missouri constructed villages of circular houses. George Catlin sketched this Arikara village on the west bank of the river. Catlin, Letters and Notes on the Manners, Customs, and Condition of the North American Indians

Trapper James Clyman recorded many of the day-to-day activities of the 1823 Ashley-Henry expedition. Library of Congress

This letter informing John S. Gardner's parents of his death in the Arikara War is the only example of Glass's writing known to exist.
South Dakota State Historical Society

Popular western publications frequently featured fanciful illustrations of Glass's encounter with the bear, such as this one from 1938. Federal Writers' Project, *A South Dakota Guide*

Bestselling novelist Frederick Manfred tried to gain firsthand experience of Glass's adventures. Here, he crawls through the Black Hills dressed as a fur trapper. *South Dakota Review*

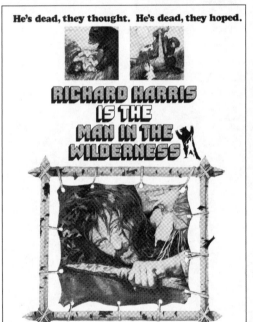

Warner Brothers distributed this poster advertising Man in the Wilderness *as part of its pressbook for the 1971 film.* James D. McLaird collection

A FILM BY *ALEJANDRO G. IÑÁRRITU*

LEONARDO DiCAPRIO TOM HARDY

BLOOD LOST. LIFE FOUND.

THE REVENANT

INSPIRED BY TRUE EVENTS

MICHAEL PUNKE SCREENPLAY MARK L. SMITH & ALEJANDRO G. IÑÁRRITU
DIRECTED ALEJANDRO G. IÑÁRRITU **JANUARY 8**

Bringing even greater recognition to the legend, Leonardo DiCaprio won the Academy Award for best actor for his portrayal of Hugh Glass in the 2015 film The Revenant. *James D. McLaird collection*

Based outside of Lemmon, South Dakota, scrap-iron sculptor John Lopez created an artistic rendition of the bear attack.
John Lopez Studio

Members of the 1874 Black Hills expedition pose with the grizzly bear they killed: from left to right are Arikara scout Bloody Knife, expedition commander Lieutenant Colonel George Armstrong Custer, Private John Noonan, and Captain William Ludlow. Photograph by William H. Illingworth. South Dakota State Historical Society

Arikara men donned grizzly bear skins to perform this bear-clan ceremony outside of Nishu, North Dakota, in 1930. State Historical Society of North Dakota

5

Life of a Trapper
1823–1833

On 15 August 1823, after the battle with the Arikaras, Ashley and Henry followed Colonel Leavenworth down the Missouri. Ashley had stored his goods at Fort Kiowa, and because the fight with the Arikaras had ended sufficiently early, he and Henry intended to send out trapping parties yet that fall. Henry left with the first party about 1 September, planning to return to his Yellowstone post, and Hugh Glass went with him. Ashley headed back to Saint Louis to arrange next spring's expedition, while Jedediah Smith, his trusted lieutenant, led another band of trappers westward from Fort Kiowa toward the Rocky Mountains. James Clyman, who accompanied Smith's group, compiled a day-to-day journal of their journey.[1]

Unfortunately, no diarist recorded Henry's movements, and it is impossible to know his exact route or the names of all those who traveled with him; even the number of men in the company is uncertain. Clyman thought that the party comprised thirteen men, whereas Daniel Potts, who had remained at the Yellowstone post during the Arikara campaign, recalled about thirty men returning in the fall of 1823. The group probably included, among others, John Fitzgerald, James Bridger, Hiram Allen, Moses ("Black") Harris, George Harris, August Néll, James Anderson, Milton Sublette, Johnson Gardner, and Hugh Glass.[2]

Despite the lack of firsthand documentation, however, Henry's progress can be reconstructed to some extent. After reaching the mouth of the Grand River a few miles south of the now deserted Arikara villages, his party began marching westward. It was during this journey, probably about 20

September, that the grizzly bear attacked Glass. Although both Potts and Clyman mentioned the mauling in their jottings, their information was secondhand and offered little detail. Sadly, no other contemporary sources document the encounter or the subsequent events that became part of the Glass legend. The question remains, then, whether the stories by James Hall, Philip St. George Cooke, Edmund Flagg, and George Yount are relatively accurate or creative tales based on a germ of truth.

Henry's party apparently traveled on foot, having acquired only a handful of horses, which they needed to haul supplies. In the aftermath of the conflict with the Arikaras, the men had to be on constant guard. They were reminded of the dangers when Indians killed two men, wounded two more, and stole two horses a few days after the party left the Missouri River. Potts, who learned of the attack after the men arrived at the Yellowstone, said that they were "fired on by the Mandanes and Groonvants [Gros Ventres] in the dead hour of the night"; the trappers returned fire, killing at least one of the Indians.[3] It was surprising that the Mandans attacked, having previously been among the friendliest nations along the Missouri.

Another document corroborates Potts's story. Later that fall, Henry dispatched three messengers, including Moses ("Black") Harris, to Fort Atkinson with messages for Ashley. They arrived at the fort on 18 December, and Colonel Leavenworth relayed Harris's news to Major General Alexander Macomb. Leavenworth's letter confirmed that the Mandans killed James Anderson and the Frenchman August Néll, wounded two others, and took two horses when they attacked Henry's party as it made its way to the Yellowstone post.[4]

Harris told Leavenworth that he and his two companions had later stopped at the villages of the Gros Ventres and Mandans on their way to Fort Atkinson. Although they "were treated in a very friendly manner," William P. Tilton, who operated a trading post there, informed them that among their hosts was the "War party of the Mandans who had fired upon Major Henry's party." Indeed, Harris spotted one of the Indians who was wounded in the fight, as well as "one of the horses which the Indians took from the Party." Harris also talked with four Arikara chiefs at the Mandan villages; they declared they were now "anxious to preserve peace with the whites, and to have traders come amongst them." However, Harris doubted the chiefs could "controul their young men, in consequence of their Towns having been burned by McDonald & Gordon." He also learned that the Arikaras "had purchased a dirt Village of the Mandans . . . about one mile below the Mandan Towns."[5]

Harris also filled Leavenworth in on Henry's activities after he and his party had arrived at the Yellowstone post. Henry learned that Blackfoot or Assiniboine Indians had stolen twenty-two or twenty-three horses during his absence, and they took seven more shortly afterward. Indians "frequently visited the Establishment of Major Henry at the mouth of Yellow Stone," Harris explained, and generally "behaved very well." However, "they would steal the horses whenever they could." Ominously, the Crow Indians had told them that "Blackfoot Indians were determined to hunt Continually for the trapping parties and destroy them, whenever it was possible to do so."[6] Faced with this prospect, Henry abandoned his post and moved his operations to the mouth of the Powder River.

Unfortunately, Harris did not mention Glass, or if he did, Leavenworth did not repeat his account. This circumstance is all the more surprising because one of Harris's two companions was John S. Fitzgerald, likely the same Fitzgerald whom Philip St. George Cooke identified as the older of Glass's two deserters. Historian Dale Morgan discovered that Fitzgerald enlisted in Company I of the Sixth Regiment on 19 April 1824, which comports with James Hall's claim that this man joined the army. The other messenger who accompanied Moses Harris was also named Harris; Morgan tentatively identifies him as George Harris, the man who in Edmund Flagg's account also disobeyed orders and went ahead of Henry's party with Hugh Glass to gather berries. If these identifications are correct, then both of Moses Harris's fellow messengers would have had all too much reason to remember Glass's savage encounter with the bear, and, perhaps, plenty of reason not to talk about it.[7]

Fitzgerald and George Harris are not the only individuals mentioned in early versions of the Glass story who also appear in contemporary documents. Hall and Cooke both claimed that the mauling occurred when Glass was sent ahead of the party to secure game, but George Yount, like Flagg, asserted that Glass encountered the bear when he wandered off against orders. In Yount's account, Hiram Allen was one of the party's designated hunters, and Leavenworth noted that Ashley selected one Hiram Allen as one of his lieutenants before the attack on the Arikara towns. If Allen was responsible enough to be an officer, Henry might well have chosen him to be the party's hunter later.[8]

Several other details in the early accounts of the Glass story also find corroboration in contemporary documents. For example, early writers claimed that after the mauling, Glass somehow traveled to Fort Kiowa and then joined a party of traders headed to the Mandan villages; in Cooke's account, a man named Longevan was their leader. Indeed, Joseph Brazeau, resident trader at Fort Kiowa, did send a party upriver around 11 October. These men were evidently associated with the French Company, and their leader, Antoine Citoleux, was nicknamed Langevin. Documents suggest that the party comprised six or seven men including Toussaint Charbonneau, formerly an interpreter for the Lewis and Clark expedition. It probably took them about six weeks to work their way upriver against the current. They were also worried about the Arikaras; on 15 October, Citoleux stopped fifteen miles south of the Bad River to write his will.[9]

Charbonneau left the party before it reached the Mandans, believing that it was safer to travel overland. He told Citoleux that he would meet them at Tilton's Fort, located near the Mandan villages. However, Citoleux never reached the fort; at some point after Charbonneau's departure, the Arikaras killed the entire party. Contemporary documents identify no other survivors besides Charbonneau, but intriguingly, Hall, Cooke, Flagg, and Yount do not mention Charbonneau and instead place Glass with this relatively obscure party. It seems likely that some frontier storyteller before Hall—maybe even Glass himself—simply substituted Glass's name for Charbonneau's, providing him another miraculous survival story. Despite the lack of contemporary evidence that Glass was with the Citoleux party, the early writers provided detailed renditions of his escape from the Arikaras, claiming that he was rescued just in the nick of time by Mandan Indians. In Cooke's version, Glass even fights an Arikara scout hand-to-hand before his rescue. Biographer John Myers Myers noticed that Cooke's story bears a suspicious resemblance to a combat in Walter Scott's popular 1810 poem *The Lady of the Lake*.[10]

Clearly, Glass reached Henry's new post at the mouth of the Bighorn River that winter, although no firsthand witnesses recorded the event. In February, Henry once again asked for messengers to carry dispatches to Fort Atkinson, and this time Glass was among them. Early writers surmise that he may have made the trip in order to confront Fitzgerald, who had gone there a few months before. According to James Hall, Glass left Henry's Fort on 29 February 1824 with four other men, whose names the *St. Louis Enquirer* later gave as Marsh, Chapman, More, and Dutton; George Yount later claimed that Lewis Dutton provided him a personal account of the trip. Instead of descending the Yellowstone, the men went up the Powder River, crossed to the Platte, and then constructed bullboats to float down to Fort Atkinson. Bullboats, made from buffalo hides stretched across willow branches, were round and difficult to steer but easy to construct and able to carry heavy loads in shallow water.[11]

Unfortunately, while descending the Platte, Glass and his companions once again encountered Arikara Indians. Chapman and More were killed, while Dutton and Marsh managed to elude their antagonists and made their way to Fort Atkinson. Not having seen Glass since the attack, they assumed that he had also been killed. Trader Louis Vasquez reported this version of events to the *St. Louis Enquirer*, which printed it along with the news that Henry had built a fort at the mouth of the Bighorn River, that a party led by Jedediah Smith had crossed the mountains, and that a "white bear" had killed trapper Holley Wheeler.[12]

Soon, however, the true outcome of Glass's encounter with the Arikaras became known. On 9 July 1824, Benjamin O'Fallon wrote William Clark that the Arikaras "recently killed two of a party of five of Ashlys & Henrys men near the black hills on the head waters of the north fork of the River Platte—the other three narrowly escaped with the loss of every thing except their lives."[13] Glass had survived. The manner of his return to Fort Atkinson is a matter of conjecture. Most writers suggest that he traveled first to Fort Kiowa, then down the Missouri. Flagg, on the other hand, claims that some hunters found Glass three hundred miles from Fort Atkinson and hauled the exhausted trapper the rest of the way. Yount suggests that Glass and Dutton traveled together to the fort, which is surprising. Yount purportedly received this information from Dutton himself, yet it contradicts Vasquez's contemporary report to the *St. Louis Enquirer*.[14]

If the various accounts are true, Glass had now escaped death four times during his year on the upper Missouri: he was wounded in the Arikaras' defeat of the Ashley party, mauled by a grizzly bear, attacked again on his way to Tilton's Fort with Citoleux, and attacked once more as he descended the Platte River. Extraordinary as these escapes may seem, they are not so surprising, considering that other trappers were enduring similarly harrowing adventures. For example, at nearly the same time that Glass was mauled, another grizzly bear wounded Jedediah Smith as he led his party of trappers westward. Smith met the bear as the men were hiking through a brushy valley in the Black Hills. His scalp was badly ripped and one ear was nearly torn off. "I got a pair of scissors and cut off his hair," wrote Clyman, who dressed Smith's wounds, and found that "the bear had taken nearly all of his head in his capcious mouth . . . and laid the skull bare to near the crown of the head leaving a white streak whare his teeth passed." Clyman stitched the wounds and his ear "through and through and over and over laying the lacerated parts togather as nice as I could with my hands." Fortunately, Smith was able to ride, and in about a mile they found water and "pitched a tent the onley one we had and made him as comfortable as circumtances would permit[.] this gave us a lisson on the charcter of the grissly Baare which we did not forget."[15]

A few months later, Clyman himself had a brush with danger. After spending the winter with the Crow Indians, Smith's party traveled to the Green River in present-Day Wyoming, where they divided into two groups. Clyman and Thomas Fitzpatrick then followed the Sweetwater River downstream to determine whether it was navigable. The two trappers then split up, planning to reconnect later with Smith's party, but when Clyman subsequently missed the rendezvous, he decided to head toward the Missouri River alone. Along the way, he saw some Arikaras chasing buffalo; "by axident I escaped them," he said. However, Clyman had another close call. Deciding that it "would be plesent to communicate with humans even though it were Indians," he stopped at a Pawnee village, where one man invited him to stay the night in his lodge. Before Clyman left the next day, his host cut off his long hair with a dull butcher knife, saying that he had saved Clyman's life by taking him in and he "wanted the hair for a memento." Other villagers robbed him, however, taking his blankets, ammunition, and flint. Now unable to hunt game, Clyman only managed to get meat by clubbing a couple of badgers to death. Exhausted, he continued walking across the prairie, until one day he raised his head and "with great surprise" saw the American flag flying over Fort Atkinson. "I swoned emmediately," he said, adding, "certainly no man ever enjoyed the sight of our flag better than I did."[16] Ten days later, Fitzpatrick and two companions arrived at the fort in even worse condition.

Their difficult experience was not without benefit to their employer. After arriving at Fort Atkinson, Fitzpatrick notified Ashley of a major discovery that Smith's party had made in March 1824. Smith and his men had wandered through South Pass, a land route through the mountains passable for wagons. Fitzpatrick also described the country as rich in beaver. Ashley could now haul supplies from Saint Louis to the mountains overland via the Platte River valley, avoiding Arikara and Blackfoot territory. It was a turning point in the fur trade.[17]

Glass, however, did not rejoin Ashley's company. Instead, he decided on a change of venue. "One would suppose, that the hardships undergone by Glass would have effectually taken from him all desire, ever again to try his fortunes in the wilderness," wrote Edmund Flagg. However, "no sooner had he regained his ordinary health and energy, than with them returned his wild—almost insane attachment to savage life. A trading party was formed to go to Santa Fe, and with it went Glass."[18] It was not an unusual decision. From the moment American merchants arrived in Saint Louis, they had attempted to open trade with the Southwest. Fearing that American incursions might lead to economic and perhaps even territorial losses, however, the Spanish authorities restricted trading activity. Some Americans had their goods confiscated, others were jailed, and a few were sent back under armed guard. The situation changed in the 1820s, as a revolution in Mexico ended Spanish control. The first American to take advantage of the new opportunity was a former military officer, William Becknell. On 25 June 1821, he placed an ad in the *Missouri Intelligencer* asking for "a company of men destined to the westward for the purpose of trading for Horses and Mules, and catching Wild Animals of every description."[19] Becknell's party left Missouri in early August and arrived in Santa Fe in mid-November. He found the trade profitable, and the provisional governor informed him that Americans were now welcome in New Mexico. Traders hauled "tobacco, buttons, knives, shoes, drugs, fruits, rice, and even spermaceti candles, to trade with the New Mexicans for silver coins, livestock, cloth, and other salable items," wrote fur-trade historian Eric Jay Dolin.[20] Others sought furs in New Mexico's rivers, most of which had not been trapped. Although southwestern beaver pelts were considered inferior to those from the north, being thinner and lighter in color, they remained in high demand.

There were noticeable differences between the fur trade in the north and in New Mexico. While nearly a thousand mountain men trapped in the northern regions, only a few hundred trapped in the Southwest. Large fur companies did not dominate the southwestern trade; instead, free trappers operated in small groups with Taos, New Mexico, as their rendezvous point. They often supplemented their income by working in the mines or by farming and ranching, and frequently, they married local women. Other factors, however, tied the two regions together. Like their counterparts on the upper Missouri, Taos trappers had a fondness for liquor, although a local brew known as "Taos lightning" seemed to be their favorite. More importantly, movement between the two regions was not uncommon. A number of Taos trappers trekked into the central and northern Rockies, even participating in the annual mountain rendezvous, and Glass was not the only northern trapper who moved to the Southwest. Indeed, Ashley's successors, Jedediah Smith, David Jackson, and William Sublette, sold out of their northern business in 1830 and reorganized to enter the Santa Fe trade. Some trappers, such as Kit Carson, moved back and forth regularly.[21]

If Glass left Fort Atkinson in the summer of 1824, as Flagg suggests, he should have arrived in Santa Fe sometime that fall or the next spring. Rowland Willard, a doctor who accompanied some Missourians on a trading expedition to Santa Fe in 1825, claimed that he met Glass in the Southwest that year. Glass and his partners had lost some of their mules and traps on their way to the upper Rio Grande, he said, and were returning to Taos for supplies. Willard hired them to provide game for his wagon train.[22]

Glass looked much older than his companions, Willard recalled. In fact, he estimated him to be about seventy-five. "These men had been several trips among the mountains for Beaver," he noted, "but it mattered little whether they got much or little, for when arriving to the settlement, would debauch until all was spent." As they conversed, Glass told the doctor about his mauling. When Willard did not believe him, Glass stripped, revealing "large chasms upon [his] right arm & shoulder blade," and wounds on his upper right thigh. The doctor concluded that by the time his companions left him on the Grand River, Glass's wounds had begun to "supperate as the inflamation gave way" and afterward slowly healed. A nearby spring provided a water supply, Willard wrote, and within a few days, Glass was able to crawl. At this point, however, Willard's account diverges from the familiar narrative. Instead of heading toward Fort Kiowa, Glass followed the trail of his fellow trappers, getting his sustenance primarily from roots. "I think he had not gone far, before he could bear his weight upon his legs and finally succeeded in overtaking the company which had commenced trapping again," the doctor said.[23]

Unfortunately, this account does not come from Willard's daily journal of his travels, but instead from a memoir that he wrote for his family when he was in his seventies or eighties. The account contains numerous errors; for example, he reports that Henry's party was en route to Saint Louis at the time of the mauling, rather than heading toward their Yellowstone post. A story that government commissioner Henry Leavitt Ellsworth heard in Oklahoma in 1832 contained the same error, suggesting that Willard may have incorporated a regionally popular tale into his reminiscence. Willard also asserted that when they met in 1825, Glass was traveling with the same three companions who had been with him at the time of the mauling. Willard named these men Stone, Andrews, and March, but these names do not jibe with those in other accounts. In addition, Willard's story gives a different context for the mauling. Glass and his companions had separated themselves from a larger party to find more beaver, said Willard, and one morning, while the others went to check their traps, Glass remained alone in camp to prepare breakfast. Suddenly, a female grizzly bear attacked Glass without provocation and threw him to the ground. Stone, wading in a nearby creek, heard the commotion and hurried back to camp. There he saw Glass with "the monster mounted upon him" and immediately killed the bear.[24] A number of factors could explain these inaccuracies; perhaps Willard met an imposter or incorporated details from other storytellers, or perhaps his memory simply failed him when he wrote his memoir.

According to George Yount, in 1825, Glass joined a trapping expedition headed by Etienne Provost, who intended to haul his pelts back to Taos and thence overland to Missouri. Yount wrote that Glass led one of Provost's parties north "into the territory of the Eutaus,"[25] while according to Flagg, Glass "joined a trapping expedition to the river Hele [Gila]," southwest of Santa Fe. Glass may have trapped in either or both of these areas, and if Yount and Flagg can be believed, on one such expedition, he survived yet another close encounter with Indians. Because he "was not yet completely in his element," Flagg wrote, he employed a Frenchman named Du Breuil to travel with him. Unfortunately, they could not find any Indians willing to exchange furs for trade goods. Then, as they ascended the river one morning, they saw a woman "upon the eastern bank digging for roots." Hoping to initiate trade, they "advanced towards her, holding out a beaver which they had caught the night previous, as a peace-offering." Beaver were considered a delicacy. However, when the woman spotted them, she screamed, "and from the neighboring bushes rushed out a powerful Indian with bow and arrows in his hands." Despite the trappers' efforts to signal their peaceful intentions, he "placed an arrow on his bow-string and raised it to his eye to launch the shaft." Glass and Du Breuil "ran with all speed for their rifles, which they had left in their skiff." As Du Breuil fired his rifle, said Flagg, "an arrow passed through his throat and he fell dead at the same moment with the Indian! Their aim had been simultaneous and deadly!" Although Glass escaped, "two or three arrows" struck him in the back.[26]

In Yount's version of this event, Glass had his rifle with him and he faced several warriors, who launched a volley of arrows. Nevertheless, Glass could have reached the boat safely if his mortally wounded companion had not asked him to reload his rifle so he could fire at the Indians as they approached. Delayed by this task, Glass was struck by an arrow as he raced back toward the boat. According to Yount, the arrow point remained in Glass's back throughout the seven-hundred-mile journey back to Taos, where a fellow trapper removed it with a razor.[27]

According to Flagg, Glass recovered from this surgery "sooner than could have been expected" and left the Southwest, and he was soon "hunting and trapping, with one companion as usual, at the head waters of the Missouri."[28]

Flagg was mistaken about Glass's departure from the Southwest, however, as Glass evidently remained in the region at least until 1827. Historian David J. Weber discovered that a man named Glass was a member of a party organized in January 1827 by Sylvestre Pratte and led by Ceran St. Vrain. The group included twenty-two men, mostly of French descent. Glass may also have joined a party that included George Yount and Hiram Allen in Arizona that spring or fall. Even so, Glass had certainly left the Southwest by 1828, for that year he was at the rendezvous in the northern Rocky Mountains.[29]

The first rendezvous, held in 1825, was mostly a business affair and lasted only a day. Subsequently, however, this annual event lasted several weeks, with trappers throughout the Rockies gathering to trade or sell their furs and bargain for needed equipment. According to Osborne Russell, who authored one of the finest mountain-man journals, a typical trapper needed at least "one Animal upon which is placed one or two Epishemores [blankets or buffalo robes] a riding Saddle and bridle a sack containing six Beaver traps a blanket with an extra pair of Mocasins his powder horn and bullet pouch with a belt to which is attached a butcher Knife a small wooden box containing bait for Beaver a Tobacco sack with a pipe and implements for making fire with sometimes a hatchet fastened to the Pommel of his saddle." A trapper might also want to purchase "a flannel or cotton shirt," or "a hat or Cap of wool."[30]

Having spent most of the year in small parties trapping beaver, the men were also ready to celebrate. According to trapper James Beckwourth, the rendezvous soon took on a carnival atmosphere. Once the suppliers arrived, "well laden with goods and all things necessary for the mountaineers and the Indian trade," the fun began. "Mirth, songs, dancing, shouting, trading, running, jumping, singing, racing, target-shooting, yarns, frolic, with all sorts of extravagances that white men or Indians could invent, were freely indulged in. The unpacking of the *medicine water* contributed not a little to the heightening of our festivities."[31]

At these and other gatherings, trappers related their experiences, real and imagined, around the campfires. Russell recalled one such occasion. After a fine dinner of elk ribs, "the jovial tale goes round the circle," he said, and "the peals of loud laughter break upon the stillness of the night. . . . Every tale puts an auditor in mind of something similar to it but under different circumstances which being told the 'laughing part' gives rise to increasing merriment and furnishes more subjects for good jokes and witty sayings such as Swift never dreamed of[.] Thus the evening passed with eating drinking and stories enlivened with witty humor until near Midnight all being wrapped in their blankets lying around the fire gradually falling to sleep one by one until the last tale is 'encored' by the snoring of the drowsy audience."[32]

According to Russell, trappers also discussed serious subjects when they met. At one gathering, "the long winter evenings were passed away by . . . entering into debates arguments or spinning long yarns until midnight in perfect good humour and I for one will cheerfully confess that I have derived no little benefit from the frequent arguments and debates held in what we termed The Rocky Mountain College and I doubt not but some of my comrades who considered themselves Classical Scholars have had some little added to their wisdom in these assemblies however rude they might appear."[33]

Another highlight was the opportunity to receive news from the states. "Joy now beamed in every countenance," Russell remembered. "Some received letters from their friends and relations[.] Some received the public papers and news of the day others consoled themselves with the idea of getting a blanket a Cotton Shirt or a few pints of Coffee and sugar to sweeten it just by way of a treat."[34]

Although no account mentions Glass sharing in these activities, he undoubtedly did. However, according to Yount, he also gained a reputation for being a loner. "The same passion for travelling alone never forsook him," said Yount, and "he would never encamp with his fellows, but always miles distant roaming solitary & sleeping in silent loneliness—Often he would not be seen by his fellow travellers during many weeks, & yet he always knew where to find them, & could at any time fly to their aid when danger threatened."[35]

In addition to the rendezvous, the northern fur trade had undergone several other changes during the years that Glass was in the Southwest. Ashley had sold his company to Jedediah Smith, David Jackson, and William Sublette. In 1827, the Columbia Fur Company merged with John Jacob Astor's American Fur Company, and instead of using the rendezvous system, the combined enterprise established a permanent post at the mouth of the Yellowstone. Built in the fall of 1828, the post was first named Fort Floyd, but it is usually known as Fort Union, the name formally adopted in 1830. To lure trappers to the post, manager Kenneth McKenzie advertised higher prices for furs than Ashley's successors paid at the rendezvous. Indeed, many trappers at the 1828 rendezvous thought that the amount they received for furs was too low, and, conversely, that prices for supplies and equipment were too high. Hoping to gain their trade, McKenzie sent Etienne Provost to lure the discontented trappers to Fort Floyd. Provost, who had evidently had a disagreement with Ashley in 1826, was a willing agent for the rival company.[36]

Despite their desire for better prices, however, most trappers did not want to travel far from the beaver sites in the Rockies, and they enjoyed the revelry of the rendezvous. Therefore, in the fall of 1828, they sent Hugh Glass to ask McKenzie to bring his goods to the gathering and compete directly with Smith, Jackson, and Sublette. McKenzie initially declined, reiterating that his company would guarantee higher prices than the competition if the trappers would bring their furs to Fort Floyd. Nevertheless, in April 1829, the American Fur Company did send a party from Saint Louis under Henry Vanderburgh to meet the free trappers. Little is known about his success, but according to fur-trade historian Hiram Martin Chittenden, "this was the beginning of the American Fur Company's participation in the fur trade of the Rocky Mountains." While it "did not prove to be an advantageous branch of the trade," it became "a source of infinite annoyance in the fierce competition which it engendered."[37]

Glass's movements after he met with McKenzie at Fort Floyd are obscure, but it is likely that he remained in that region for the remaining years of his life. Indeed, Chittenden claimed that Glass "was at one time employed as hunter for the fort and used to hunt for bighorns on the bluffs opposite the post. These bluffs are still known as Glass' Bluffs."[38] During the winter of 1832–1833, news arrived at the fort that Indians had killed Glass and two others near Fort Cass, or Tulloch's Fort, established for the Crow Indian trade and located about three miles below the mouth of the Bighorn River on the east bank of the Yellowstone. Details about Glass's death emerged piecemeal. Prince Maximilian of Wied, who was then visiting McKenzie at Fort Union, wrote that on 14 May 1833, they spotted four men arriving in a canoe. These men informed McKenzie that Indians had "killed seven of his men." A week later, Maximilian learned that only three men had actually been killed, and that the Arikaras were responsible, not the Blackfeet as first rumored. According to Maximilian, those killed included "a certain Glass," Edward Rose, and a man named Menard. They had been "dispatched on the Yellowstone River from Fort Cass to Fort Union. In the forest at the Missouri, they met a war party of eighty Arikaras, and all three of them were killed."[39]

Maximilian also learned that other trappers had already avenged Glass's death. A band of Arikaras met with eighteen trappers encamped at the headwaters of the Powder River with a large number of horses, and some of the Arikaras entered the camp, pretending to be friendly. Suddenly, according to Maximilian, "all of them ran out," scattering the horses and stealing many of them. However, the trappers captured three of the Arikaras. Recognizing "the rifle of old Glass as well as the knife of another of the three slain men," they realized that the men who had taken their horses belonged to the same party that had killed Glass, and they decided to execute the captives unless the horses were returned. One of the prisoners managed to cut his bonds with a concealed knife and got away. While the others began chanting "their death songs," the Arikaras outside the camp shouted that the captives "had to help themselves, since they could not give up the horses." Maximilian concluded his account saying, "the two Indians were killed, and I own the scalp of one of them." He received the scalp from one of McKenzie's clerks, Francis A. Chardon. In a later journal entry, Maximilian recorded the details slightly differently: the Arikara captive who "cut himself loose and tried to escape" was caught and killed in the thickets, and it was this man whose scalp Maximilian received. He meant to display the scalp when he returned to Germany, but it evidently was destroyed in a boat fire on the way home.[40]

The next year, as Maximilian descended the Missouri, he learned that a trapper named Johnson Gardner was paddling "a poor, heavily loaded canoe" not far ahead. Advised that Gardner was a "reliable helmsman" who would be a great asset in negotiating the river, Maximilian invited him aboard. Gardner happily joined them on the steamboat. As they visited around the campfire that evening, Maximilian learned that it was Gardner who had killed the Arikaras who were deemed guilty of Glass's death, and Gardner provided further details about the incident. "Old

Glass went beaver hunting with two companions from Fort Cass on the Yellowstone River," Maximilian reported, and "as they crossed the ice of the Yellowstone farther down-river, all three of them were shot, scalped, and robbed by a war party of about eighty Arikaras hidden on the opposite bank." Afterward, these Indians traveled to the headwaters of the Powder River, where Gardner was camped with about twenty men.[41]

The Arikaras tried to deceive him, Gardner said, by greeting him in the Hidatsa language. Unfortunately for them, a Hidatsa woman in Gardner's party identified them as Arikaras. Realizing that they might be after his horses, Gardner watched the visitors closely. Thus, when the Indians began scattering the herd, the trappers were able to capture three warriors. When the others tried to negotiate their release, Gardner told them that if they "did not immediately return the horses, the prisoners would die." One prisoner managed to escape, while the other two, "foreseeing their deaths, started their death songs." One of these men "had old Glass's knife," and other Indians in the party had the rifles of the other murdered trappers. Later that day, the prisoners asked to relieve themselves and then tried to escape in the dense brush. One was immediately stabbed to death, and the other was shot several times. "Both [were] scalped," wrote Maximilian.[42]

Gardner may have disguised the truth, however, for Flagg's 1839 account includes a different version of the executions. According to Flagg, Glass had been "hunting and trapping, with one companion as usual, at the head waters of the Missouri." Then, for several months, nothing was heard of him. Later, "a party of four Erickeraw Indians came to the encampment of a company of hunters on the banks of the Powee [Powder] river, and on one of these was seen several articles of clothing, which, from their peculiar character, were known to have belonged to Glass." The Indians were taken captive, but they insisted that they knew nothing about Glass. Finally, Gardner released one, telling him "that unless he returned within twenty-four hours with Glass in safety, his three companions who remained as hostages should be burned at the stake." The freed prisoner never returned, "and, being now sure that the unfortunate hunter had been murdered by the savages then in their hands, the order was given . . . to burn them alive!" And, said Flagg, "to the disgrace of civilization and humanity this command was obeyed!" Later, according to Flagg, the Arikaras exacted their revenge, capturing Gardner and inflicting "upon him the same dreadful death."[43]

Trapper James Beckwourth, who typically exaggerated and placed himself at the center of events, claimed that he witnessed both the immolation of the captives and Glass's burial. After he arrived at Fort Cass in company with two hundred Crow warriors, Beckwourth said, three men left the fort for Gardner's camp eighteen miles downriver to notify him of their arrival so that they could trade. That was the night that Arikara Indians stole Gardner's horses, and soon afterward, the butchered bodies of the three messengers were discovered. Beckwourth and the Crows rode in pursuit; stopping at Gardner's camp, they learned that his men had taken two captives. "They had bound them with trap-chains, and were in the act of throwing them into a tremendous log fire," he said. "There was a terrible struggle for a moment; then all was still." Riding on, the Beckwourth party spotted a party of four hundred Arikaras, and in the subsequent battle killed 172 of them. Returning to Fort Cass, they sent word to the rest of the Crow village "to help us mourn for the three white men who had recently been killed on the ice, and who were yet unburied." One of these was Hugh Glass. "The crying was truly appalling," Beckwourth remembered, because the three men were highly regarded by the Crows. "When their bodies were lowered to their last resting-place, numberless fingers were voluntarily chopped off and thrown into the graves; hair and trinkets of every description were also contributed, and the graves were finally filled up."[44]

Glass's death roughly coincided with the beginnings of a decline in the fur trade. Cutthroat competition caused fur companies to take every beaver they could, meanwhile searching for other locations where the animals remained numerous. Indeed, this relentless quest for new beaver sites was one reason why many trappers became known as important western explorers. Trappers were fully aware of the decline in the beaver population and what it meant for their future. As Osborne Russell noted in the mid 1830s, "the trappers often remarked to each other as they rode over these lonely plains that it was time for the White man to leave the mountains as Beaver and game had nearly disappeared."[45] Although these men may have assumed that beaver numbers would rebound over time, they made no effort to ensure that result. Fortunately for the beaver, the price of pelts dropped significantly in the early 1830s. As John Jacob Astor noted to Pierre Chouteau, Jr., in 1832, "I very much fear Beaver will not sell well very soon unless very fine, it appears that they make hats of silk in place of Beaver."[46] Although the fur trade continued for the remainder of the decade, trappers faced a significant transition in their livelihood. Eventually, buffalo robes, not beaver pelts, came to dominate the fur industry.

Had Glass lived, he would have had to adjust to a new lifestyle, just as many of his former companions did. William Ashley returned to Saint Louis after selling out of his fur business in 1826. He continued to supply his successors with goods for several years, but finally severed all connections to the fur trade, remarried, and built a fine house. In 1831, he was elected to fill a new seat in the United States House of Representatives, and he successfully retained his seat in 1832 and 1834. Although a Jacksonian Democrat, he split from President Jackson in 1836 and ran for governor of Missouri as a Whig Party candidate. He lost this election but planned to run for Congress again in 1838. Instead, he died of pneumonia that year at the age of sixty. He emancipated his eight slaves and, having no children, left his wife a sizeable estate. Interestingly, in 1827 he had promoted the unpopular notion that mountain regions should not be trapped for about five years in order to allow beaver numbers to rebound.[47]

Andrew Henry was less successful. He made his last trip down the Missouri River in the fall of 1824 and ended his partnership with Ashley. According to an acquaintance, he had "suffered much and met with many misfortunes" in the mountains, and he also missed his wife and children, providing another reason to leave the trade.[48] Unfortunately, he withdrew from the business a year before the company made significant profits. He spent the remainder of his life at his home in Washington County, Missouri, working at his mines. A private man, he struggled to make ends meet, began drinking heavily, and died in 1832. According to a notice published at that time, Henry was "much respected for his honesty, intelligence and enterprise."[49]

Jedediah Smith became one of the partners who succeeded Ashley and Henry after they sold out of their fur business. Smith ran out of supplies while searching for new beaver streams southwest of the Great Salt Lake and traveled to California, where he ran afoul of Mexican authorities for entering the territory without permission. After caching their beaver pelts in California, Smith and two other trappers arrived at the 1827 Rocky Mountain rendezvous, surprising his partners, who assumed that he was dead. That summer, Smith led a party back to California to fetch his furs. On the way, Mojave Indians killed most of his new recruits, and once he arrived, he again found himself in trouble with Mexican officials. The disasters continued: on the way home, Indians in Oregon slaughtered all but two of his party. Smith finally returned via the Columbia River, and in 1830, he and his partners sold out of the fur business. Smith profited sufficiently to purchase a fine house in Saint Louis, where he planned to write his memoirs and complete his maps of the West. However, he decided to rejoin his former partners once more and left on an expedition to Santa Fe on 10 April 1831. Comanche Indians killed Smith while he was searching for water in the Cimarron Desert; he was just thirty-two years old. His extensive explorations and contributions to mapping the West made him one of the most significant figures of the fur-trade era. Indeed, biographer Barton H. Barbour characterized him as "a supernova in the galaxy of mountain men who roamed the Rockies."[50]

Edward Rose, who met his death with Glass on the Yellowstone, had an interesting and controversial career. He grew up in the vicinity of Louisville, Kentucky; his father was a white trader, and his mother was Cherokee and African American. When about eighteen years of age, Rose went to New Orleans as a deckhand on a keelboat, and in the next few years, he gained a reputation as an outlaw. By 1806, he had moved to Saint Louis, and the next year he joined Manuel Lisa's expedition to the upper Missouri. Sent to trade with the Crow Indians, he evidently dispensed his trade goods too freely in order to gain acceptance, leading to a quarrel with his employer. Although he lived with the Crows for a couple of years, Andrew Henry found him living with the Arikara Indians in 1809. Rose also traveled with Wilson Price Hunt's overland expedition in 1811 and later lived with the Omaha Indians. He evidently rejoined the Arikaras in about 1820, and he emerged as a key figure during Ashley's battle with the tribe. Rose also accompanied Jedediah Smith's party in 1823 as a guide and interpreter. He reportedly was living with the Crows again before his death in the winter of 1832–1833.[51]

Daniel T. Potts trapped in the Rocky Mountains from 1822 to 1828, participating in the first rendezvous in 1825. In his letters home, he became the first to describe—and perhaps named—the Great Salt Lake. In 1826, he also made the first confirmed visit by a European American to the region of present-day Yellowstone National Park and described that unique area in a letter. The next year, deciding that the fur trade was too risky, he switched careers and began to ship horses and cattle from Texas to New Orleans. Sadly, this work did not offer security either. According to his family, he died when his ship sank in the Gulf of Mexico.[52]

James Clyman worked as a trapper only from 1823 to 1827. After a successful hunt with William Sublette, David Jackson, Robert Campbell, Jim Bridger, and Daniel T. Potts, Clyman left the mountains, selling his furs to Wilson Price Hunt for $1,257. Afterward, he purchased land in Illinois and volunteered in the Black Hawk War, serving in the same company as the young Abraham Lincoln. He then purchased land in Wisconsin, where he narrowly escaped being killed by Indians. After developing a chronic cough in 1843–1844, he again left for the West, joining a caravan headed for Oregon. In 1845, he continued on to California, where he married and settled on a large ranch near Napa. He grew fruits, including the highly desired "Clyman plum," as well as walnuts, berries, vegetables, hay, grain, and cattle. He died there on 27 December 1881.[53]

Like Clyman, Jim Bridger lived a long and fruitful life. After working for Ashley and his successors, Bridger bought the firm in 1830 with his partners Thomas Fitzpatrick, Milton G. Sublette, Henry Fraeb, and Baptiste Gervais, creating the Rocky Mountain Fur Company. A year or two later, Bridger was wounded in a fight with Indians, and he carried a metal point in his back until 1835, when the missionary Marcus Whitman removed it on his way to Oregon. In 1834, Bridger, Fitzpatrick, and Sublette bought out their partners, but they had difficulty making sufficient profits because of increased competition. By 1838, Bridger was affiliated with the American Fur Company. He was well known and had his portrait painted by artist Alfred J. Miller, who had accompanied the Scottish traveler William Stewart to the West.

Between 1838 and 1840, as the fur trade declined, Bridger and his partner, Louis Vasquez, constructed Fort Bridger on Blacks Fork of the Green River to serve western emigrants. From 1850 to 1865, he worked as a guide for numerous government expeditions, as well as the hunting expedition of the Anglo-Irish sportsman George Gore. Finally, in 1866, he purchased a home near Westport, Missouri, where he died on 17 July 1881. Bridger's name is widely commemorated in the West; he is the namesake of Fort Bridger State Park, Bridger Creek, Bridger Lake, Bridger Mountain, Bridger National Forest, Bridger Pass, Bridger Wilderness, and the city of Bridger, Montana. He obviously suffered no ill effects from being named as one of the men who deserted Hugh Glass.[54]

The lives of Glass and his associates seem typical of the men associated with the fur trade. Using the 292 biographies written for *The Mountain Men and the Fur Trade of the Far West,* edited by LeRoy R. Hafen, Richard J. Fehrman discovered that traders and trappers had amazingly long life spans, averaging sixty-four years. Although Indians killed 11 percent of them, 77 percent had non-violent deaths. As Hafen noted, however, these figures are probably skewed because those who died relatively young did not have sufficient accomplishments to warrant a biography. Indeed, after examining the careers of 446 mountain men, historian William H. Goetzmann found that 182 of them were killed while in the fur trade. Regardless, and importantly for a study of Hugh Glass, Fehrman discovered, "loss of life from the grizzly bear was minimal." Fehrmann also learned that 1805 was the average year of birth for the men in his sample, suggesting that Glass, who may have been born in 1775, was older than most trappers. Although little evidence exists to determine the trappers' levels of education, "where the information was available," Fehrman noted, "the majority could at least read and write."[55] Indeed, according to historian Don D. Walker, an extraordinary number of these men kept journals. Finally, of those who survived, 30 percent later became farmers or ranchers, 10 percent became businessmen, 10 percent worked in government-related careers, and 22 percent became miners, guides, interpreters, teachers, carpenters, surveyors, writers, and so forth. The remainder (28 percent) of the men in Fehrman's sample either took up no other occupation after retiring from the fur trade or died in the mountains.[56]

Why these men became trappers has been hotly debated. According to Goetzmann, two prevailing stereotypes of mountain men dominated early studies. Some imagined them as "outcast banditti, veritable misanthropes of the plains and Rockies who loved only the freedom of the hunt and the chase, and scorned civilization." In contrast, others pictured them as "the saddest of all American heroes," members of "the backwoods proletariat enslaved and exploited by ruthless company masters."[57] This contrast is evident in the works of two of the writers who examined Glass's career. According to biographer John Myers Myers, Glass's story "is undiluted by . . . the desire for wealth, an ambition for honors, or any other feelings with one eye cocked for applause or envy." He was, as a result, "the purest known example of the American in buckskin."[58] Historian Jon T. Coleman, on the other hand, claims that Glass's "absence from the written record confirmed his status as a regular guy. Ordinariness hid him in the crowd of working-class males."[59]

Goetzmann believed that both stereotypes contained a grain of truth. However, he decided that most trappers resembled "the common business-oriented people of the time all across the country. It was this set of values that General Ashley was counting on when he made his appeal to them as men of 'enterprise.'"[60] In this conclusion, Goetzmann agreed with historian Richard Hofstadter's description of the Jacksonian man as "an expectant capitalist, a hardworking, ambitious person for whom enterprise was a kind of religion." Hofstadter's exemplars included "the master mechanic who aspired to open his own shop, the planter or farmer who speculated in land, the lawyer who hoped to be a judge, the local politician who wanted to go to Congress, the grocer who would be a merchant."[61] Like them, said Goetzmann, the free trapper "went out to the frontier . . . to seek his fortune. In short, though he may have looked quaint or even outlandish, the mountain man was no simple primitive. . . . He too was an expectant capitalist." Though primarily interested in the fur trade, the mountain man "remained alert for other possibilities that would make his fortune, whether it be farming, the mines of Mexico, the transportation and supply business, or simply real estate."[62]

Although few documents reveal Glass's thoughts and beliefs, his behavior to some degree fits Goetzmann's description. He responded to the advertisement by Ashley and Henry for "men of enterprise," perhaps hoping to elevate his station in life. Rather than seeking refuge in Saint Louis after being mauled by a grizzly bear, he rejoined his companions. Although revenge may have motivated him, it is clear that he also meant to remain in the fur trade; after reaching Fort Atkinson, he set out for the Southwest, changing locations rather than leaving the business. Later, upon his return to the upper Missouri region, he attempted to negotiate with McKenzie for lower prices for goods and higher prices for furs, clearly hoping for monetary gain.

Don Walker has described mountain men in a way that might reconcile the opposing views. He has criticized western scholars for oversimplifying mountain men as being "moved by the simplest of drives: the need to escape, a curiosity about the other side of the mountain, and, most important, the chance to gather a modest wealth in beaver plews. This man has sometimes seemed to come into the West with an almost empty head, a mind like a blank tablet, putting down or remembering the places he has seen, the bears and Blackfeet he has encountered, the other men he has known, and finally maybe his gains or losses in the trade."[63] Fur traders such as Glass were probably more complex than any of the theories about the motivations of mountain men would suggest. Glass probably shared the feelings expressed in the journals and letters of Potts, Clyman, and Smith, enjoying the scenery, being intrigued by Indian customs, and perhaps even reading a newspaper—in other words, he was typically human. Like other mountain men, he probably liked telling tall tales, as well. In the decades following his death, however, Glass's tale would grow into a western legend.

6

Creating a Western Legend
1823–2016

In late July 1923, members of the John G. Neihardt Club drove from Nebraska to the Grand River, fourteen miles southwest of Lemmon, South Dakota, to commemorate the hundredth anniversary of the encounter between Hugh Glass and the grizzly bear. Members of the party were all "devotees" of Neihardt, poet laureate of Nebraska and author of *The Song of Hugh Glass* (1915), who accompanied the party. Julius D. Young, principal of the school in Murdo, South Dakota, thought Neihardt had written "a towering and absorbing piece of literature."[1] Young and his new wife had interrupted their honeymoon to join the festivities. Between twenty and thirty people joined them, including Julius T. House, author of *John G. Neihardt: Man and Poet* (1920); Justice Samuel Polley of the South Dakota Supreme Court; Lawrence K. Fox, assistant director of the South Dakota State Historical Society; and the editor of the *Lemmon Tribune*, who provided press coverage.[2]

As they arrived at the forks of the Grand River, said House, they became "absorbed with tracing parallels between the poem and what must have been the actual experiences of Glass." House acknowledged that although Neihardt strove for realism in his epic, not "all details of his poem [were] true to facts." Nevertheless, from reading *The Song of Hugh Glass*, House felt that he "already had a mental photograph" of the landscape, and now he found "it was really so."[3] The group had driven Model Ts up the primitive roads to a bluff south of the forks of the Grand in search of an appropriate site to locate a monument. Enraptured by Neihardt's poem, they sought a spot similar to the one described in his book.

"Local features were found to fit the story 'like a glove,'" Young declared. "This was the place!"[4]

Local rancher Otto Weinkauf, who had donated land for the monument, brought a "rustic, homemade mixer" to make concrete, which they "poured into a wooden form to shape a frustum of a pyramid with ample footing below ground." Everyone pitched in, including Justice Polley, who wore coveralls and wielded a shovel. Finally, they attached a bronze plate to the structure: "This altar to courage was erected August 1, 1923 by the Neihardt Club in honor of Hugh Glass[,] who, wounded and deserted[,] here began his crawl to Fort Kiowa in the fall of 1823."[5] Completing their work on 31 July, they planned to dedicate the marker formally the next day.

That afternoon, however, the weather turned cold, and they decided not to wait. "Soon the Model T's again growled in low gear up the steep new trail for the dedication," and the party built a campfire for warmth. Young remembered feeling "an inner presence . . . in the silence." House began the ceremony in this mystic atmosphere, reading passages from Neihardt's poem that "fit the mood and place."[6] As he recited the lines "wolfish corybants / Intoned their wild antiphonary chants," coyotes began yowling nearby, as if in imitation.[7] "The 'coincidence' was perfect, the effect was eerie," Young recalled.[8]

Sixteen years later, Neihardt returned to South Dakota to dedicate another Hugh Glass monument. Nearly two thousand people gathered for the event on 19 August 1939 in the small town of Bison. The community had just finished building a new school, and the Perkins County Old Timers' Association had decided to construct a Hugh Glass memorial on the school grounds as a "tribute to an historical event important as an early milestone in the progress of the white settlers into this country."[9] Neihardt gave a dedication speech, while Fred Jennewein, president of the Old Timers' Association, paraded as Hugh Glass.

The crowd "stood enthralled" as Neihardt told Glass's story. He also spoke about the Indians of the region, "and brought his talk to a fitting and appropriate climax when he asked the audience to face the west, raise their hands and bow their heads while he besought the blessing and divine direction of 'Grandfather Great Spirit' in the Indian fashion." Then, as the monument to Glass was unveiled, he urged the attendees "to emulate the characteristics that brought fame to the pioneer hero."[10]

As these incidents show, Neihardt did more than anyone to popularize the Hugh Glass legend in the first half of the twentieth century. In 1912, he had begun working on a "cycle of heroic *Songs*, designed to celebrate the great mood of courage that was developed west of the Missouri River in the nineteenth century."[11] *The Song of Hugh Glass* (1915) was the first of his "hero tales in verse,"[12] followed by *The Song of Three Friends* (1919), relating the Mike Fink story; *The Song of the Indian Wars* (1925); *The Song of the Messiah* (1935), about the Ghost Dance; and *The Song of Jed Smith* (1941). When completed, they were republished together as *A Cycle of the West* (1949). "The series was dreamed out, much of it in detail, before I began," Neihardt said, "and for years it was my hope that it might be completed at the age of 60—as it was." He intended to tell the story of "a genuine epic period, differing in no essential from the other great epic periods that marked the advance of the Indo-European peoples out of Asia and across Europe. It was a time of intense individualism, a time when society was cut loose from its roots, a time when old culture was being overcome by that of a powerful people driven by the ancient needs and greeds."[13]

Before writing, Neihardt traveled through the region to study the terrain and wrote to geographers and geologists to obtain information about trees, shrubs, and rocks. Although he depended upon fur-trade histories and trappers' journals for his account of Hugh Glass, he also talked with old timers. He once met a friend of Jim Bridger. "Such intimate contacts with soldiers, plainsmen, Indians and river men," he said, "were an integral part of my life for many years."[14]

The poet also boated down the Missouri River from Montana, a trip he recounted in *The River and I* (1910). "On the upper river the country was practically unchanged," he said, and "it was no difficult feat of the imagination to revive the details of that time—the men, the trails, the boats, the trading posts where veritable satraps once ruled under the sway of the American Fur Company."[15] Later, in *The Splendid Wayfaring* (1920), Neihardt gave a nonfictional account of the travels of Jedediah Smith and other trappers associated with Ashley and Henry, including Hugh Glass. He also reproduced the letter that Glass had written to the parents of John Gardner.[16]

Neihardt's fascination with this history was longstanding. "My interest in that period may be said to have begun at the age of six when, clinging to the forefinger of my father, I discovered the Missouri River from a bluff top at Kansas City," Neihardt said. The river was for him "what the sea must have been to the Greek boys of antiquity. And as those ancient boys must have been eager to hear of perils nobly encountered on the deep and in the lands adjacent, so was I eager to learn of the heroes who had travelled my river as an imperial road."[17]

Indeed, Neihardt's *Cycle of the West* has been compared to epics from ancient Greece and Rome, although Neihardt was quick to differentiate his poems from those classics. "There has been no thought of synthetic *Iliads* and *Odysseys*," he said, "but only of the richly human saga-stuff of a country that I knew and loved."[18] Nevertheless, the influence of ancient sagas is evident in his poetry. He fell under the spell of the classics while attending the Nebraska State Normal College at Wayne, but he came to view his own region's history in even grander terms. "The history of the American fur trade alone makes the Trojan War look like a Punch and

Judy show!" he exclaimed. However, he lamented, "we have not Homer."[19]

Critics have debated the suitability of Neihardt's characters as subjects for epic poetry. "The real Glass scarcely typified the classical hero," wrote Neihardt biographer Lucile F. Aly, for he "could not claim noble birth, handsome appearance, nor youth." Nevertheless, "he had courage and the capacity for both physical and moral heroism." In Neihardt's poem, "Old Hugh, seasoned trapper and hunter," serves as a parent figure for "his young friend Jamie, a character for whom Neihardt gives no specific historical source."[20] Though Neihardt may have derived the name from James Bridger, Jamie is fictional, and he is central to Neihardt's story; the poem is as much about Jamie as it is about Glass.

The opening section of *The Song of Hugh Glass*, "Graybeard and Goldhair," describes Old Glass and his parental relationship with Jamie. Indeed, Glass's companions had begun calling him "Mother Hugh." He risked his life to rescue the reckless youth during the battle with the Arikaras and was wounded in the hip. Later, when Glass did not return after being sent out to secure game for Henry's party as it marched along the Grand River, a worried Jamie rode ahead to see what was delaying him, hoping that Glass had killed a buffalo. Instead, he discovered that a grizzly had mauled him. Jamie managed to kill the bear with a single shot and then cared for Glass until the rest of the party arrived. Naturally, when Major Henry asked for two men to remain with Glass, Jamie volunteered. The other man who agreed to stay was Jules Le Bon, a fictional character who was interested only in the monetary reward. The moment Henry departed, the villainous Le Bon began playing on Jamie's fears, highlighting the likelihood that Arikara Indians would discover them. Finally, when Jules told Jamie that he saw Arikaras coming, the two men departed with Glass's rifle and supplies.

Part two, "The Awakening," begins as Glass regains consciousness. Finding evidence that Jamie was one of two men who had left him, he vowed to exact vengeance. The third portion of the poem, "The Crawl," is the longest, relating Glass's struggle to get to Fort Kiowa. Dragging his injured leg behind him, Glass survived on berries, plums, and an occasional bit of meat taken from wolf kills. On one occasion, he hid from a band of Arikaras led by Elk Tongue. Afterward, he noticed that they had left an old woman behind to die alone. He considered killing her for her food and supplies, but refrained, suggesting a higher morality than that of his former companions. Eventually, he found a flint and broken knife blade, enabling him to make fire, cook, and warm himself. Finally, when he reached the Missouri River, he built a primitive raft and drifted down to Fort Kiowa.

Afterward, Glass accompanied a trading party to the Mandan villages, then continued alone, struggling against snow and cold weather to Henry's post on the Bighorn River. When he banged on the gates, none other than Jules Le Bon opened the door. Glass could have killed Le Bon on the spot, but considered him unworthy of the effort; after all, he had remained with Glass only for the money, whereas Jamie had betrayed their friendship. Jamie, however, had left for Fort Atkinson before Glass arrived at Henry's camp, so when Henry asked for men to carry dispatches there, Glass immediately volunteered. His trek was uneventful, but when he arrived at the fort, Jamie was no longer there either. Learning that his old friend had somehow survived, Jamie's deep guilt and remorse led him to leave and search for Glass. Now Glass departed, searching for Jamie. Meanwhile, Jamie, who still carried Glass's rifle, was blinded when it misfired. Piegan Blackfoot Indians took him in and went to find a "black robe," or priest, so that he might confess his sins before death. Finally, a man arrived, listened to his tale of desertion, and granted him forgiveness. The sightless Jamie did not realize that the man was Hugh Glass.

Neihardt invented characters and changed facts to fit his epic tale of vengeance and forgiveness, but his poem proved popular, and the Hugh Glass story quickly spread to schoolbooks and popular histories. However, although he was the most responsible for the story's rise in prominence, Neihardt had many predecessors who had kept the tale alive through the nineteenth century. Besides the important narratives of James Hall, Philip St. George Cooke, Edmund Flagg, and George C. Yount, several other writers had published secondary accounts of Glass's adventures. One of the first was Warren Angus Ferris, a member of the American Fur Company in the 1830s, who summarized previous accounts in his memoirs, printed in the *Western Literary Messenger* of Buffalo, New York, in 1843 and 1844.[21]

As the story was retold, other versions appeared. Henry Leavitt Ellsworth, one of three government commissioners sent to Oklahoma in 1832 "to study the country, to mark the boundaries, to pacify the warring Indians, and, in general, to establish order and justice," heard one of these variant accounts.[22] Today, Ellsworth's party is mostly remembered because it included the writer Washington Irving, who afterward described their travels in *A Tour on the Prairies*. Irving did not mention the Glass story, but in his own account of the trip, Ellsworth included a thorough rendition that he heard from Captain Jesse Bean of the mounted rangers.

"Stories about bears are always interesting," Ellsworth began, "so I'll tell you one mentioned this evening by Capt Beans who knows the characters concernd personally." The incident involved one of Ashley's men "on the upper waters of the Missouri." The unnamed trapper wounded a grizzly bear, which responded by attacking. The trapper's companions, hearing his cries for help, "found him in possession of a huge white bear, and expiring aparently in the last agonies of death." After killing the bear or driving it away, the party carried the trapper back to camp. Although the wounded man "was able to talk somewhat inchoherently, and begged them not to forsake him," Ellsworth claimed that the men were in a hurry to resume their journey home to Saint Louis—not to the Yellowstone country, an error repeated in some subsequent accounts including Rowland Willard's—and felt that they could not wait. "It was finally agreed that a purse should be made up of two hundred dollars and this sum given to the two persons who should stay with the wounded, untill he should recover, or as was most probable untill he should die, and then give him a decent burial." Two men volunteered, not because they cared about the injured man, but because "avarice is a strong motive." A few days later, the two men killed a deer, laid a portion beside the wounded man, and departed.[23]

After the men returned to Saint Louis, "often was the story told of the death of one of their number in consequence of the wounds inflicted by a bear." They did not realize that the man was still alive. "For several days he ate nothing," then began eating the raw venison beside him. Finally, he gained enough strength to crawl to a nearby stream and worked his way to the Missouri River. There, finding "a dry crooked log," he pushed it into the river and floated "untill he arrived opposite the fort at St Louis." There, a sentinel spotted him and sent a boat out to get him. His former companions were shocked when they learned he was alive. "Oh! the curses reeked upon the two men who deserted him in one hour of peril," Ellsworth concluded. "Flight only saved them from claws worse than a bears, which would have rent them in pieces."[24]

Rufus B. Sage provided a different version of the Hugh Glass tale in *Scenes in the Rocky Mountains* (1846), along with several other "thrilling stories of frightful encounter with that proud monarch of the mountains, the grizzly bear." Born in Connecticut in 1817, Sage learned the printing trade, and in 1841, he decided to travel westward and write an account of his experiences. He returned from the West in 1844 and published his book two years later. "Several years since," Sage began, "an old trapper by the name of Glass" and his companion "came upon a large grizzly bear." The two men fired, and the bear, "as usual, rushed towards his uncivil assailants, who broke from him with all possible despatch." Unfortunately, Glass stumbled as he ran, and almost immediately, "the infuriated beast was upon him." A "death-struggle" then began; firing both of his pistols, Glass hit the bear in the breast and back. "Smarting and maddened by the pain of additional wounds, the bleeding monster continued the conflict with the fury of desperation," wrote Sage. Glass next fought with his knife, but the loss of blood made him "unable to oppose further resistance." Luckily, the bear also weakened, falling next to him.[25]

Glass's companion, finding him "apparently lifeless and half-torn to pieces," took his "arms and every other valuable . . . and, mounting his horse, started immediately for the nearest trading post." There, he announced Glass's death, "and the name of Glass found place upon the long catalogue of those who had fallen a prey to wild beasts and savage men." Six weeks later, a "poor, emaciated form of a man, half-naked, and covered with wounds and running sores, and so torn the fleshless bones of his legs and thighs were exposed to view in places," was seen standing before the post. It was Glass: "A veritable ghost suddenly appearing upon the spot could not have occasioned greater wonder!"[26]

After his wounds had been treated, Glass related his tale. For three days, he had fed on "the raw flesh of the carcase at his side," until it became too putrid to eat. Then he started for the post, crawling the seventy miles "upon his hands and knees,—subsisting, for the meanwhile, only upon insects." Sage did not mention any confrontation between Glass and the man who stole his belongings. Instead, he incorrectly concluded, Glass "still lives in the town of Taos, New Mexico, and frequently repeats to wondering listeners the particulars of this terrific and painful adventure."[27]

In the 1840s, George Frederick Ruxton related yet another variation of the Hugh Glass story. After attending and being expelled from the Royal Military Academy in Sandhurst, England, Ruxton traveled throughout Europe, served in Canada as an officer in the British army, and visited Morocco, South Africa, and Mexico City. Eventually, he headed north to Santa Fe and into Colorado before dying in Saint Louis in 1848. During his travels in the American West, Ruxton published colorful stories in English periodicals. He "was the first writer to depict the Old West realistically," wrote historians Bessie and Edgar Haynes, "often using the rough jargon of this rough tribe of men, so that his writings literally breathe life."[28] Among his tales was an account of Glass and the grizzly bear, replete with errors, including Glass's name.

"Some years ago a trapping party was on their way to the mountains, led, I believe, by old Sublette, a well-known captain of the West," wrote Ruxton. "Amongst the band was one John Glass, a trapper who had been all his life in the mountains, and had seen, probably, more exciting adventures, and had had more wonderful and hairbreadth escapes, than any of the rough and hardy fellows who make the West their home." While along a stream running out of the Black Hills, Glass spotted a grizzly bear, and he and his companion crept within twenty yards of the animal and fired their rifles. Both men hit the bear, but the wounds were not fatal. "'Harraw, Bill!' roared out Glass," as the animal charged, "'we'll be made meat of as sure as shootin'!'" The two men "bolted through the thicket" with the bear in close pursuit.[29]

Their only hope was to reach a nearby bluff, but Glass stumbled on a rock and fell. Yelling to his partner to reload, Glass fired his pistol. "The bear, with blood streaming from its nose and mouth, knocked the pistol from his hand with one blow of its paw, and, fixing its claws deep into his flesh, rolled with him to the ground." Glass then fought with his knife, while the bear, "with tooth and claw," ripped into his body, "baring the ribs of flesh and exposing the very bones." Finally, "weak with loss of blood," Glass "sank down insensible, and to all appearance dead." The bear died beside him.[30]

Glass's companion, "not having had presence of mind even to load his rifle, fled with might and main back to camp." There, he told the party of Glass's fate. The captain sent him back with another man to remain with Glass "if still alive, or to bury him if, as all supposed he was, defunct, promising them at the same time a sum of money for so doing." Surprisingly, Glass was still breathing. However, certain that he could not live for long, the two men gathered his belongings and returned, claiming, "Glass was dead, as probably they thought, and that they had buried him."[31]

Several months later, "a lank cadaverous form with a face so scarred and disfigured that scarcely a feature was discernible," approached the party. "Hurraw, Bill, my boy!" he shouted to his former companion. "You thought I was gone under that time, did you? But hand me over my horse and gun, my lad; I ain't dead yet by a dam sight!" The trappers gathered around Glass and listened to his story. He had eaten from the carcass of the bear to regain his strength and then crawled along the river to the fort. There, he recovered "and was, to use his own expression, 'as slick as a peeled onion.'"[32]

These and other tales published in newspapers and periodicals kept the Hugh Glass story alive through mid-century. In 1840, the *St. Louis Western Atlas and Saturday Evening Gazette* added a fictionalized version of the story titled "Old Glass," and in 1860, novelist Emerson Bennett published a short story in his collection *Forest and Prairie* based on Ruxton's account. The story appeared less frequently in the second half of the nineteenth century, which is surprising, given the rising popularity of dime novels focusing on western characters. Hugh Glass was never the subject of a dime novel, perhaps because his known adventures were limited to his encounter with the bear and subsequent quest for revenge. Kit Carson and Jim Bridger had longer careers, making them more adaptable for the dime-novel form. Moreover, as the fur trade declined, public interest shifted toward Indian conflicts and problems of law and order in the West. Individuals such as George Armstrong Custer, Wild Bill Hickok, Buffalo Bill Cody, and Billy the Kid now gained prominence at the expense of characters like Glass. By the end of the nineteenth century, popular histories featuring western heroes frequently neglected Glass. For example, E. G. Cattermole's *Famous Frontiersmen, Pioneers and Scouts* (1883) failed to mention him. A similar publication by Frank Triplett, *Conquering the Wilderness* (1888), described the mauling, but the story occupies only four paragraphs in a chapter about trapper Bill Gordon. George Yule of Colorado, who also had a fight with a grizzly bear, received equal coverage.[33]

Fortunately for the Glass legend, interest in the fur trade revived in the twentieth century. Hiram Martin Chittenden's monumental *The American Fur Trade of the Far West* (1902) included a thorough account of Glass's mauling. "Among the anecdotes that have come down to us of wild life on the plains," wrote Chittenden, "none is better authenticated than that of the escape of Hugh Glass from the very portal of death at the hands of a grizzly bear." Chittenden titled his chapter "Miraculous Escape of Hugh Glass," indicating the epic nature of the event. The story "has survived in oral tradition and is well known by the older men of the mountains and plains who still live," Chittenden wrote. Although these men told other exciting tales about the fur trade, the story of Hugh Glass "must have been considerably more noteworthy than the average or it would not have survived so long."[34]

Chittenden gained some of his information about Glass from one of these storytellers, steamboat captain Joseph La Barge. Although La Barge never met Hugh Glass, he was on the Missouri River in 1831 when Glass was still alive, and undoubtedly talked with people who knew him. However, Chittenden mostly relied on previously published sources, especially an article from the *Missouri Intelligencer* of 18 June 1825. Chittenden was unaware of its authorship, but it was a reprint of the *Port Folio* article by James Hall. "It is . . . evidently the most correct in all its details," Chittenden claimed.[35] The other two sources he acknowledged were Rufus Sage's *Scenes in the Rocky Mountains* and Philip St. George Cooke's *Scenes and Adventures in the Army*.

Chittenden's work led to a revival of interest in Hugh Glass. South Dakota historian Doane Robinson immediately included the story in his *History of South Dakota* (1904), essentially summarizing Hall's account. Abraham L. Van Osdel included a version in *Historic Landmarks* (1915), but he misidentified one of the deserters as Fitzpatrick and suggested that he and Bridger fled from Henry's post after hearing from Indian scouts that Glass had survived. When Glass finally caught up to his deserters at Fort Atkinson, both men were "protected by the United States army," Van Osdel wrote, and although the commander and soldiers provided Glass with a new outfit, he could not carry out his vengeance.[36]

Neihardt's publication of *The Song of Hugh Glass* in 1915, however, was the true watershed for the Glass saga. The story subsequently began to appear in children's books, schoolbooks, and general histories. Effie Florence Putney's *In the South Dakota Country* (1922) was typical of accounts for younger readers. She described Glass as "large-boned, deep-chested, gray-bearded, and gray crowned," and wrote that the grizzly attacked him without provocation.[37] Revenge motivated Glass to find the two men who deserted him, but when he arrived at Henry's Yellowstone post, he found that they had gone to Saint Louis to join the army, and there Putney's account ends. Prominent western artist Charles M. Russell included a sketch of Glass among his illustrations for the anthology *Back-Trailing on the Old Fron-*

tiers (1922); the article on Glass proclaimed that the event was "one of the most sensational happenings of the frontier a hundred years ago, and has survived . . . because of the amazing facts involved in it that have to do with treachery and a man's grim fight to live to be revenged."[38] In *Stories for Young Dakotans* (1942), Jeannette A. Vanderpol and Lynn Paley McCain wrote that Glass never again saw the two men who deserted him, "which perhaps was just as well, for the old man was very bitter toward them."[39] In *When the West Was Young* (1942), Shannon Garst essentially recapitulated Neihardt's poem in prose form: "old Hugh Glass," with his "leathery, weather-beaten face," looks after "the sandy-haired, blue-eyed boy," Jamie.[40]

South Dakota schoolbooks included the tale, as well. In addition to a brief summary, the 1919 edition of Willis E. Johnson's *South Dakota: A Republic of Friends* reprinted Glass's letter to the parents of John Gardner. In *Our State: A History for the Sixth Grade* (1937), Matilda Tarleton Barker mistakenly wrote that Glass was a member of "the expedition sent out by John Jacob Astor," but she emphasized his endurance: "he was able to withstand the pain and hunger and to get back to a settlement." Barker did not include any act of forgiveness, however, saying that Glass "felt very bitter toward those who left him, and he tried to find and punish them, but he never did; or at least if he did the story has not been told."[41] Herbert S. Schell, in *South Dakota: Its Beginnings and Growth* (1942), offered a more satisfying conclusion in which Glass finally forgave his deserters; he also noted that Glass was "a widely sung hero of both prose and poetry," adding that "the best story about Hugh Glass is told by John G. Neihardt."[42] Neihardt's poem, too, was available to students; a special edition with an extended introduction by Neihardt and notes by Julius T. House first appeared in 1919.[43]

During the Great Depression, members of the Federal Writers' Project in South Dakota also collected the story for their publications. In *Both Sides of the River* (1942), Hugh Glass encountered a grizzly bear fifteen miles south of present-day Lemmon, South Dakota. Glass managed to get the muzzle of his gun close enough to kill the bear as it tore into him, while a companion killed its cubs. Two men remained with Glass for five days before the older man persuaded the younger one to desert him. After crawling and floating a hundred miles to Fort Kiowa, Glass finally reached Henry's post in February 1824, where he forgave one deserter. Glass did not find the second man when he arrived at Fort Atkinson in June, for in a scene reminiscent of Neihardt, this man "had repented of his desertion. His remorse had led him to the scene of Glass's encounter with the grizzly. Glass finally found and forgave him."[44] *A South Dakota Guide* (1938) also included the Hugh Glass story, replete with an illustration of Glass on his knees, knife in hand and dripping blood, with a grizzly standing before him, her cubs in the background. Glass set "a record for grit and endurance,"[45] the writers concluded and, quoting Neihardt, affirmed that Glass's forgiveness of those who deserted him raised his story "to the level of sublimity."[46]

The account in *A South Dakota Guide* piqued the interest of novelist Frederick Manfred, who immediately borrowed a copy of Neihardt's poem from the University of Minnesota library. "I sat on a hard little bench and examined it," he said, and after reading "a couple dozen pages . . . found myself not liking it too well." He thought that Neihardt had written "in imitation of Homer, and in English it didn't come off well." Manfred, already considering writing something on Glass, did not want to be influenced by Neihardt. "I wanted to make my own wriggle down that muddy road of the unknown," he later wrote. "So I snapped *A Cycle of the West* shut and handed it back."[47]

Like Neihardt, Manfred "had read the Greeks," and when he first encountered the Glass story, he said, "it struck me that we, too, in our American past had had an Achilles." Indeed, because Glass "had forgiven his deserters," he was an even greater hero. Moreover, "Hugh Glass had performed his heroics while completely alone," Manfred said, whereas "Achilles always had a contingent of Greek warriors near by."[48]

In 1954, Manfred published his own rendition of the Hugh Glass story in *Lord Grizzly*, the first tale in his five-volume Buckskin Man series. He had previously published several novels under the name Feike Feikema, but *Lord Grizzly* was the first work of fiction he published as Frederick Manfred. It was also his first novel on a historical topic and the first to sell well, remaining on the national bestseller list for six weeks. *Lord Grizzly* is a "real, rich, bright novel," wrote Richard Sullivan in the *Chicago Sunday Tribune*, and it deserves the "warm applause of all who, like the author, value the legends of America and believe in both their perpetuation and their interpretation."[49] Similarly, V. P. Hass wrote in the *New York Times*, "there is a ranginess, a free-wheeling robustness, an engaging lustiness of style and expression" not apparent in Manfred's earlier works. *Lord Grizzly*, he concluded, "is a heady mixture of history made into first-rate fiction."[50] Manfred's choice for the book's title served him well. "The grizzly is the lord of the animal world on this continent," Manfred said. "And Hugh Glass, after his heroic crawl, was the lord of all mountain men. Using that title as a bull's-eye helped me keep my eye on the main thrust of the story."[51]

Manfred's preparations for writing *Lord Grizzly* were extensive. "The librarians at the university soon caught on that I was going to do something about the Hugh Glass story," he said, and they began finding books for him. "I don't know how many I read. More than a hundred perhaps," he said. Two of them especially grabbed his attention: *Life in the Far West* by George Frederick Ruxton, and *Wah-to-yah and the Taos Trail* by Lewis Garrard. He liked these, not because they discussed Glass, but because in his opinion they offered "the truest account" of how mountain men actually talked. The dialogue in these books became a model for him. He also observed grizzly bear behavior at the zoo and fired a replica of Glass's rifle. Later, he made a splint, tied it to his leg, and crawled over the ground near his home in Bloomington, Minnesota, to simulate Glass's experience. "The perspective from that low point of view was astonishing," he said. "Eyes a foot off the ground, I found it to be a new way of looking at life."[52] It undoubtedly was, for Manfred stood six feet, nine inches tall.

Manfred and his wife Maryanna also drove their old Ford to western South Dakota so that he could examine the terrain for himself. A resident of Lemmon showed them the Hugh Glass monument and the spot "where local talk placed the mauling." The next morning, Manfred used some maps to explain to his wife, "now, I'm going to walk from this spot here to that spot there. Since there are no roads in this part of Dakota, you'll have to drive back to the main highway, go across to here, and then come down to here. I should be there in about three or four hours." At that point, he said, "she slowly turned purple."[53]

Manfred said that he "walked from near Lemmon on the Grand River, past Thunder Butte," and down to the Moreau River, where Maryanna waited. "The next day she once again took the long way around," he said, "while I climbed he next hogback, past Rattlesnake Butte, down to where Cherry Creek poured into the Cheyenne River." He took careful notes as he hiked, and he carried "a gunnysack and some one hundred small wax-paper bags. Every time I saw something interesting—a flower, some grass, what a farmer would call a weed—I would clip it, mark it on the map, and then put it into the wax bag. . . . Why invent grasses or flowers when nature was far more inventive than I might be?"[54]

Afterward, Manfred traveled to Pierre to visit historian Will Robinson at the South Dakota State Historical Society.

"Robinson became intrigued with my project," Manfred said, but "hoped that I wouldn't go about it the way Neihardt did." Robinson told Manfred how he had taken Neihardt for a drive to locate Glass's route. Suddenly, Neihardt told him to stop. "Ah," whispered Neihardt, "Hugh went along here. On hands and knees." When Robinson asked, "How do you know?" Neihardt responded, "I can just feel him having been here."[55] Robinson also showed Manfred the letter that Glass had written to John Gardner's parents. Manfred was skeptical, wondering whether Glass actually wrote it.

Literary critic John R. Milton thought that all these experiences helped Manfred "project the story through the mind of his main character, in most cases keeping himself as a writer out of the story." He allowed readers to observe "exactly the same things that Hugh sees, no more and no less," making *Lord Grizzly* a powerful novel with "a remarkable fusion of style and theme, of rhythm and form, of biblical allusions and mountain man history, and of myth-symbolism and down-to-earth realism."[56]

Despite all his research, Manfred clarified that *Lord Grizzly* was "a novel—not a history," and in some instances, he admitted, he did not follow "what some claim as fact or the most plausible legend."[57] According to Manfred, the changes he introduced were an important part of the creative process. "Historians can't tell us much beyond such facts as they find," he asserted. "They can speculate some, but it had better be done guardedly, with much qualification. The novelist, however, can fill in the gaps with speculation based on his or her general knowledge of human nature."[58] Manfred admitted to creating one fictional person, Bending Reed, a Sioux woman living with Glass. He justified the addition by noting that many trappers had Indian wives. In his novel, Bending Reed was the Sioux woman whose escape from her Arikara captors resulted in the shooting deaths of two Arikaras by fur trappers, raising tensions that culminated in the Arikara attack on Ashley's party later that year. Bending Reed calls Glass "White Grizzly," suggesting a similarity between Glass and the grizzly bear.[59]

To make Glass more heroic, Manfred also magnified his place in Ashley's 1823 party, placing him on guard duty the night of the Arikara attack. In this invented role, Glass is able to criticize Ashley's decisions during the battle. Manfred also makes Glass the partner of Johnnie Gardner, the man killed during the attack, clarifying why he was asked to write the letter to Gardner's parents. Manfred even invents a relationship between Glass and Mike Fink; when Henry informs the party about Fink's death, Glass is pleased, for he and Fink had been enemies.[60]

Following Gardner's death, Manfred has Glass partner with Fitzgerald and Bridger. While hunting buffalo, the three barely escaped an ambush set by Arikara warriors who disguised themselves with buffalo robes. Despite Glass's warning, the inexperienced Bridger fell for their ruse and had to be rescued. In another instance, Glass learned that his new companions had slept on guard duty, allowing Mandan Indians to enter the camp and kill two men. Glass lied to Henry to cover up their mistake and thought that this favor should have made them more indebted to him. On the other hand, their failures also indicated that Fitzgerald and Bridger were not trustworthy. Manfred even invented a new reason for Glass to be hunting alone ahead of the party. Indians preferred to kill and scalp trappers who wore beards, wrote Manfred, and Glass's facial hair placed the entire party in jeopardy. Henry ordered Glass to shave, and when Glass refused, Henry removed him from hunting duty. Glass angrily sneaked off to hunt by himself.[61]

After Glass's mauling, Fitzgerald and Bridger remained with him while the rest of the party continued to the Yellowstone. Manfred's Fitzgerald was more educated than the other trappers, so like most educated people in Manfred's view, he was incapable of making quick and appropriate decisions. Thus, Fitzgerald concluded that the only way he and Bridger could save themselves from Indians was to leave. Speaking in a delirium, Glass himself made their decision easier by telling them not to risk their lives. He also described how he had once unwittingly consumed human flesh, making him a cannibal. In addition, his companions learned that he had deserted his wife and two sons. These admissions made it easier for Fitzgerald and Bridger to leave him and, later, made it difficult for Glass to hold them accountable, for he, too, had been guilty of disobedience and desertion.[62]

After his novel became a bestseller, Manfred attempted to adapt it for film. In 1964, he completed a screenplay, which was optioned by Screen Gem Studios. However, the studio decided not to produce it. Manfred believed that the decision rested on problems inherent in the script: Glass's crawl demanded that audiences watch a single actor on the screen for more than half an hour. However, historian Jon T. Coleman suggested that there were other problems with Manfred's script, including scenes from his novel depicting a grizzly bear licking maggots from the festering wounds on Glass's back and a spirit grizzly appearing in the closing scene.[63]

What Manfred did for Hugh Glass in fiction, John Myers Myers did in biography. His *Pirate, Pawnee, and Mountain Man* (1963), the first book-length study of Glass, presented the trapper as an authentic hero deserving national attention. "Deep in the medicine bag of every nation is the tale of a warrior pitted against a beast of dread proportions," he wrote. "In the lore of America, this alpha of epics takes the form of a struggle between a mountain man called Hugh Glass and an outsize grizzly." The only difference, he added, is that with Glass, the fight with the bear "is of less moment than his feat of surviving, after being abandoned in the wilderness by men who were sure his watch couldn't be wound again." Indeed, Myers claimed, Glass was "the purest known example of the American in buckskin," surpassing even Daniel Boone. While Boone worked on the edge of settlement and wanted to be a "great landholder," Glass "functioned when and where settlement wasn't yet dreamed of, and he had no more use for a tie to any piece of real estate than he had for the leg-irons of organized society." Thus, Glass's story "springs only from a hard-mouthed will to thrive again, in the face of cataclysm."[64] According to Myers, there is nothing like it in ancient literature.

In setting Glass up as a great hero, Myers felt obligated to defend him against criticism. Thus, he rebutted the accusations made by J. Cecil Alter, biographer of James Bridger, who concluded that most of the Glass story was fiction. To prove his argument, Myers assembled every source he could find on Glass. Unfortunately, he accepted stories of dubious veracity, such as Glass being captured by pirates and Pawnees. As Myers said, his purpose was only to assemble the accounts, and "whether or not any of these can also be styled 'facts' will be the book's secondary concern."[65]

By the mid-twentieth century, the Hugh Glass story was reaching a peak in its popularity, being featured not only in histories, poetry, fiction, children's books, school texts, and biography, but also in newsstand magazines, comics, television programs, and even sheet music. The August 1951 issue of the comics magazine *Gunsmoke* included Stephen Kirkel's story "Hugh Glass: Fighting Firebrand of the Frontier." According to Kirkel, "Indians hated, feared and yet respected Hugh Glass, a strapping six footer, the most fabulous frontiersman who ever lived." Kirkel's Glass weighed two hundred twenty pounds, and "no man, white or red, ever questioned his courage after . . . he crawled 210 miles, on hands and knees, more dead than alive, to get aid after being left for dead following a fight with a ferocious grizzly bear." Although he asserted that his comic was "a true story," Kirkel named Tom Fitzpatrick as one of Glass's deserters; claimed that Bridger was Glass's adopted son; had

Glass give up on revenge in order to set an example to others; and finally killed Glass off four years later as he was "heroically helping settlers attacked by Indians."[66] In *Famous Heroes of the Old West* (1957), written for younger readers, author William Moyers claimed that it would be "difficult to find a story of endurance and recovery equal to that of Old Hugh Glass and his incredible journey."[67] In 1966, the television series *Death Valley Days* featured John Alderson as Hugh Glass in an episode called "Hugh Glass Meets the Bear," and the same year, Harold B. Lambert's song "The Hugh Glass Story" versified, "The food that he found was nothing to relish; Slugs, beetles and snakes and ev'rything hellish!"[68]

Popular magazines such as *Saga*, which advertised its articles as "True Stories for Men," featured more creative writing than research. J. Eugene Chrisman's "He Lived for Revenge" (1954) described Glass as "a giant whose great strength was legendary in the West." He could put his "massive shoulder to the rear wheel of a heavily loaded freight wagon and by sheer strength release it from the viscous clutch of Red River mud."[69] Likewise, *True West* declared that its articles were "All True—All Fact." Nevertheless, it published E. Gorton Covington's "Alone and Left to Die!" (1962), which opened with an invented order that Henry gave on the morning before Glass met the grizzly. "Hugh Glass will ride ahead to hunt," Henry purportedly said. "He will go alone because he can take care of himself and because he knows the country. If he sees Indian sign he can turn back and warn us. Otherwise we will meet him this evening at the base of yonder butte." According to Covington, Glass was actually hunting the grizzly that attacked him. This bear, however, was "a rogue, carrying in its groin an Indian arrowhead which turned the grizzly into an unpredictable foe more prone to charge than run."[70] In a 1964 article in *Real West*, author Bob Young noted spuriously that the Grand River "was notorious for the fierce, brutish grizzly bears which prowled the territory in packs of two or three. Since they had never been consistently hunted, they had no fear whatever of the white man and actually attacked him as fair game whenever they roamed in numbers." Young also claimed that Glass eventually met his death at the hands of Arikara Indians while he was hunting; he was "so intent upon his quarry that he had let his guard down." Young asked rhetorically, "What had he been hunting? Why, grizzly bears, of course."[71]

Some popular magazines even doctored information to illustrate their stories. In the February 1969 issue of *Great West*, Emily H. Lewis captioned a well-known drawing of an anonymous trapper thus: "Old Glass looked cautiously around for Indians in hiding before starting into the thicket." This caption is deceptive, as no likeness of Glass is known to exist. Worse, George Catlin's famous painting of the Mandan O-kee-pa ceremony, showing young Mandan men hanging from the ceiling of a lodge with hide thongs thrust through their skin, is captioned: "When Indians tortured his comrades, Hugh Glass soon realized he could not trust them in spite of their professions of friendship."[72]

The Glass legend also made it into academic works. In *South Dakota: A Bicentennial History* (1977), John Milton called it "the one amazing story which cannot be debunked. . . . It is not uncommon to pit man against beast, in folklore or in fiction," he said, "but the importance of the Glass story comes not so much from his single-handed battle with a grizzly bear as it does from his act of survival afterward."[73]

However, times were changing. Beginning in the sixties, interest in western heroes declined dramatically and "westerns" virtually disappeared from television and movie screens. It was an age marked by civil-rights marches, antiwar protests, demands for women's rights, and environmental activism. The "winning of the West" was less often viewed as a heroic achievement of civilization and progress.

Instead, western "heroes" were criticized for destroying both American Indian culture and the environment. Depictions of conflicts between powerless working people and strong political and economic authorities began to rise in popularity.

In 1971, *Man in the Wilderness*, starring Richard Harris, reached movie screens. Threatened with lawsuits over copyright infringement by Neihardt and Manfred, the producers had changed the story. Hugh Glass became Zachary Bass, and much of the film strangely featured a large boat, the "Moby Richard," that the men hauled across the prairie. In her review of the movie, critic Judith Crist wrote, "an unfortunate thing happened on its way to or from the cutting room. The backbone of the plot and the point of the film got lost." Nevertheless, it provided a decent survival story, she said, and Richard Harris gave "an excellent performance."[74]

In the story, Captain Filmore Henry (John Huston) hauls the boat across the prairie using a wagon pulled by horses. Zachary Bass, a member of Henry's party, is hunting nearby with an inexperienced companion named Jamie. After Jamie wounds a deer, Bass pursues the injured animal and is attacked by a grizzly bear. Jamie rushes to camp to inform Henry, who hurries to the scene with his men and kills the bear. Although the men drag Bass back to camp, Henry tells them that the party must continue toward its destination, and he asks two men to remain with Bass until he dies. After the party moves on, the two men desert Bass, having spotted Indians in the distance. When they catch up with the party, they explain to Henry that they left Bass because Indians were breathing down their necks. Although the younger man says they could return, Henry nixes the idea, claiming that they are on an expedition important to America. "I know he would be proud of my decision," Henry says of Bass.

Much of the film centers on Bass's efforts to survive. He also experiences numerous flashbacks, revealing that he was married and that after his wife's death, he left their baby with others. He feels guilty about his decision, even while pursuing Henry for his desertion. Meanwhile, Henry somehow realizes that Bass is following him to exact revenge and often stares into the distance, watching for him. In the final scene, the boat is mired down in the mud by the Missouri River, and the Arikara Indians are attacking. When Bass arrives, the Indians cease fighting and watch quietly while Bass goes to take his vengeance. However, Bass only demands the return of his rifle and walks away. Rather than fighting, he has decided to go home. The rest of the men follow him, leaving the boat and the Arikara warriors behind. The antiwar theme and the slap at the notion of dying for one's country were a far cry from earlier portrayals of Glass's heroism.

A more recent work, John T. Coleman's *Here Lies Hugh Glass: A Mountain Man, a Bear, and the Rise of the American Nation* (2012) shows even more dramatically how depictions of western heroes have changed. Coleman, who asserts that "as a writer and a historian," he is "on a prolonged expedition to see how much I can get away with in the company of somber academics," admits to having an "antiauthoritarian" streak. According to Coleman, biographers share a "central conceit . . . that individual human lives tower above all else." Thus, writers telling Glass's story have made him into "America's Odysseus, a laughable honorific for a working-class guy whose major talent, accident proneness, made him more Homer Simpson than Homeric." Indeed, "Glass was a loser by most measures. Estates and fortunes evaded him. He appears to have impressed people with his physical endurance and storytelling skills, but there's no evidence that his confidants loved or admired him." Coleman found Glass to be a kindred spirit. "I picked a biographical companion," he said, "who suited my personality."[75]

Coleman used Glass's story as a vehicle for a wide-ranging commentary on early nineteenth-century American society; the portion of his book dealing with Glass himself is piecemeal and occasionally inaccurate. For example, he carelessly named one of Glass's deserters as Fitzpatrick (rather than Fitzgerald) and did not mention that Fitzgerald was one of the three messengers sent by Henry to Fort Atkinson in 1823 or that his enlistment in the Sixth Regiment has been confirmed.[76]

However, Coleman's work is clearly not meant to be straightforwardly biographical. Instead, he considered Glass to be a typical member of the working class exploited by employers. "The Americans' gamble to equip bands of their own hunters and send them west to kill beavers was a disaster for the men contracted to do the job," he asserted. Survival stories such as Glass's crawl "hinted at their bewilderment and communicated their shared sense of powerlessness." Instead of focusing on their own weakness and exploitation, trappers related stories about being mauled by bears or attacked by Indians. These stories celebrated their endurance and gave them power.[77]

Despite the changed attitudes about western heroes exhibited in Coleman's work and elsewhere, romanticized accounts of the Hugh Glass story have not vanished. In fact, a resurgence of such stories occurred near the end of the twentieth century. In 1987, for example, Douglas W. Ellison penned an account called "Hugh Glass: The Survivor" for *South Dakota Magazine*, describing the story as "one of the most incredible true-life dramas ever recorded."[78] Likewise, Nancy M. Peterson wrote "Hugh Glass' Crawl into Legend" for the June 2000 issue of *Wild West*. In her article, Glass reached Henry's post just after New Year's Day, 1824, and the men immediately celebrated his return, except for "Young Jim Bridger," who "stood frozen in shock and fear." Indeed, Bridger became "such a piteous sight that Glass could not bring himself to cock his rifle" and decided that Bridger's "punishment would come from his own conscience."[79]

Novelists, too, continued to find Glass a suitable subject. In *Hugh Glass* (1995), Bruce Bradley created a Glass who was a skilled frontiersman even before Ashley hired him. "He was an expert tracker and hunter; he knew how to survive out on the open plains or in the hills," Bradley wrote. "In addition to all this, Glass was educated. . . . Ashley knew that one could never tell when that might come in handy."[80] Michael Punke's *The Revenant* (2002) contrasted Glass, a responsible, trusted member of Henry's party, with Fitzgerald, a disreputable villain. Glass sympathizes with trapper William Anderson, whose brother was killed by the Arikaras, whereas Fitzgerald tells Anderson that the coyotes were probably dragging parts of his brother's body around the prairie. When Glass prevents Fitzgerald from harming Anderson during the ensuing confrontation, Fitzgerald vows to get even with him. Thus, Punke provided a reason for Fitzgerald's desertion of Glass after the mauling. Larry McMurtry also used Glass as a significant background character in his novel *The Wandering Hill* (2003), which opens with Glass attacking Bridger and the incorrectly named Tom Fitzpatrick for deserting him. Later, when the trappers listen to Glass tell his story of survival, they assume it is merely a tall tale and only pretend to believe him. Nevertheless, one of them is certain that the story "would be told around Western campfires for years to come," having "the makings of a play, or an opera even."[81]

New works for younger readers have also appeared. Robert M. McClung's novel *Hugh Glass, Mountain Man* (1990) asserted that Glass, "because of his exploits and his incredible fortitude, endurance, and determination, became a legendary hero of the Old West."[82] Andrew Glass, in his *Mountain Men: True Grit and Tall Tales* (2001), admitted that Glass was disobedient, never being "much for taking orders," but considered his story of survival worthy of attention.[83] Margie La Due, author of *Crawl into the Night: A Story about Hugh Glass* (2008), was inspired to write by Neihardt's "beautifully written epic poem."[84] The Hugh Glass story also became part of Carl W. Hart's *Amazing Stories from History* (2009), a special text published for school children by the University of Michigan Press. The book employs "high interest stories" to make students "want to read, want to finish, want to understand."[85]

The Glass tale even found its way into a new genre: survival literature. For example, Edward E. Leslie's *Desperate Journeys, Abandoned Souls: True Stories of Castaways and Other Survivors* (1988) included a thorough discussion of Glass's adventures. Glass also made an appearance in the inaugural issue of *American Frontiersman* (2012). "A frontiersman has the spirit, mindset, and grit to strike out on his own where others fear to tread," the editor declared.[86] Among other articles describing how to build a dugout canoe or a cabin, how to tan furs and butcher big game, and how to make a muzzle-loader appears Jim Spencer's article on Hugh Glass, John Colter, and John ("Liver Eating") Johnston. According to Spencer, Glass's survival after being mauled is "one of the most remarkable feats of endurance known to man."[87]

Meanwhile, the monument that the John G. Neihardt Club built to honor Hugh Glass in 1923 was slowly deteriorating and had even been vandalized. Finally, in 1964, the South Dakota State Historical Society, the Department of Game, Fish, and Parks, and the Lemmon Chamber of Commerce placed a new marker about half a mile south of the earlier monument. It asserted that Glass, "a habitual 'loner,'" was abandoned by Bridger and Fitzgerald, who "probably" believed him dead. Upon waking, Glass made his way "by an uncertain route" to Fort Kiowa. "That much is verified history," the marker proclaimed; "whatever the details, it was a marvelous show of strength and courage."[88]

On the one hundred fiftieth anniversary of Glass's encounter with the bear, the town of Lemmon celebrated the "Hugh Glass Odyssey" to "commemorate the exploits of the man who was mauled by a grizzly bear" and "crawled to civilization to survive."[89] During these 1973 festivities, Governor Richard Kneip and Julius Young of the John G. Neihardt Society dedicated Hugh Glass State Park, located on the shores of Shadehill Reservoir. The members of an interim class on Hugh Glass being taught at the University of South Dakota were also in attendance. Neihardt himself had made his last trek to the site in September 1967, accompanied by Young and his wife. It was the first time "since the memorable event in 1923" that they had made the journey together. Reflecting on the endurance of Glass's story, Young had asked rhetorically, "A really big observance is planned for August 1, 2023. Will you attend?"[90]

Remarkably, it seems likely that the two-hundredth-anniversary commemoration of the Glass mauling will be larger than any previous celebration. The film *The Revenant*, based on Michael Punke's novel and starring Leonardo DiCaprio as Hugh Glass, was released in December 2015 and January 2016. DiCaprio, who has appeared in movies such as *Titanic*, *The Wolf of Wall Street*, *The Great Gatsby*, *J. Edgar*, *Blood Diamond*, *The Aviator*, and *Catch Me If You Can*, brought significant attention to the Hugh Glass story. In October 2015, a *Washington Post* reporter noted that *The Revenant* was "based on a true story" and would feature "a transformed Leo, complete with dirty, stringy hair, tortuously chapped lips and bad teeth."[91]

Well before the film was released, enthusiasts in Lemmon, South Dakota, held "the first annual Hugh Glass rendezvous" in August 2015. As local newspaper publisher LaQuita Shockley noted, the town "was sitting on a little gold nugget," and as soon as the movie was released, there would be "global attention," and people would "want to walk upon the very spot" where Hugh Glass struggled with the bear.[92] *Bismarck Tribune* reporter Lauren Donovan explained that the word "revenant" is French "for one who has returned from the dead," an appropriate epithet for the man who was mauled by a grizzly, deserted by his companions, and "crawled, mauled and broken, to seek revenge." Donovan predicted that the film's release would "put Lemmon and the nearby Shadehill Reservoir on the nation's map like nothing ever has."[93]

According to Donovan, however, the town of Lemmon was not solely dependent on DiCaprio's acting to advertise the Glass story: "It has its own nationally renowned scrap iron sculptor John Lopez to do that." Lopez, whose studio is located on the outskirts of Lemmon, has created a monumental sculpture weighing about a thousand pounds and visualizing "that horrific encounter between Glass and the grizzly." It portrays Glass "with the hot breath of a raging carnivore in his face."[94]

Lopez created the sculpture with local heritage in mind. "You come to Lemmon and Shadehill and there's no imagery of the grizzly bear or Hugh Glass," he remarked, "so we definitely need to flesh out some kind of visual. It's a cool part of our history."[95] Lopez had already created numerous scrap-iron sculptures featuring the region's history, which are catalogued in *John Lopez Sculpture: Grand River Series* (2014). He had considered adding Hugh Glass to his series long before DiCaprio's film was announced. "I've been dreaming and scheming about this piece for a long time," said Lopez.[96] According to Donovan, Lopez finally decided to depict "those seconds just before the grizzly tore claw and teeth into the man's flesh." Glass appears to be facing certain death in the sculpture, where his "prized German-made black powder rifle is out of reach," although he does hold an "upraised knife," suggesting that there is hope. Lopez's new sculpture was appropriately unveiled at the Grand River Museum in Lemmon on 29 August 2015, during the first Hugh Glass Rendezvous. According to Donovan, Lopez hoped that the rendezvous would continue, "fueled by the movie's release, in the same way Kevin Costner's role in 'Dances With Wolves' sparked a new national romance" with the region in the 1990s.[97]

There were other indications of renewed interest in the Glass story, as well. Mitchell, South Dakota, artist Lyle Miller, Sr., who spent part of the summer of 2015 as artist-in-residence at the Crazy Horse Memorial near Custer, South Dakota, planned his painting *Lord Grizzly* prior to the announcement of the DiCaprio film. Likewise, work on this biography began several years ago, independently of other commemorative efforts (*see* the Acknowledgments). Despite occasional lapses in popularity, it appears that the saga of Hugh Glass will continue to attract a diverse regional and national audience well into the future.[98]

7

And
What about
the Bear?

Today, no grizzly bears live along the Grand River in South Dakota. Those in the prairie region were killed off within decades after Glass was mauled, and the grizzlies in the Black Hills were gone by the turn of the century. Of the eighteen states where grizzly bears originally lived, only five are still known to have them within their borders: Alaska, Montana, Wyoming, Idaho, and Washington. "Once in a while one of the other thirteen western states will hopefully announce the sighting of a grizzly," remarked wildlife administrator Frank Dufresne in 1955, but such reports were not confirmed. In fact, Dufresne concluded, "more than ninety-nine percent of the original grizzly populations of the United States [were] destroyed."[1] Between one thousand and fifteen hundred grizzly bears remain in the contiguous United States, many in national parks.

Today, it is difficult even to estimate how many grizzly bears lived in the American West prior to European American settlement. "Any figure arrived at can at best be little more than something between an estimate and a wild guess," noted bear expert Harold McCracken. Nevertheless, after studying the journals and records of early travelers and the reports of game and wildlife services, he calculated that at least one hundred thousand grizzlies lived between the Mississippi River and the Pacific coast in 1850. "That is really a lot of grizzly bears, although it is apt to be an underestimate of the actual number," he concluded.[2]

Writers telling the Hugh Glass story have usually portrayed Glass as a heroic survivor and the grizzly bear as a ferocious predator. In stark contrast, most naturalists portray humans as the predators and grizzly bears as the victims. McCracken, for example, made this point forcefully. "The most dangerously destructive creature that ever lived on this fair continent of ours, taken collectively as a species, certainly is the white man of our western pioneer era," he wrote. European Americans "virtually exterminated the grizzly bears throughout most of their native haunts," he said, making them, not the grizzly bear, "the bravest, boldest, and most dangerous of all—the real American *king of beasts!*"[3]

Early western travelers, however, commonly depicted grizzly bears as monsters. The grizzly bear "is the enemy of man; and literally thirsts for human blood," wrote Henry M. Brackenridge in 1814, adding that this bear "seldom fails to attack." Although Brackenridge had accompanied Manuel Lisa's expedition up the Missouri River in 1811, his information about grizzly bears was mostly secondhand. Lisa had informed him, for example, that some of these bears weighed in excess of twelve hundred pounds and were so powerful that they tore "to pieces the largest buffaloe." No wonder Brackenridge concluded that grizzly bears were the "monarch of the country," comparable to lions and tigers in Africa and Asia. He also claimed that, for American Indians, killing a grizzly bear gave a hunter "greater renown than the scalp of a human enemy." When they entered wooded areas frequented by grizzly bears, Brackenridge wrote, Indians made "a loud and continued shout, in order that the bears, if there be any, may either come forth to attack them, or retire."[4]

Most Americans were familiar with the smaller and less aggressive black bear, common in the eastern half of the continent. Grizzly bears, however, were a new phenomenon. Although there had been rumors about a different kind of bear in the West, no one described the grizzly bear's behavior and habits thoroughly before the expedition led by Meriwether Lewis and William Clark between

1804 and 1806. Indeed, for the next half-century, Lewis and Clark's field notes became the primary source of information about these animals. Not until 1815, a decade after the expedition, was the grizzly bear officially designated a new species. George Ord, who has been called "the father of North American zoology," published his account in the second American edition of William Guthrie's *New Geographical, Historical, and Commercial Grammar.*[5] Ord named the new species *Ursus horribilis*, suggesting that he shared popular conceptions of its ferocity. Although Ord cited observations made by Lewis and Clark and used hides and skulls that they collected for his scientific classification, his description of the animal was largely a quotation from Henry Brackenridge.[6]

Some early observers believed that there might actually be several species of large bears in the West. Lewis and Clark found the grizzly bears in the Far West to be less ferocious than those in the Missouri River region, and the color of their fur varied between black, brown, and red. Although Lewis still considered them to be the same species as those along the Missouri, on 14 May 1806, he wrote, "perhaps it would not be unappropriate to designate them as the variagated bear."[7]

Indeed, one later scientist, after examining the different colors, sizes, and behaviors of these bears, concluded that there were many unique species. Clinton Hart Merriam, a respected biologist and author of *Review of the Grizzly and Big Brown Bears of North America* (1918), listed eighty-six different species of grizzly bears. Merriam was a "splitter," as opposed to a "lumper"; that is, he "tended to make more and more species based on finer and finer distinctions between individual animals."[8] Although most of his designations were based on skull measurements, his descriptions of these bears also noted color differences. Today, scientists generally accept that there are only two species of bears in North America: black bears (*Ursus americanus*) and grizzly bears (*Ursus arctos*). Indeed, genetic research indicates that *Ursus arctos* is the only grizzly species in the world. Some naturalists suggest that two subspecies occur in North America: *Ursus arctos horribilis* in the American West, and *Ursus arctos middendorffi* in Alaska.[9]

Trappers such as Hugh Glass probably heard stories about grizzly bears before ascending the Missouri River. Many of these tales came from Lewis and Clark, whose accounts helped to shape American perceptions of grizzly bears. The captains first encountered grizzly bears along the Missouri River and its tributaries in North and South Dakota, not far from where Glass was later mauled. This was, indeed, grizzly bear territory. Because hunters later eliminated the bears from the Great Plains region, modern Americans often assume that they had always confined their residence to the Rocky Mountains. However, as naturalist Paul Schullery observed, "the historic range of the grizzly bear at the time of the first Euro-American settlement . . . more or less followed the one hundredth meridian from north to south."[10] This range included most of western North and South Dakota, Nebraska, and Kansas.

In his instructions to Lewis and Clark, President Thomas Jefferson had requested that the captains describe "the animals of the country generally, & especially those not known in the U.S."[11] Thus, the captains wrote detailed descriptions of grizzly bears and their behavior and, when possible, sent back specimens. In their journals, they usually referred to grizzly bears as "white bears," probably because of the whitish hair along the bears' faces and upper backs. However, they also called the animals brown bears, based on their general color. The captains described almost every encounter they had with bears during their trip. As soon as they began their ascent of the Missouri from their winter camp along the Mississippi River, upstream from Saint Louis, Clark reported that one of the men "Saw three Bar on the other Side of the Prarie."[12] These, of course, were black bears, not grizzlies. The captains' notes on black bears were "brief and matter-of-fact," observed Schullery, but their comments changed dramatically when they encountered grizzly bears.[13]

Evidence of grizzly bears appeared long before Lewis and Clark spotted the animals themselves. At the end of August 1804, they noticed the Yankton Sioux wearing necklaces made of grizzly bear claws. Then, on 7 October, Clark spotted large bear tracks at the mouth of the Moreau River and, two weeks later, "Saw Several fresh tracks of that animal double the Sise of the largest track I ever Saw." One of the men, Pierre Cruzatte, actually shot and wounded a "white bear" on 20 October. He was so frightened at the bear's appearance that he then dropped his gun and ran, and when he returned, he discovered "that the bear had taken the opposite rout."[14] Evidently, he was the only member of the expedition to see a grizzly bear that year.

Lewis and Clark spent the winter of 1804–1805 near present-day Bismarck, North Dakota, close to the Mandan villages. Bears are inactive during the winter months, so the men did not encounter any during their stay. However, when they resumed their westward journey on 7 April 1805, they soon discovered evidence that grizzlies were nearby. On 10 April, John Ordway observed "the track of a verry large white bare,"[15] and on 13 April, near the Little Missouri River, Lewis reported "many tracks of the white bear of enormous size, along the river shore and about the carcases of the Buffaloe, on which I presume they feed." Although they had "not as yet seen one of these anamals," he added, the men were "anxious to meet with some of these bear."[16]

Their desire to see these bears stemmed in part from stories told by the Indians, who, according to Lewis, provided "a very formidable account of the strength and ferocity of this animal," which they "never dare to attack but in parties of six eight or ten persons; and are even then frequently defeated with the loss of one or more of their party." Lewis speculated that the Indians were obliged to come danger-ously close to the bears in order to hunt "with their bows and arrows and the indifferent guns with which the traders furnish them."[17]

With typical skepticism, Lewis discounted much of this information. Despite seeing "immence quantities of game in every direction around us as we passed up the river," he wrote on 17 April 1805, the only bears were "at a great distance generally running from us." Thus, he concluded grizzly bears were "extreemly wary and shy." His perception began to change after his first personal encounter with a grizzly on Monday, 29 April 1805, near the mouth of the Yellowstone River. While walking with another member of the party at about eight o'clock in the morning, he spotted two grizzly bears, "both of which we wounded." Although one bear escaped, the other one chased Lewis "seventy or eighty yards." Fortunately for Lewis, it had been hurt so badly that he was able to reload his gun and kill it. The bear, a young male, weighed about three hundred pounds, and Lewis immediately noted several differences between it and the more familiar black bear. Its "tallons and tusks" were "incomparably larger and longer"; it was yellowish brown in color, with "small, black, and piercing" eyes; and its fur was "finer thicker and deeper than that of the black bear." Finally, he concluded, "it is a much more furious and formi-dable anamal, and will frequently pursue the hunter when wounded." Still, Lewis judged, "in the hands of skillfull ri-flemen they are by no means as formidable or dangerous as they have been represented."[18]

Subsequent encounters cast doubt on this conclu-sion. On Sunday, 5 May 1805, Clark and George Drouillard "killed the largest brown bear this evening which we have yet seen." Despite having "five balls through his lungs and five others in various parts," the bear swam to a sandbar and survived another twenty minutes. Although the bear did not attack, it "made the most tremendous roaring from the moment he was shot." Clark estimated its weight at five hundred pounds, but Lewis believed it to be at least a hundred pounds heavier than that. Since the bear "was in good order," they divided its meat among the men. They also boiled the fat and stored the resulting oil in a cask for use in cooking. The immense size and endurance of this bear "staggered the resolution" of some of the men, Lewis said, but other members of the party continued to be "keen for action with the bear."[19]

They did not have long to wait. Late in the afternoon of 11 May 1805, Lewis saw "one of the Party runing at a distance towards us and making signs and hollowing as if in distress." He ordered the pirogues to stop, and the man, William Bratton, soon caught up with them. He had shot a brown bear about a mile and a half down the river, and it "immediately turned on him and pursued him a considerable distance but he had wounded it so badly that it could not overtake him." Following the trail of blood, Lewis and seven other men went "in quest of this monster." They found the bear "concealed in some very thick brush" and immediately killed the "monstrous beast." According to Lewis, it had "remarkably long fine and rich" fur, and "the flece and skin were as much as two men could possibly carry." The carcass also produced about eight gallons of oil.[20]

Even though Bratton had shot the bear "through the center of the lungs," it had "pursued him near half a mile and had returned more than double that distance" and then "prepared himself a bed in the earth of about 2 feet deep and five long." This endurance, Lewis admitted, was somewhat intimidating, and he decided he would "reather fight two Indians than one bear." The only way to kill these animals, he said, was "by shooting them through the brains, and this becomes difficult in consequence of two large muscles which cover the sides of the forehead and the sharp projection of the center of the frontal bone, which is also of a pretty good thickness."[21]

On Tuesday evening, 14 May 1805, the men once again experienced the difficulty of killing these animals. Lewis recorded the encounter. Spotting "a large brown bear lying in the open grounds about 300 paces from the river," six men, "all good hunters," worked their way to within forty paces of the bear. Four of them "fired nearly at the same time and put each his bullet through him." Nevertheless, the bear "ran at them with open mouth." Now, the two men "who had reserved their fires discharged their pieces at him." One shot broke the bear's shoulder, yet it continued to pursue the men, who "took to flight." Two jumped in a canoe, while the others hid in a clump of willows. Each man fired when able, and although they hit the bear "several times[,] . . . the guns served only to direct the bear to them." Finally, in desperation, two men jumped into the river. "Altho' the bank was nearly twenty feet perpendicular," Lewis wrote, the enraged bear "plunged into the river only a few feet behind the second man." Eventually, one of the hunters on shore "shot him through the head."[22]

Another frightening incident occurred on 2 June 1805, when Lewis and several others went ashore to hunt. They killed six elk, several bison, and some deer, and shot at a grizzly bear, which almost caught George Drouillard and then "pursued Charbono who fired his gun in the air as he ran." While Toussaint Charbonneau hid in a thicket, Drouillard killed the bear "by a shot in the head." Lewis was now even more convinced that a shot to the head was the only way to kill these "tremendious anamals."[23] Unfortunately, the men could not always get any shot at all. On 4 June 1805, Clark reported, a "white Bear" almost caught Joseph Fields, "who could not fire, as his gun was wet." The bear got so close that "it Struck his foot."[24]

For Lewis, the most frightening and perplexing encounter occurred on Friday, 14 June 1805, near the Great Falls of the Missouri. Lewis had taken his rifle and espontoon—a type of halberd issued to officers—to look for a portage around the rapids. Spotting some buffalo, Lewis shot one, but he carelessly neglected to reload his rifle. Almost immediately, he spotted a grizzly bear "briskly advancing" toward him. Being on "an open level plain, not a bush within miles nor a tree within less than three hundred yards of me," and with "no place by means of which I could conceal myself from this monster untill I could charge my rifle," he decided to retreat. As he began moving away, the bear charged, "open mouthed and full speed." It gained on him rapidly, and in desperation, he jumped into the river. When "about waist deep," he turned and pointed his espontoon toward the grizzly bear, now only twenty feet away. To Lewis's surprise, the bear "wheeled about as if frightened, . . . and retreated with quite as great precipitation as he had just before pursued me." While Lewis hurried to shore to reload his rifle, the bear continued to run across the open plain for about three miles, going "at full speed, sometimes appearing to look behind him as if he expected pursuit." Lewis could not explain the bear's strange behavior. Nevertheless, he was "gratifyed" that the bear "declined the combat," and he was determined never again to forget to reload his rifle.[25]

In his book *Lewis and Clark among the Grizzlies*, Paul Schullery explained the behavior that mystified Lewis. Noting that grizzlies are much faster than humans, he pointed out that the bear could easily have caught Lewis if it had wanted to. He suggested that the bear probably approached Lewis out of curiosity, became alarmed, and then made a "bluff charge" in order to intimidate him. Running, Schullery added, was the worst possible reaction, for it triggered the bear's instinct to pursue. As soon as Lewis confronted the animal in the river, it retreated.[26]

Grizzly bears became increasingly troublesome. On the night of 26 June 1805, one "came within thirty yards" of camp to eat some buffalo meat hanging from a pole. Two days later, Lewis noted that the bears now "come close arround our camp every night but have never yet ventured to attack us and our dog gives us timely notice of their visits." He required the men "to sleep with their arms by them . . . for fear of accedents," and he no longer thought it "prudent to send one man alone on an errand of any kind, particularly where he has to pass through the brush." However, the men had also learned much about the behavior of grizzlies, helping them to escape harm. On 27 June 1805, Lewis wrote, "it is worthy of remark that these bear never climb." That day, after a violent thunderstorm, Drouillard and Fields had spotted tracks in the brushy area along the river. They quietly landed and climbed about twenty feet up a tree. From this position of safety, they hollered loudly, "and this large bear instantly rushed forward to the place from whence he had heard the human voice issue." Drouillard immediately "shot him in the head."[27]

Lewis and Clark's stories of frequent and dangerous encounters with bears naturally led readers to believe that grizzlies were ferocious monsters, and subsequent writers capitalized on this impression. Given "the public's great appetite for lurid stories," wrote Paul Schullery, it was impossible for popular writers to ignore the potential for "all that delicious dread and gore."[28] For example, John Davidson Godman's *American Natural History* (1826) described two grizzly bear cubs caged at Peale's Museum (later renamed the Philadelphia Museum). "When first received they were quite small," wrote Godman, but as they grew, they "gave indication of that ferocity for which this species is so remarkable." Indeed, they "became exceedingly dangerous, seizing and tearing to pieces every animal they could lay hold of, and expressing extreme eagerness to get at those accidently brought within sight of their cage, by grasping the iron bars with their paws and shaking them violently, to the great terror of spectators." The bears were killed when only half grown, because "their ferocity became so alarming as to excite continual apprehension lest they should escape."[29]

However, many of these commonly held perceptions were inaccurate. Hunter and naturalist William Wright, who studied grizzly bears for twenty-five years and authored the first significant work on the species, observed that they generally avoided trouble, and that human provocation was an element in most bear attacks. They fight "when they think they have to," Wright wrote, and "I would no more provoke one, unarmed, or rashly venture upon any action that my experience has taught me they regard as calling for self-defence, than I would commit suicide."[30] Likewise, South Dakota scientists William H. Over and Edward P. Churchill asserted that grizzly bears, "unless wounded or molested while with their young, are not offensive and are eager enough to amble off and be let alone."[31]

Careful examination of encounters between western travelers and grizzly bears supports these assertions. Explorer Zebulon M. Pike, who purchased the cubs that ended up in the Philadelphia Museum from Indians, wrote that at first his men carried the animals "in their laps on Horse back." Later, they hauled them in a cage on a mule, but they always let the cubs out when the expedition halted. "By this treatement they became extreamely Docile," Pike wrote, and when freed from their cages, they followed his men "like dogs through our camps, small villages; and the forts where we halted." As long as they were well fed, they "would play like young puppies," he said, "but the instant they were shut up and put on the Mule they became cross." Similarly, said Pike, the grizzly bears he saw in their natural habitat were less vicious than popularly perceived. "Whilst in the Mountains we sometimes discovered them at a distance, but in no instance was ever able to come up with one, which we eagerly sought, and *that* being the most inclement season of the Year, induces me to believe they seldom or ever attack a man, unprovoked, but defend themselves courageously."[32]

Later naturalists agreed. "The grizzly was not a malignant man-killer," Harold McCracken asserted. Although "guilty of occasionally staining his chops with the taste of human conquest, resulting from unprovoked aggression," the grizzly bear, he said, "was not, as a species, a confirmed diabolist." Generally, bear attacks were "inspired by circumstances which would make justifiable homicide a proper verdict if the affair had been between man and man." Attacks almost always were "a case of meeting an enemy in a counterattack, rather than seeking whomsoever he might tear to pieces and devour." McCracken would likely have suspected that Hugh Glass's own behavior led to his mauling. "The pioneer trappers and others who avoided putting themselves in belligerent relations with the grizzly seldom got into serious difficulties with him," McCracken insisted.[33]

Nevertheless, popularly held notions prevailed, and chronicles of western adventures regularly featured encounters between people and ferocious bears. For example, in his autobiography, frontiersman Kit Carson described leaving camp one day to "kill something for supper." After shooting an elk, he heard a noise behind him and, upon turning around, "saw two very large grizzly bears making for me." Carson had not reloaded his rifle, so he raced to some nearby trees. He dropped his gun while climbing and had to wait "till the bears found it convenient to leave." When the last bear finally departed, he hurried back to camp without supper. Carson wrote that he was never "so badly scared in my life."[34]

If a famous westerner did not have an authentic encounter with a bear, then later writers invented one for him. In *Heroes of the Plains* (1881), author J. W. Buel claimed that Wild Bill Hickok encountered a cinnamon bear with two cubs while he was hauling freight through the mountains for "Majors & Russels" in 1859. This bear, "moved entirely by her maternal instincts, boldly disputed his passage, and with further advance of the team she growled fiercely and showed her intention to attack him." Hickok was not overly concerned, having two pistols and a bowie knife with him.

Although his first pistol shot struck her "squarely in the forehead," the hit only made the bear angrier, said Buel, "for the cinnamon, like the grizzley, has a brain protection so thick that the ball from an ordinary rifle will produce no impression on it." After Hickok fired a second time, "the bear reared on her hind legs and grappled him." Hickok pulled out his knife, and the ensuing struggle "was one of the most desperate ever known." By the time the fight ended, said Buel, Hickok "had literally disemboweled the dangerous animal," but "it was difficult to decide which presented the more horrifying spectacle, Bill or his dead antagonist." A friend transported him to Santa Fe, where a doctor had him able to travel in two months. Nevertheless, said Buel, Hickok carried the scars "to his grave."[35] The scars were figurative, of course, since the bear fight never occurred.

Such depictions of bears as monsters prevailed in popular culture. "During the childhood days of most of us, bears played a formidable part in our fears," wrote William Over and Edward Churchill in 1941. "Some of this apprehension was justified but more often it was due to imagination on the part of parents or sensational story writers."[36] Theodore Roosevelt, famous as a hunter as well as a politician, thought that grizzly bears should be renamed grisly bears, "in the sense of horrible, exactly as we speak of a 'grisly spectre.'"[37] He even titled one of his books *Hunting the Grisly*.

In some ways, the grizzly bear's fearsome reputation became a self-fulfilling prophecy during the nineteenth century. "The white pioneers, even before they had seen a grizzly, were prepared to meet a dragon," wrote William Wright. Consequently, they tended to shoot when they spotted them, and after they had "peppered a tough old bear or two with their pea-gun ammunition, they found their expectations realized." Grizzly bears were formidable antagonists for people "armed with the muzzle-loading smooth-bores of small calibre and still smaller penetration." People seldom acknowledged that they initiated the attack, wrote Wright, or mentioned that "for every bear that stayed to fight them, there were one or more that ran away."[38]

Indeed, inadequate firepower bolstered the perception of the grizzly bear's ferocity and endurance. Even though Lewis and Clark made their trip at the beginning "of an era of incredibly swift evolution in firearms," noted Paul Schullery, "they were just a little too early to reap the benefits of technological advances that within half a century would place in the hands of mountain men, explorers, and settlers weapons powerful enough to kill both grizzly bears and bison with far less risk." Most members of the Lewis and Clark expedition carried relatively new smooth-bore muskets, "adequate for medium-sized game, perhaps even elk, up to fifty yards, and lethal if progressively less accurate beyond that up past one hundred yards."[39] However, these weapons took about thirty seconds to reload, too long when a grizzly bear was charging. Several expedition members probably carried British-made fusils, popular among trappers and Indians in the upper Missouri region, but generally ineffective against large, dangerous game. Given the number of grizzly bears they shot at, Schullery notes, it is surprising that no members of the expedition were killed or seriously mauled.[40]

Theodore Roosevelt, who categorized the grizzly bear as the only truly dangerous game animal in the United States, agreed. Hunters in the early nineteenth century had only "the long-barrelled, small-bored pea-rifle," he noted, and although these weapons were "marvellously accurate for close range, and their owners [were] famed the world over for their skill as marksmen," the combination was still relatively ineffective against grizzly bears. By the time Roosevelt began hunting, improved weaponry made shooting these bears "much safer than it was at the beginning of [the nineteenth] century."[41]

Roosevelt, an expert outdoorsman, did not fail to notice that grizzlies were more likely to run than to fight. However, instead of concluding that earlier writers had overstated the animals' ferocity, he suggested that the temperament of the species had changed over time. He also ascribed this change to advances in weaponry; the bears altered their behavior as they came to experience "the death-dealing power of men." Over time, the bears' knowledge became hereditary. "No grizzly will assail a man now unprovoked," said Roosevelt. Still, if a bear "is wounded or thinks himself cornered he will attack his foes with a headlong, reckless fury that renders him one of the most dangerous of wild beasts.[42]

Francis Parkman, in the 1892 edition of his classic account *The Oregon Trail*, disagreed. "It is said that [the grizzly bear] is no longer his former self, having found . . . that his ferocious strength is no match for a repeating rifle." However, "one may be permitted to doubt if the blood-thirsty old savage has really experienced a change of heart," Parkman said, "and before inviting him to single combat, the ambitious tenderfoot, though the proud possessor of a Winchester with sixteen cartridges in the magazine, would do well to consider not only the quality of his weapon, but also that of his own nerves."[43]

In fact, the idea that bears had unhesitatingly attacked humans in the past but had now become "shy" because they feared modern firepower was based on false impressions. Grizzly bears had seldom attacked humans without provocation in the first place. After carefully examining the journals of Lewis and Clark, Paul Schullery noticed that expedition members "were rarely attacked, and only occasionally even approached, by grizzly bears unless the bears were shot first."[44] Fred R. Gowans, author of *Mountain Man and Grizzly* (1986), made a statistical analysis of recorded fights between grizzly bears and mountain men. He found seventy instances where humans initiated attacks on grizzlies, whereas bears initiated violence only fourteen times. Even in those fourteen cases, however, mountain men usually surprised the grizzly bears at close range, encountered a sow with cubs, moved too close to a bear feeding on a carcass, or inadvertently lured a bear to camp with the scent of meat. In only one or two instances did a grizzly bear attack a man unprovoked. Likewise, William Wright, in his classic work *The Grizzly Bear* (1909), noted only one instance during the nineteenth century in which "a grizzly attacked a man without provocation," and he concluded that this bear probably attacked because the man had a dog with him.[45] As Schullery noted, these studies do not support "the notion that [grizzly bears] harbored a constant craving for human blood." Instead, he added, on close examination, nineteenth-century grizzlies "sound a great deal like the bears in modern national parks."[46]

In his account of his experiences as a trapper from 1834 to 1843, Osborne Russell had provided an outstanding counterexample to the then-current notion that bears attacked unprovoked. "In going to visit my traps a distance of 3 or 4 mils early in the morning I have frequently seen 7 or 8 [grizzly bears] standing about the clumps of Cherry bushes on their hind legs gathering cherries with surprising dexterity not even deigning to turn their Grizzly heads to gaze at the passing trapper but merely casting a sidelong glance at him without altering their position." Once, he and a Canadian companion surprised a grizzly in a bushy area. It leaped at Russell's companion, "and placing one forepaw upon his head and the other on his left shoulder pushed him one side about 12 ft." Luckily, the Canadian was uninjured; only his coat was torn. However, "it was hard telling which was the most frightened," said Russell, "the man or the Bear." Later, they spotted another grizzly eating a buffalo calf. Rather than defending its prey, "the bear on seeing us dropped the calf & took to his heels into the brush."[47]

The notion that grizzly bears had once been more aggressive was only one of several misconceptions that permeated popular accounts. Indeed, naturalists writing about grizzlies have spent much of their time correcting inaccurate information. "When I first began actually to hunt the grizzly," wrote William Wright, "I found that much of what I had read about him and most of what I had heard was fiction." After listening to hunters relate personal experiences, he decided, "like the Psalmist, that all men were liars." Some storytellers, said Wright, were simply "stuffing the tenderfoot," and he forgave them: "When a man can neither read nor write, and lives most of his life alone on fresh venison and flapjacks, he is entitled to some amusement."[48] However, he could not tolerate superstitions passed on as truth.

One popular misconception was that grizzly bears would put their "fore legs around an antagonist and 'hug' him to death." According to Wright, "there is no truth whatever in this idea, beyond the fact that a grizzly, in attacking a large animal like a steer, will sometimes hold it with one paw while he strikes it or rips it open with the other." Likewise, Wright challenged the notion that bears attack people while walking upright. "I have never yet seen a charging grizzly stand on his hind legs and thus walk up to his antagonist," he said. To the contrary, attacking grizzlies "rush on all-fours; sometimes with a bawl and a snort and with champing of the jaws, but never with open mouth." They would "bite and rend with their teeth, sometimes holding down the object of their wrath with their fore paws while they tear and bite." Although Wright observed bears rearing up "on their hind feet to deliver a blow," they never did so "until they were near enough to strike."[49]

Grizzly bear behavior was misunderstood simply because most early observers were more likely to shoot at the animals than study them. Weighing more than five hundred pounds, standing five feet tall at the shoulder, with claws measuring an incredible seventy-five to one hundred fifty millimeters, shaggy brown coats, and humped shoulders often bearing a silvery mark, these bears appeared ferocious. However, grizzlies do not specialize in hunting large game. They are omnivorous, using their claws to dig up roots, rip into rotten logs for grubs, or make a winter den. In the fall, they devour berries and other seasonal fruit and even eat grass, bark, and mushrooms. Although strong enough to kill any North American land animal, they are so large that pursuing hoofed animals for long distances is difficult, even though they are able to run at speeds up to thirty miles per hour. Their meat diet is primarily carrion, fish, and small mammals such as marmots and ground squirrels. Although they sometimes cache food, grizzlies consume everything they can in the late summer and fall in order to build body fat for the winter. They spend winters in dens, but they do not actually hibernate; their body temperature remains high enough so that they are easily wakened if disturbed. Entering their dens in October or November, they usually emerge in April or May.[50]

Mating typically occurs in mid-July, and the young, usually twins, are born during the winter. They are blind and weigh only a pound and a half at birth; they weigh about six pounds when they leave the den. The cubs begin eating solid foods at four to six months of age but remain with their mother for their first two winters. Yearling bears weigh between one hundred and two hundred pounds. Grizzlies do not attain full growth until they are eight to ten years old.[51]

Interestingly, grizzly bears had "no particular habitat preference," wrote the authors of *Mammals of the Northern Great Plains*. The animals ranged freely "through most kinds of ecosystems, following their noses and propelled by their appetite." On the Northern Great Plains, they fed "on the carrion provided by the great herds of bison."[52] Today, however, they are found almost solely in mountain forests. Grizzly bears no longer inhabit the prairie region because humans killed almost every bear they spotted. Sometimes travelers killed them for food; the men with the Lewis and Clark expedition shot them, as Paul Schullery observed, "not because the men had anything against the bears; they just needed the resources that the bears carried in their bodies, and if any additional incentive for shooting was needed, it was provided by the thrill of the chase."[53] They also killed some bears to obtain specimens for scientific study.

Indeed, the amount of game that western travelers killed is amazing. According to Schullery, the thirty-three members of the Lewis and Clark expedition who traveled from Fort Mandan to the Pacific coast had to hunt constantly to have sufficient food. Clark estimated that the men needed four deer, an elk and a deer, or one bison every day to satisfy the party's demand for meat. After carefully studying the expedition's journals, researchers Ken Walcheck and Raymond Darwin Burroughs determined that expedition members killed 1,001 deer, 396 elk, eighty-five pronghorn antelope, thirty-five bighorn sheep, forty-three grizzly bears, and twenty-three black bears. As Schullery observed, the constant shootings in the journals are "pretty bruising" for modern readers. "We must resist cramming our own values down the throats of people who lived in a very different world," he added, but "after a while it's hard not to wince when the sentence begins, 'They saw a large bear.'"[54]

Other western visitors sought grizzly bears as trophies. George Armstrong Custer, for example, whose 1874 Black Hills expedition is remembered today for the discovery of gold, seemed equally excited at the time about his hunting conquests. On 15 August, he wrote to his wife Elizabeth, "I have reached the highest round on the hunters ladder of fame I have killed my grizzly after a most exciting hunt & combat."[55] The expedition's photographer, William H. Illingworth, commemorated the event in an image showing Custer, Captain William Ludlow of the engineers, the Arikara scout Bloody Knife, and an orderly all posed around the dead bear. Although Custer was justifiably proud of his achievement, having shot the bear twice, Ludlow and Bloody Knife also hit the bear three times. According to the expedition's zoologist, George Bird Grinnell, Custer's bear was "a very old male," whose canine teeth were "mere broken stumps." Many of the incisors were missing, and the molars were worn almost to the gums. The bear also bore many scars, most notably a rugged ten-inch gash on its back, that were probably "the result of battles with some rival during the rutting season," Grinnell concluded.[56]

The grizzly bears encountered by the Custer expedition behaved normally. "I saw no evidences of any great ferocity in any of the specimens killed by the party," wrote Grinnell. "None made any attempt at defense unless so badly wounded as to be unable to escape by flight." For example, two Indian scouts killed a sow and her two half-grown cubs, and "the old female . . . continued to run after both her cubs had been disabled." Grinnell seemed more impressed by their swiftness than their ferocity, noting, "it took several hours' hard riding to overtake the three last mentioned."[57]

Theodore Roosevelt, who ranched in western North Dakota during the 1880s, related numerous accounts of his own hunting exploits. *Hunting Trips on the Prairie*, first published in 1885, included a thorough discussion of his efforts to shoot a grizzly bear. "But few bears are found in the immediate neighborhood of my ranch," he noted, although he had "once or twice seen their tracks in the Bad Lands." To get his trophy, he had to travel to the Bighorn Mountains of Wyoming, where after a long search, Roosevelt and his guide finally discovered the "huge, half-human footprints" of a grizzly. When located, the bear "reared up on his haunches" to look at them, then "dropped down again on all fours, the shaggy hair on his neck and shoulders seeming to bristle." Roosevelt raised his rifle, aimed at a spot "between his small, glittering, evil eyes," and fired. "The huge beast fell over on his side in the death throes," he said, "the ball having gone into his brain, striking as fairly between the eyes as if the distance had been measured by a carpenter's rule." The entire episode had taken only twenty seconds. Roosevelt estimated the animal's weight at twelve hundred pounds. He also described it as an old bear, with "teeth and claws being all worn down and blunted," though "as fat as a prize hog."[58]

Although humans nearly exterminated grizzly bears in the American West, neither trophy hunters such as Custer and Roosevelt nor expedition members seeking food were responsible. The primary cause of the grizzly bear's decline was the arrival of settlers and cattlemen, who blamed grizzly bears for killing livestock. While he admitted that a few "outlaw bears" did kill cattle, Harold McCracken asserted that grizzlies were generally charged with crimes they never committed. "Whenever a head of stock was found dead in a rough part of the range, and there were signs that a grizzly had been feeding upon the carcass, the cattlemen quickly jumped to the conclusion that the bear had done the killing," McCracken wrote.[59] This assumption was frequently not correct. Cattle and sheep often died from disease or accidents, and wolves and mountain lions sometimes killed stock. Grizzly bears ate the carcasses when they found them. McCracken agreed with naturalist Enos A. Mills, who asserted, "perhaps ninety-nine out of every hundred grizzlies never kill any stock or big game."[60]

In their war on grizzly bears, hunters used high-powered repeating rifles and packs of trained hunting dogs. Simultaneously, western settlement reduced the area available to the bears, depleting their food supply. Soon, "cash bounties for the random killing of any grizzly were offered by cattle and sheep growers associations, as well as local and state governments," said McCracken, and "the use of poison and sufficiently heavy steel traps was introduced." The result was "the most consistent and intensive campaign that has ever been carried out for the willful extermination of a species." In fact, McCracken concluded, "not even the rattlesnake has had such a determined and widespread campaign of destruction waged against them as a species."[61]

During the period from 1840 to 1900, Americans considered killing predators to be "part of the necessary job of civilizing the country," observed Paul Schullery, and the grizzly bear was then "a prominent symbol of evil wilderness." Even in the twentieth century, these bears still were "widely perceived as vermin of the worst sort." To some degree, this attitude still persists. "I am sure that in my own neighborhood in northwestern Wyoming and southwestern Montana there are still a fair number of people who would just as soon shoot a grizzly bear on sight," Schullery noted, because they perceive grizzly bears as dangerous and a threat to their commercial interest.[62]

Interestingly, American Indians had a more positive image of grizzly bears, even though they respected them as dangerous adversaries. For many tribes, noted ethnologist David Rockwell, animals were models "to be understood and emulated . . . as a source of wisdom," and various animal species came to symbolize human qualities and characteristics. Some Great Plains tribes regarded the grizzly bear as a "bestower of the secrets and mysteries of plants." The association of bears with plants was logical, for berries, roots, and nuts represent a large portion of the grizzly bear's diet. According to Rockwell, seeing the bear "using its claws instead of a digging stick," it was natural to characterize it as "that wise old animal person digging roots on the sunbaked hillsides." It also became "the mysterious herbalist collecting medicines in the dense undergrowth of the wet bottomlands."[63]

The influence of grizzly bears was evident in various aspects of American Indian society and culture. Many plains tribes had grizzly bear societies that performed bear dances and participated in rituals such as the one that James Clyman witnessed during the attack on the Arikara towns in 1823. Individuals painted representations of grizzly bears on tipis and wore grizzly bear claw necklaces. In many mythologies, including that of the Arikaras, bears and humans often interacted. In one Arikara story, a fourteen-year-old girl turned into a bear, then chased her brothers and sisters.

To escape, they stood on a large stone that began to grow upward. Their sister clawed at the rock as it rose, leaving distinct claw scars on its surface. This story explained the origin of Devils Tower, or Bear Lodge, a unique geological formation in northeastern Wyoming. In another Arikara myth, a male bear mated with a woman. Their son eventually killed his father and returned to his people with his mother. He had extraordinary powers, having inherited the strength of the bear, as well as his human qualities. Eventually, he defeated all of his competitors and became chief of the village.[64]

American Indians, of course, also killed grizzly bears. Before doing so, however, some tribes performed rituals designed both to guarantee success in the hunt and to appease the bear's spirit. When killing a bear for food or for ceremonial reasons, they asked for the bear's forgiveness so that it would allow them to hunt successfully again in the future.[65]

As grizzly bears were pushed into more remote and distant areas, images of bears in European American culture, too, became more favorable. "In less than two hundred years," observed Paul Schullery, "the grizzly has gone from being the symbol of everything in nature that is evil and in need of destruction, to being the opposite. Today, the grizzly bear, at least in the Rocky Mountain West's energetic conservation community, has become one of the foremost symbols of all that is good and deserving of our protection and affection in wild country."[66]

The story of Theodore Roosevelt and the "Teddy Bear" illustrates this change in attitude. In 1902 in Mississippi, according to biographer Edmund Morris, Roosevelt declined to shoot a "stunned, bloody, mud-caked runt" of a black bear that his hunting companions had tied to a tree, wanting to be certain that the president got his bear. The story of his sportsmanlike refusal to shoot led to national publicity, including "bear cartoons." Eventually, Morris noted, cartoonist Clifford Berryman of the *Washington Post* depicted the bear as "smaller, rounder, and cuter," making it even more popular.[67] Within the year, stuffed bear cubs bearing the president's nickname, "Teddy," were on the market, and millions of children have enjoyed playing with them since then.

Many other positive images of bears have emerged in popular culture, including Smokey the Bear, Yogi Bear, Winnie the Pooh, Gentle Ben, Goldilocks's three bears, and gummi bears. The more favorable image of grizzly bears is evident, Paul Schullery wrote, "in art galleries overflowing with portraits, sculpture, and every other form of fine and commercial iconography that can be applied to wildlife; in local businesses beyond counting that somehow incorporate the bear into their name or trademark; in high school and college athletic teams known as bears, grizzlies, or bruins; and in an overwhelming flood of books, articles, and calendars that keep the bear in front of us and drive it ever more firmly into our consciousness and our consciences."[68] Sometimes the change has been subtle. Although the opening scene of *Man in the Wilderness* depicted a bear tearing "Zachary Bass" to pieces, an inspection of the credits reveals that "Peggy the Bear" played the role. It is difficult to imagine a bear in Hugh Glass's era being named Peggy.[69]

Today, rather than hunting grizzly bears, people travel long distances to observe them in their natural environment. Bear watching occurs mostly on public lands, such as Yellowstone, Glacier, Denali, and Katmai national parks. Indeed, some people now travel longer distances to see grizzly bears than Lewis and Clark journeyed on their expedition through the West. "Once in sight, the bears are objects of great wonder," noted Schullery. "They are described as magnificent, beautiful, breathtaking, gorgeous, lovely, grand."[70]

Observing grizzly bears too closely, of course, can be dangerous, as Timothy Treadwell, "the man who wanted to become a bear, and died trying," proved. Passionately believing that he could freely associate with grizzly bears, Treadwell somehow survived for more than a decade camping near them during summers in Alaska. He refused to carry bear spray or to protect his campsite with a portable electric fence. Finally, in 2003, he and his partner Amie Huguenard were killed and partially devoured. Now, like Hugh Glass before him, Treadwell is becoming a legendary figure. As biographer Nick Jans noted, "there's little doubt the story will be retold around campfires, bars, and boardrooms, discussed, argued, and altered until it passes into the pantheon of Alaskan mythology."[71]

In the years since Glass survived his mauling, scientists have carefully examined the behavior and genetics of grizzly bears and know how best to preserve them. In their classic study *The Grizzly Bears of Yellowstone* (1995), John J. Craighead, Jay S. Sumner, and John A. Mitchell concluded: "The fundamental threat to the grizzly bear's survival is not a lack of biological knowledge, nor a lack in knowing how to apply this information. Rather, it is the threat from our politico-economic system that demands unsustainable use of our public land and water resources, whether these resources are forage, timber, fish, or minerals." In order to preserve grizzly bears, "we need . . . large areas of near-pristine environment." However, the authors conceded, "if special interest groups and their political supporters prevail in dictating the use of public lands, it will become extremely difficult, if not impossible, to maintain the grizzly in perpetuity as a free-roaming member of the western landscape."[72] Changed attitudes have prevented the extermination of grizzly bears. New policies in national parks, such as Yellowstone and Glacier, have stabilized their numbers by removing them from daily contact with humans. Still, there are few grizzly bears left, and they might easily vanish from the scene in the future as the human population increases and expands into even the most remote regions.

From the grizzly bear's perspective, it would have been better had European Americans not arrived in the West. Cowboy-artist Charles M. Russell captured this sentiment in a speech to a booster committee. "I have been called a pioneer," he said. "In my book a pioneer is a man who comes to a virgin country, traps off all the fur, kills off all the wild meat, cuts down all the trees, grazes off all the grass, plows the roots up, and strings ten million miles of wire. A pioneer destroys things and calls it civilization. I wish to God that this country was just like it was when I first saw it and that none of you folks were here at all."[73] The grizzly bear would have agreed, but would have preferred it if Russell and Hugh Glass had not arrived either.

Conclusion

James O. Pattie's *Personal Narrative*, published in 1831, described his trapping adventures in the Southwest between 1824 and 1830. Although his memoir is packed with unverifiable adventures, it remains an important account of the fur trade in that region. One of his many tales describes an encounter with a grizzly bear. The animal attacked his party's horses during the night, and despite the darkness, Pattie managed to kill it. However, the bear had already mauled one of Pattie's fellow trappers. "The flesh on his hip was torn off, leaving the sinews bare," said Pattie, and "his breath came through the openings" in his side, as well as "from both sides of his windpipe, the animal in his fury having placed his teeth and claws in every part of his body." No one believed it possible for him to survive, including the injured man himself, who remained conscious despite his wounds. He "desired us from the first to leave him," said Pattie, "as he considered his case as hopeless." Nevertheless, they stayed with him for three days; finally, not "seeing any change for the worse or better," they paid two men a dollar a day to care for him until he died.[1] Several weeks later, the two men caught up with the main party, carrying the man's gun and ammunition and reporting that he had expired the fifth day after Pattie and his men had left.

Portions of this story are so similar to the Hugh Glass story that it seems likely that Pattie or his editor, Timothy Flint, simply appropriated Glass's tale for their own use. "For students of the American West, Pattie's book has always been one of the greatest puzzles," wrote historian William H. Goetzmann. "It is difficult to assess its true historical value because no one knows for certain just how much of Pattie's adventure was true and how much was the characteristic elaboration of the teller of tall tales."[2]

The same, of course, can be said of the many narratives about Hugh Glass himself. Besides incorporating popular tales into their adventures, mountain men frequently stretched the truth, making it difficult to separate fact from fiction. As Frances Fuller Victor noted in her biography of trapper Joe Meek, each man "claimed to own the best horse; to have had the wildest adventures; to have made the most narrow escapes; to have killed the greatest number of bears and Indians; to be the greatest favorite with the Indian belles, the greatest consumer of alcohol, and to have the most money to spend." Not surprisingly, then, stories told by and about mountain men contain exaggerated tales of heroic feats and dangerous encounters.[3]

Nineteenth-century writers complicated the situation further. As historian Kent Ladd Steckmesser observed, although a few mountain men wrote accounts of their own adventures, such stories were more often propagated by aspiring professional authors. "These writers had a casual attitude toward the truth and often held imaginative appeal to be of more importance than the facts," Steckmesser wrote. Following popular literary conventions of that era, they "erected a grand edifice of legend upon the slender foundation of fact."[4]

Later authors were prone to this practice, as well, and the lack of verifiable information about Glass's mauling became a boon for them. Literary critic John R. Milton noted several factors that made the Hugh Glass story so attractive to novelists such as Frederick Manfred. Much about Glass "remains a mystery," Milton asserted. His obscure origin story, the fight with the Arikara Indians, and his encounter with the grizzly bear all provide fertile ground for novelists. "From here on, until the actual death of Glass about ten years later, the story is vague," Milton wrote, "allowing the imagination of the novelist full play." Novelists could ponder questions such as: "What was it like, being left for dead? How did Hugh Glass feel about the two men who left him? How did he manage to survive, alone in the wilderness? Why did he not get revenge on his deserters? What motivated him during each phase of his life in the West?"[5] However, while it is normal for novelists to create an interesting story based on meager evidence, the same practice does not result in good history. Unfortunately, like these novelists, many nonfiction writers telling Glass's story employed as much time in creative speculation as they did in research.

The varying reactions to the identification of Jim Bridger as one of Hugh Glass's deserters provide examples of this speculation, and they also show how authors' viewpoints color their interpretations of fact. Concerned about the vilification of their hero, Bridger's biographers have attempted to deny or explain his alleged misconduct. J. Cecil Alter, who wrote the first thorough account of Bridger's life, decided that Glass invented the entire story. However, even if the mauling had occurred and Bridger had deserted Glass, Alter wrote, Bridger would have been justified in taking Glass's rifle and equipment because "it would have been imprudent . . . to leave a good gun . . . beside the body of a dead man."[6] Unlike Alter, biographer Louis O. Honig accepted the story that Glass was mauled and left alone to die, but he argued, "history has not been able to prove that Jim Bridger was one of the wretches who deserted Glass." Considering Bridger's "well-known courage as he matured into manhood and the fact that he was a man of great dependability in times of danger, it is very unlikely that he had any connection with the incident," Honig concluded.[7] Writer J. Eugene Chrisman decided that there must have been two men named Jim Bridger, and that the one who deserted Glass was not the one who later became famous. Finally, biographer Stanley Vestal declared all these conclusions invalid. He conceded that Bridger was indeed one of the deserters. Although some have "objected that Bridger's behavior in deserting Hugh Glass is not in character with his later life," Vestal asserted, it actually "only makes his behavior the more probable—for this early mistake affords the most satisfying explanation of his later splendid character and achievements." Indeed, he concluded, "sometimes a bad mistake in early life proves to be the making of a man—*if* he has the makings of a man."[8] That four writers arrived at such different conclusions about a specific detail indicates that they were speculating from their own opinions, not deducing the facts from historical evidence.

Similar discrepancies are apparent in other aspects of the Hugh Glass story. Even the earliest writers, who had access to informants who might have more reliable knowledge of the events, disagreed on crucial details. For example, James Hall and Philip St. George Cooke claimed that Glass encountered the grizzly bear while securing game as a designated hunter for the Henry party. On the other hand, Edmund Flagg and George Yount said that Glass disobeyed his orders and met the bear after leaving the party to pick berries. This disagreement is critical; was Glass a steadfast team member or a disobedient scoundrel? The way in which different writers described this point often determined how they evaluated the behavior of Glass's deserters, who had to put their lives at risk to remain with him.

Other differences reveal how writers exaggerated. For example, all early accounts agree that two men stayed with Glass to await his death or recovery, but there the agreement stops. Hall claimed that these men were offered an "extravagant reward."[9] Cooke gave the amount as eighty dollars; Flagg, three hundred; and Yount, four hundred. The two men remained with Glass for two days, five days, or six days, and the mauling occurred more than two hundred miles, or three hundred miles, or perhaps three hundred fifty miles from Fort Kiowa.

Likewise, writers disagreed about Glass's route and method of travel. Many reported him crawling his way directly across the prairie to Fort Kiowa. Cooke, however, said that he first made his way to the abandoned Arikara villages along the Missouri, then followed the river to the trading post. Both Cooke and Flagg wrote that Sioux Indians found him partway through his journey and transported him the rest of the way to the post, but Hall and Yount did not mention the Sioux. After reading John G. Neihardt's extended description of the crawl in *The Song of Hugh Glass*, South Dakota historian Doane Robinson playfully penned his own little doggerel: "I guess if Hughie made his way / From Shade Hill to Fort Kiowa, / He did not crawl, but first and last / He traveled by some water-craft."[10] As Robinson's verse suggests, there is no way to ascertain how Glass traveled or the route he took. Yet, those describing the crawl have provided intimate details, including the berries, rattlesnake meat, insects, and buffalo carcasses that Glass consumed en route.

According to Hall, Glass left Fort Kiowa to seek revenge even before his wounds healed. Cooke, on the other hand, claimed that Glass remained at Fort Kiowa two months to allow his wounds to mend, and Yount asserted that he passed the entire winter there. In a remarkable moment of unanimity, all of the early writers mentioned that he ascended the river with a trading party that was later attacked by Arikara Indians, but they diverge once again in the details of his escape. The accounts of his confrontations with his deserters offer further discrepancies. Hall did not describe any meeting between Glass and the younger deserter and only briefly mentioned the older man, who had enlisted in the army at Fort Atkinson. In Cooke's account, Glass met the younger man at Henry's fort but let him off because of his youth, then postponed his pursuit of the other deserter. In Flagg's account, no confrontation occurred at all; indeed, when he arrived at Fort Atkinson, Glass did not even look up the man who purportedly left him to die. Finally, Yount provided detailed descriptions of both confrontations, right down to Glass's words of reproach.

"People . . . have a right to know whether they are reading fact or fiction," asserted Kent Steckmesser in his landmark study *The Western Hero in History and Legend*, "and the historian has a responsibility to draw the line which separates the two."[11] This task becomes difficult, however, when the earliest accounts provide such different details. Further complicating the effort, much of the historical background in the stories is indeed true. For example, contemporary documents verify that both Glass and a man named Fitzgerald were with Andrew Henry's party in the fall of 1823, and that they followed the Grand River toward their Yellowstone post. A party led by a man often called Langevin did indeed ascend the Missouri River later that fall, and Arikara Indians did kill most of them. Similarly, documents attest that Glass and several companions left Henry's post for Fort Atkinson during the winter, and that two of the men were killed on the journey. Because these aspects of the story are verifiable, it is tempting to assume that other claims made about Glass are equally true. But which claims?

In fact, rather than proving that the tales about Glass are true, these documented incidents prove only that early storytellers were familiar with events on the upper Missouri in 1823 and framed their stories within actual occurrences. It is important to remember that there are no eyewitness accounts describing the mauling, the desertion, Glass's epic crawl, or his forgiveness of those who left him. Moreover, it is likely that the storytellers injected other historical incidents into the tales even though Glass may have had no part in them. For example, contemporary records indicate that Toussaint Charbonneau narrowly missed the massacre of Langevin and his traders, but no surviving documents mention Hugh Glass being with the party. Early storytellers might simply have substituted Glass for Charbonneau, creating another miraculous—but unfortunately, false—escape.

Adding to the difficulty, later writers cherry-picked from earlier accounts, mixing details freely without citing their sources. It makes a difference whether the information came from James Hall in 1825 or from George Yount in 1855. Moreover, the original authors' sources of information are often unclear in themselves. In Yount's narrative, for example, it is difficult to determine whether particular facts come from Hiram Allen, Lewis Dutton, or Glass himself, and whether the interpretations are Yount's own or those of his assistant, Orange Clark. Interestingly, the account related by James Clyman is seldom cited. Since Clyman knew Glass and likely gained his information from men who had been with Henry's party, his account may be among the most reliable, and it indicates that Glass disobeyed orders and may have provoked the attack by shooting the bear. Unfortunately for lovers of legend, Clyman does not relate anything about a desertion, epic crawl, or forgiveness.

Early writers also typically failed to assess the careers of the two men who are supposed to have deserted Glass, John S. Fitzgerald and Jim Bridger. No evidence suggests that their companions shunned them after their alleged act of desertion, nor do their reputations seem to have suffered. After carrying messages for Henry to Fort Atkinson, Fitzgerald joined the army. Listed as a carpenter, he seems to have been a decent soldier, serving as a member of the 1825 Atkinson-O'Fallon expedition up the Missouri River. He left the army in 1829 after successfully completing his enlistment. Bridger had a distinguished career, becoming one of the partners who purchased the Ashley and Henry company. Later, he frequently served as a scout for the army. Neither man is known to have provided any explanation of the Glass incident.[12]

Rather than attempting to separate fact from fiction, most storytellers exaggerated Glass's deeds, making him comparable to the heroes of ancient classics. According to Steckmesser, this exaggeration was not unusual. Biographers of Kit Carson, for example, compared him to Hercules and Hannibal. Like Carson, Hugh Glass was made to "personify traits which Americans have always admired," including "courage, self-reliance, and physical prowess," as well as his moral qualities. Glass demonstrated his courage and physical strength in his crawl, and he became a symbol of moral strength through his acts of forgiveness. While it is easy for historians to chastise these writers for inventing heroes, they were simply supplying what readers demanded. "Romance and legend . . . are warm and colorful, representing the ideal in human aspirations," Steckmesser explained. That no documents prove these acts occurred "is of little relevance in the legend."[13]

If stories about Glass are regarded as legend rather than documented history, he bears many similarities to such cultural heroes as Kit Carson, Billy the Kid, Wild Bill Hickok, and George Armstrong Custer. The stories told about these figures often reveal more about how legends are made than about their purported subjects. Such tales typically passed through cycles, including "biographies, histories, novels, juveniles, movies, and television plays." As Steckmesser noted, "it is the range of mediums in which the legend appears over a period of time which entitles the hero to legendary stature." Like other western heroes, Glass cleverly outwitted his "frontier adversaries," especially Indians, and as in many such tales, there are no witnesses to affirm or deny the truth of his exploits. These incidents, Steckmesser noted, are mostly "imaginative versions of what might have happened." Besides miraculously escaping Indian attacks several times, Glass, like other Western heroes, is given "exceptional ability in such frontier skills as trailing, marksmanship, and hand-to-hand combat with Indians and wild beasts." Some writers portray him as among the best marksmen in Henry's party, and he "overcomes tremendous odds" by crawling back to civilization after being mauled by a grizzly bear.[14]

Once a heroic tale was published, it became extremely difficult to correct it. Subsequent writers repeated the story, and "by simple repetition," it was "accepted as truth." Indeed, "people seem to believe that proof of the reliability of a story lies in the number of times it has been repeated," Steckmesser observed, "without stopping to consider the source from which it came." After extensive research, historians sometimes prove these tales to be more fiction than fact, but destroying "the beauty of a perfected legend" can be unpopular. "There is something cold and abstract about truth," Steckmesser acknowledged, and people sometimes dislike historians who "manage to spoil a good story."[15]

Historians themselves have reacted in different ways to the legendary aspects of western history. Discussing the fur-trade era, David J. Wishart concluded, "probably no other period of the American past has been represented so much by lore and so little by systematic analysis."[16] Likewise, Ray Allen Billington, reflecting on the need to make Western history more professional, asserted that historians should discuss "the economic results of the fur trade rather than repeat the tale of Hugh Glass and the grizzly bear."[17] Believing that Glass and other heroic figures have been granted undeserved historical significance, many historians omit these popular stories from their accounts. Like Billington, they want to discuss larger issues, such as how the fur trade operated, the marketing of furs, the competition between companies, and the impact of the trade on American Indians and the environment. Others continue to embrace the legends.

A comparison of historical accounts of the fur trade by academic historians and popular writers reveals this difference in approach. Billington, of course, excluded Glass from his *Westward Expansion* (1960). Although Hugh Glass received attention in Herbert S. Schell's grade-school text, he does not appear in the *History of South Dakota* (1961) that Schell wrote for a scholarly audience. Glass receives no mention in David J. Wishart's *Fur Trade of the American West, 1807–1840* (1979) or Richard White's history of the West, *"It's Your Misfortune and None of My Own"* (1991).[18]

In contrast, more popular accounts have continued to romanticize mountain men as important and heroic figures. Don Berry's history of the Rocky Mountain Fur Company, *A Majority of Scoundrels* (1961), provides an extended account of Hugh Glass and the bear. In his work on mountain men, *Give Your Heart to the Hawks* (1973), Winfred Blevins not only provided a lengthy account of Hugh Glass but also noted that he did not enjoy professional histories focusing on "large movements . . . like mercantilism, imperialism, or Manifest Destiny." For him, history should deal with "actual people and actual doings." Moreover, Blevins wanted to show "how they felt about what they did," which meant "a certain amount of creating."[19] Likewise, George Laycock included a colorful chapter on Hugh Glass in *The Mountain Men* (1988). In his introduction to Laycock's book, Paul Schullery explained that while historians spend "more and more of their time wondering about" environmental issues and ethnocentrism, "most people are still interested in the mountain men primarily because of their adventures."[20] Interestingly, although he excluded Glass from his study of the fur trade, David Wishart still believed that historians should not overlook fur-trade lore, and he made the Hugh Glass tale the centerpiece of his entry on the subject in the *Encyclopedia of the Great Plains*.[21]

The repetition of the Glass tale has continued to impact subsequent generations. Gregory J. Lalire, editor of *Wild West* magazine, remembered the impression the story made on him as a child. In the fourth grade in an Ohio school, he and his classmates were "required to read a short story based on the Glass legend." The tale "moved me to the edge of my seat. Reading could be fun!" Afterward, he read everything he could on the West. "And so I owe a lot to Hugh Glass," Lalire concluded, "and to the writer of that short story, whoever he or she was."[22]

Still, readers might ask, how much of the Hugh Glass story is true? It is, of course, impossible to be certain about the truthfulness of the tales about Glass's mauling, desertion, survival, and forgiveness. But as William Goetzmann reminded us in his discussion of James Pattie's *Personal Narrative*, the question of authenticity misses the main point. Such works are, "above all else . . . documents of American mythology," belonging "with John Filson's work on Daniel Boone, Henry T. Bonner's *The Life and Adventures of Jim Beckwourth*, and Davy Crockett's autobiography." Like them, Pattie "presents us with an authentic culture hero. He is Odysseus or Beowulf."[23] The same is true of Hugh Glass. Whatever the truth of his story, he stands as a significant legendary figure embodying traits that Americans revere.

Notes

INTRODUCTION

1. Milton, *South Dakota: A Bicentennial History* (New York: W. W. Norton & Co., 1977), p. 23.

2. Wishart, "Fur Trade Lore," in *Encyclopedia of the Great Plains*, ed. Wishart (Lincoln: University of Nebraska Press, 2004), p. 302.

3. John R. Milton, "Foreword," in Frederick Manfred, *Lord Grizzly* (1954; repr., Lincoln: University of Nebraska Press, 1983), p. vii.

4. Coleman, *Here Lies Hugh Glass: A Mountain Man, a Bear, and the Rise of the American Nation* (New York: Hill & Wang, 2012), p. x.

5. Alter, *James Bridger, Trapper, Frontiersman, Scout and Guide: A Historical Narrative* (1925; repr., Columbus, Ohio: Long's College Book Co., 1951), p. 553.

6. McClung, *Hugh Glass, Mountain Man* (New York: Morrow Junior Books, 1990), pp. 161–62.

7. Walker, "The Mountain Man Journal: Its Significance in a Literary History of the Fur Trade," *Western Historical Quarterly* 5 (July 1974): 307.

8. *See* [James Hall], "The Missouri Trapper," *Port Folio* 19 (Mar. 1825; collected ed., Philadelphia: Harrison Hall, 1825), pp. 214–19; John Myers Myers, *Pirate, Pawnee, and Mountain Man: The Saga of Hugh Glass* (Boston: Little, Brown & Co., 1963), pp. 3–4, 238; and Frederick Feikema Manfred, "The Making of *Lord Grizzly*," *South Dakota History* 15 (Fall 1985): 201.

CHAPTER 1. THE WITNESSES AND THE TESTIMONY

1. Potts to Thomas Cochlen, 7 July 1824, quoted in *The West of William H. Ashley: The International Struggle for the Fur Trade of the Missouri, the Rocky Mountains, and the Columbia, . . . 1822–1838*, ed. Dale L. Morgan (Denver, Colo.: Old West Publishing Co., 1964), pp. 79–80. For full copies of Potts's letters, *see* Jerry Bagley, *Daniel Trotter Potts, Rocky Mountain Explorer, Chronicler of the Fur Trade and the First Known Man in Yellowstone Park* (Rigby, Idaho: Old Faithful Eye-Witness Publishing, 2000), pp. 270–88.

2. Convalescing at the Yellowstone post, Potts missed participating in both the battle with the Arikara Indians and the westward march during which Hugh Glass met the grizzly bear. Thus, he did not learn about the mauling until several months after it occurred. Gerald C. Bagley, "Daniel T. Potts," in *The Mountain Men and the Fur Trade of the Far West*, ed. LeRoy R. Hafen, 10 vols. (Glendale, Calif.: Arthur H. Clark Co., 1965–1972), 3:253–54.

3. Charles L. Camp, ed., *James Clyman, Frontiersman: The Adventures of a Trapper and Covered-Wagon Emigrant as Told in His Own Reminiscences and Diaries* (Portland, Ore.: Champoeg Press, 1960), p. 15.

4. [James Hall], "The Missouri Trapper," *Port Folio* 19 (Mar. 1825; collected ed., Philadelphia: Harrison Hall, 1825), pp. 214–19. Hall reprinted the story in *Letters from the West; Containing Sketches of Scenery, Manners, and Customs; and Anecdotes Connected with the First Settlements of the Western Sections of the United States* (1828; repr., Gainesville, Fla.: Scholars' Facsimiles & Reprints, 1967), pp. 293–305. For Hall's authorship, *see* Edgeley W. Todd, "James Hall and the Hugh Glass Legend," *American Quarterly* 7 (Winter 1955): 362–70; and Randolph C. Randall, "Authors of the *Port Folio* Revealed by the Hall Files," *American Literature* 11 (Jan. 1940): 379–416.

5. *See* Randolph C. Randall, *James Hall: Spokesman of the New West* ([Columbus]: Ohio State University Press, 1964); and John T. Flanagan, *James Hall, Literary Pioneer of the Ohio Valley* (Minneapolis: University of Minnesota Press, 1941).

6. Hall, *Letters from the West*, p. 5.

7. [Hall], "Missouri Trapper," p. 215.

8. Ibid., p. 216.

9. Ibid.

10. Ibid., pp. 216–17.

11. Ibid., p. 217.

12. Ibid.

13. Ibid., pp. 217–18.

14. Ibid., p. 218.

15. Reported ibid., pp. 218–19.

16. Ibid., p. 219.

17. Todd, "James Hall and the Hugh Glass Legend," p. 369. *See also* [Hall], "Missouri Trapper," p. 214.

18. Haines, "Hugh Glass Tells His Story," in *Historical Essays on Montana and the Northwest*, ed. J. W. Smurr and K. Ross Toole (Helena: Western Press, Historical Society of Montana, 1957), pp. 23–24. The article includes an English translation of von Wrede's account of Hugh Glass on pp. 24–40. *See also* Cooke, *Scenes and Adventures in the Army; or, Romance of Military Life* (1857; repr., New York: Arno Press, 1973), pp. 135–52.

19. Quoted in Haines, "Hugh Glass Tells His Story," pp. 24–25.

20. Von Wrede eventually did settle in Texas, but in 1843, he returned to Germany, where he wrote his book as a guide for potential emigrants. Besides the Hugh Glass story, von Wrede included various reports and excerpts from his diary. The next year, von Wrede returned to Texas to help German immigrants and probably stayed. Ibid., pp. 22–25. *See also* Haines, "Hugh Glass," in *Mountain Men*, ed. Hafen, 6:168–69.

21. Haines, "Hugh Glass," 6:164n6, 170–71. When Haines learned that he had been mistaken about the original authorship of Cooke's Hugh Glass story, he issued a retraction in his essay in Hafer's *Mountain Men*.

22. Thomas M. Spaulding, "Cooke, Philip St. George," in *Dictionary of American Biography*, ed. Allen Johnson and Dumas Malone, 20 vols. (New York: Charles Scribner's Sons, 1928–1937): 4:389.

23. Cooke, *Scenes and Adventures*, pp. 16–17, 94–95. Although Cooke refers to the military post as Fort Leavenworth, it was actually known as Cantonment Leavenworth while he was there.

24. Ibid., pp. 134–35, 148.

25. Ibid., p. 138.

26. Ibid., pp. 138–39.

27. Ibid., pp. 139–40.

28. Ibid., pp. 140–41.

29. Ibid., p. 142. Cooke says that the trading post was near "the mouth of the Little Missouri," a contemporary name for the Bad River.

30. Ibid., pp. 142–43.

31. Ibid., p. 143.

32. Ibid., pp. 144–45.

33. Ibid.

34. Ibid., pp. 146–47.

35. Ibid., pp. 147–49.

36. Ibid., pp. 149–50.

37. Reported ibid., pp. 150–51.

38. Ibid., p. 152.

39. Edmund Flagg, "Adventures at the Head Waters of the Missouri," *Louisville Literary News-Letter* 1 (7 Sept. 1839): 326–27; John D. Wade, "Edmund Flagg," in *Dictionary of American Biography*, ed. Johnson and Malone, 6:447–48.

40. Flagg, "Adventures," p. 326.

41. *The North American Journals of Prince Maximilian of Wied*, ed. Stephen S. Witte and Marsha V. Gallagher, trans. William J. Orr, Paul Schach, and Dieter Karch, 3 vols. (Norman: University of Oklahoma Press, 2008–2012), 3:6–7. *See also* 3:3n2. For biographical information about Hamilton, *see* Ray H. Mattison, "James A. Hamilton (Palmer)," in *Mountain Men*, ed. Hafen, 3:163–66. Apparently Hamilton's real name was Archibald Palmer. Flagg wrote that his information came from "an adventurer in the same expedition" as Glass ("Adventures," p. 326). Hamilton was not on the 1823 expedition, and supposing that he was indeed Flagg's informant, Flagg may have been referring to Hamilton's meeting with Glass in the winter of 1832–1833. More likely, given the errors in his account, Flagg simply invented this detail in order to make his story more convincing.

42. George Catlin, *Letters and Notes on the Manners, Customs, and Condition of the North American Indians*, 2 vols. (1841; repr., Minneapolis, Minn.: Ross & Haines, 1965), 1:21.

43. Maximilian, *North American Journals*, 3:7.

44. Washington Matthews, quoted in Charles Larpenteur, *Forty Years a Fur Trader on the Upper Missouri: The Personal Narrative of Charles Larpenteur, 1833–1872*, ed. Elliott Coues, 2 vols. (1898; repr., Minneapolis, Minn.: Ross & Haines, 1962), 1:85n11.

45. Larpenteur, *Forty Years*, 1:85–86.

46. Matthews, quoted ibid., 1:84–85n11. *See also* Mattison, "James A. Hamilton (Palmer)," 3:166; and Walter Hough, "Washington Matthews," in *Dictionary of American Biography*, ed. Johnson and Malone, 12:420.

47. Mattison, "James A. Hamilton (Palmer)," 3:166.

48. Flagg, "Adventures," p. 326. Flagg calls the nearby river the "Chian" (Cheyenne), but the incident actually occurred on the Grand River.

49. Ibid.

50. Ibid.

51. Ibid.

52. Ibid. *See also* p. 327.

53. Alter, *James Bridger, Trapper, Frontiersman, Scout and Guide: A Historical Narrative* (1925; repr., Columbus, Ohio: Long's College Book Co., 1951), p. 553. Alter overstated his case; both Daniel Potts and James Clyman mentioned the mauling in their letters and journals, and documents prove there was a trapper named Fitzgerald with Henry's party. For information on John S. Fitzgerald, *see* Henry Leavenworth to Alexander Macomb, 20 Dec. 1823, in *The West*, ed. Morgan, pp. 68, 248n210.

54. Alter, *James Bridger*, p. 29. *See also* p. 36.

55. Charles L. Camp, "George C. Yount," in *Mountain Men*, ed. Hafen, 9:411–20.

56. Charles L. Camp, ed., *George C. Yount and His Chronicles of the West, Comprising Extracts from His "Memoirs" and from the Orange Clark "Narrative"* (Denver, Colo.: Old West Publishing Co., 1966), p. xiv. Yount's narrative was first published in "The Chronicles of George C. Yount, California Pioneer of 1826," ed. Camp, *California Historical Quarterly* 2 (Apr. 1923): 3–66.

57. Camp, ed., *George C. Yount*, p. 203.

58. Ibid., p. xvii.

59. Reported ibid., p. 199. For a biographical sketch of Dutton, *see* Rex W. Strickland, "Lewis Dutton," in *Mountain Men*, ed. Hafen, 9:147–52.

60. Camp, ed., *George C. Yount*, pp. 199–200.

61. Ibid., p. 200.

62. Ibid., pp. 201–2.

63. Ibid., p. 202.

64. Ibid., pp. 201–2, 204.

65. Ibid., p. 208.

66. Ibid., p. 200.

CHAPTER 2. HUGH GLASS BEFORE 1823

1. "Six Pence Reward," *Pittsburgh Gazette*, 23 Apr. 1795. Henry J. Kauffman reprinted the advertisement in *The Pennsylvania-Kentucky Rifle* (New York: Bonanza, 1960), p. 240. *See also* Don Baird, "Hugh Glass, Fugitive Gunsmith," *Muzzle Blasts* 24 (June 1963): 7.

2. Baird, "Hugh Glass," pp. 7–8; Kauffman, *Pennsylvania-Kentucky Rifle*, p. 240.

3. Kauffman, *Pennsylvania-Kentucky Rifle*, p. 146.

4. Ibid., pp. 142–46, 363–65; Baird, "Hugh Glass," pp. 7–8.

5. Quoted in Milo Milton Quaife, "Historical Introduction," in *Kit Carson's Autobiography*, ed. Quaife (Chicago: R. R. Donnelley & Sons Co., 1935), p. xvi.

6. J. Cecil Alter, *James Bridger, Trapper, Frontiersman, Scout and Guide: A Historical Narrative* (1925; repr., Columbus, Ohio: Long's College Book Co., 1951), pp. 2–6.

7. [James Hall], "The Missouri Trapper," *Port Folio* 19 (Mar. 1825; collected ed., Philadelphia: Harrison Hall, 1825), pp. 214–19; Willard, "Autobiography," sec. 2, p. [11], Rowland Willard-Elizabeth S. Willard Papers, 1822–1921, WA MSS S-2512, box 1, folder 1, Beinecke Library, Yale University, New Haven, Conn.; Charles L. Camp, ed., *George C. Yount and His Chronicles of the West, Comprising Extracts from His "Memoirs" and from the Orange Clark "Narrative"* (Denver, Colo.: Old West Publishing Co., 1966), pp. xvii-xviii, 197–99.

8. Camp, ed., *George C. Yount*, p. 197.

9. Ibid., pp. 197–98.

10. Ibid., pp. 198–99.

11. Washington Irving, *Astoria; or, Anecdotes of an Enterprise beyond the Rocky Mountains*, ed. Edgeley W. Todd (1836; repr., Norman: University of Oklahoma Press, 1964), pp. 223, 225. *See also* John Myers Myers, *Pirate, Pawnee, and Mountain Man: The Saga of Hugh Glass* (Boston: Little, Brown & Co., 1963), pp. 41, 46; and Aubrey L. Haines, "Hugh Glass," in *The Mountain Men and the Fur Trade of the Far West*, ed. LeRoy R. Hafen, 10 vols. (Glendale, Calif.: Arthur H. Clark Co., 1965–1972), 6:161–62. Like Myers, fur-trade historian Aubrey Haines also accepted Yount's account of Glass's encounters with pirates and Pawnee Indians. Myers, however, went a step further and declared that because he was literate, Glass was likely the *captain* of the captured ship!

12. Camp includes Dana's notes on the Glass story in *George C. Yount*, p. xvii. *See also* Jon T. Coleman, *Here Lies Hugh Glass: A Mountain Man, a Bear, and the Rise of the American Nation* (New York: Hill & Wang, 2012), pp. 60–61.

13. Myers, *Pirate, Pawnee, and Mountain Man*, p. 56.

14. Ibid., p. 67; George E. Hyde, *Pawnee Indians* ([Denver, Colo.]: University of Denver Press, 1951), chaps. 5–6; Albert Watkins, ed., "Notes of the Early History of the Nebraska Country," *Publications of the Nebraska State Historical Society* 20 (1922): 14–15, 17.

15. Myers, *Pirate, Pawnee, and Mountain Man*, pp. 67–68.

16. Camp, ed., *George C. Yount*, p. 198. *See also* [Hall], "Missouri Trapper," p. 218; and Myers, *Pirate, Pawnee, and Mountain Man*, pp. 180–84.

17. Morgan, *Jedediah Smith and the Opening of the West* (Lincoln: University of Nebraska Press, 1964), pp. 20, 22.

18. Paxton, *St. Louis Directory and Register, Containing the Names, Professions, and Residence of All the Heads of Families and Persons in Business . . .* (Saint Louis, Mo.: n.p., 1821), pp. [8–10, 14]. *See also* Morgan, *Jedediah Smith*, p. 22.

19. Paxton, *St. Louis Directory and Register*, p. 14.

20. Writers' Program, Work Projects Administration, *Missouri: A Guide to the "Show Me" State*, American Guide Series (New York: Duell, Sloan & Pearce, 1941), p. 300. In one such confrontation, future United States senator Thomas Hart Benton shot and killed his opponent, Charles Lucas.

21. Writers' Program, *Missouri*, p. 300.

22. Quoted in Walter B. Stevens, *Centennial History of Missouri (The Center State): One Hundred Years in the Union, 1820–1921* (Saint Louis, Mo.: S. J. Clarke Publishing Co., 1921), p. 8.

CHAPTER 3. THE FUR TRADE

1. Herbert S. Schell, *History of South Dakota*, 4th ed., rev. John E. Miller (Pierre: South Dakota State Historical Society Press), pp. 30–36.

2. Ibid., p. 39; Gary E. Moulton, ed., *The Journals of the Lewis & Clark Expedition*, 13 vols. (Lincoln: University of Nebraska Press, 1983–2001), 2:5, 8:157.

3. David J. Wishart, *The Fur Trade of the American West, 1807–1840: A Geographical Synthesis* (Lincoln: University of Nebraska Press, 1979), p. 42; Robert M. Utley, *A Life Wild and Perilous: Mountain Men and the Paths to the Pacific* (New York: Henry Holt & Co., 1997), pp. 11–16; Richard Edward Oglesby, *Manuel Lisa and the Opening of the Missouri Fur Trade* (Norman: University of Oklahoma Press, 1963), pp. 40–63.

4. Wishart, *Fur Trade*, pp. 42–46; Oglesby, *Manuel Lisa*, pp. 56, 67–98, 115–16; Harrison Clifford Dale, *The Ashley-Smith Explorations and the Discovery of the Central Route to the Pacific, 1822–1829, with the Original Journals*, rev. ed. (Glendale, Calif.: Arthur H. Clark Co., 1941), pp. 29–32; Utley, *Life Wild and Perilous*, pp. 18–24.

5. Wishart, *Fur Trade*, pp. 46, 116–19; Utley, *Life Wild and Perilous*, pp. 24–34; Dale, *Ashley-Smith Explorations*, pp. 32–33, 36–39. Washington Irving's *Astoria* made Hunt's travels famous; for a thorough examination, *see* James P. Ronda, *Astoria & Empire* (Lincoln: University of Nebraska Press, 1990).

6. Dale, *Ashley-Smith Explorations*, p. 54

7. Ibid., pp. 54–55; Eric Jay Dolin, *Fur, Fortune, and Empire: The Epic History of the Fur Trade in America* (New York: W. W. Norton & Co., 2010), pp. 266–67. For a favorable view of the factory system, *see* Hiram Martin Chittenden, *The American Fur Trade of the Far West: A History of the Pioneer Trading Posts . . . and of the Overland Commerce with Santa Fe*, 3 vols. (New York: Francis P. Harper, 1902), 1:12–16.

8. Dolin, *Fur, Fortune, and Empire*, pp. 268–69; Dale, *Ashley-Smith Explorations*, pp. 54–55; Wishart, *Fur Trade*, p. 121.

9. *St. Louis Enquirer*, reprinted in *Missouri Intelligencer* (Franklin), 17 Sept. 1822, in *The West of William H. Ashley: The International Struggle for the Fur Trade of the Missouri, the Rocky Mountains, and the Columbia, . . . 1822–1838*, ed. Dale L. Morgan (Denver, Colo.: Old West Publishing Co., 1964), p. 19.

10. Wishart, *Fur Trade*, pp. 47–50; Dale, *Ashley-Smith Explorations*, pp. 55–56; Utley, *Life Wild and Perilous*, p. 44.

11. *Missouri Gazette & Public Advertiser* (Saint Louis), 13 Feb. 1822, in *The West*, ed. Morgan, p. 1.

12. Dale, *Ashley-Smith Explorations*, pp. 55–62; Harvey L. Carter, "William H. Ashley," in *The Mountain Men and the Fur Trade of the Far West*, ed. LeRoy R. Hafen, 10 vols. (Glendale, Calif.: Arthur H. Clark Co., 1965–1972), 7:23–25. For a thorough account of Ashley's life before entering the fur trade, *see* Richard M. Clokey, *William H. Ashley: Enterprise and Politics in the Trans-Mississippi West* (Norman: University of Oklahoma Press, 1980), pp. 3–57.

13. Louis J. Clements, "Andrew Henry," in *Mountain Men*, ed. Hafen, 6:173.

14. Ibid., 6:173–79; Linda Harper White and Fred R. Gowans, "Traders to Trappers: Andrew Henry and the Rocky Mountain Fur

Trade," *Montana the Magazine of Western History* 43 (Winter 1993): 58–65, (Summer 1993): 54–63.

15. *Missouri Intelligencer*, 29 Oct. 1822, in *The West*, ed. Morgan, p. 19.

16. Dale, *Ashley-Smith Explorations*, pp. 62–63.

17. O'Fallon to Calhoun, 9 Apr. 1822, in *The West*, ed. Morgan, p. 6.

18. Dale, *Ashley-Smith Explorations*, p. 63; Utley, *Life Wild and Perilous*, pp. 11–12, 26–27; Dolin, *Fur, Fortune, and Empire*, pp. 223–27.

19. Hempstead to Pilcher, 3 Apr. 1822, in *The West*, ed. Morgan, pp. 3–4.

20. Dale, *Ashley-Smith Explorations*, p. 63; Utley, *Life Wild and Perilous*, pp. 62–64; Dolin, *Fur, Fortune, and Empire*, pp. 225–27.

21. Hempstead to Pilcher, 5 May 1822, in *The West*, ed. Morgan, p. 9.

22. Hempstead to Pilcher, 3 Apr. 1822.

23. *St. Louis Enquirer*, 13 Apr. 1822, in *The West*, ed. Morgan, pp. 6–7.

24. *Missouri Saturday News* (Saint Louis), 14 Apr. 1838, ibid., p. 7.

25. Potts to Thomas Cochlen, 7 July 1824, ibid., pp. 7–8. *See also* Potts to Robert Potts, 16 July 1826, p. 8.

26. Hempstead to Pilcher, 5 May 1822.

27. Dale L. Morgan, *Jedediah Smith and the Opening of the West* (Lincoln: University of Nebraska Press, 1964), p. 29; Morgan, ed., *The West*, p. 9.

28. Maurice S. Sullivan, *The Travels of Jedediah Smith: A Documentary Outline Including the Journal of the Great American Pathfinder* (Lincoln: University of Nebraska Press, 1992), p. 1.

29. Ibid., pp. 1–2.

30. Bompart, journal, 2 June 1822, in *The West*, ed. Morgan, p. 10.

31. *Missouri Republican* (Saint Louis), 5 June 1822, ibid., p. 11.

32. *St. Louis Enquirer*, 3 June 1822, ibid.; Morgan, *Jedediah Smith*, p. 34.

33. Sullivan, *Travels*, p. 2.

34. Potts recounted that he "met with Gen. Ashley, on a second expedition with whom I entered the second time, and arrived at the mouth of the Yellow Stone about the middle of October" (Potts to Potts, 16 July 1826, p. 8). One imagines that Potts must have recovered from his earlier surfeit.

35. Sullivan, *Travels*, p. 3.

36. Ibid. *See also* Chittenden, *American Fur Trade*, 2:768–69.

37. Sullivan, *Travels*, pp. 3–5.

38. Ibid., p. 6.

39. Ibid., pp. 6–7.

40. Ibid., p. 7.

41. Ibid., p. 8; Clark to Calhoun, 16 Jan. 1823, ibid., pp. 19–20; Morgan, *Jedediah Smith*, p. 378; Morgan, ed., *The West*, p. 8. *See also* Andrew Henry and William H. Ashley, account of property lost to Indians, enclosed in Clark to Calhoun, 14 Jan. 1824, ibid., p. 70.

42. Potts to Potts, 16 July 1826, p. 14.

43. Sullivan, *Travels*, p. 8.

44. Morgan, *Jedediah Smith*, pp. 42, 44–45.

45. Sullivan, *Travels*, pp. 8–9. *See also* Morgan, *Jedediah Smith*, p. 44.

46. Sullivan, *Travels*, pp. 9–10.

47. Ibid., p. 10.

48. Potts to Cochlen, 7 July 1824, p. 40.

49. Brown, "Mike Fink," in *The Reader's Encyclopedia of the American West*, ed. Howard R. Lamar (New York: Thomas Y. Crowell Co., 1977), p. 369.

50. *Missouri Republican*, 16 July 1823, in *The West*, ed. Morgan, pp. 46–47. For biographical information on Fink and for a collection of legendary tales about him, *see* Walter Blair and Franklin J. Meine, eds., *Half Horse, Half Alligator: The Growth of the Mike Fink Legend* (Chicago: University of Chicago Press, 1956), pp. 3–14.

51. Potts to Cochlen, 7 July 1824, p. 40.

52. Utley, *Life Wild and Perilous*, p. 47. *See also* Hugh Johnson, deposition, 13 Jan. 1824, in *The West*, ed. Morgan, p. 72.

53. William Gordon to [Pilcher], 15 June 1823, extracted in Pilcher to O'Fallon, 23 July 1823, in *The West*, ed. Morgan, p. 49. *See also* O'Fallon to Clark, 3 July 1823, ibid., pp. 44–45; and Pilcher to Hempstead, n.d., ibid., pp. 50–51.

54. William H. Ashley to *Missouri Republican*, 4 June 1823, ibid., p. 25; *Missouri Republican*, 15 Jan. 1823, ibid., p. 19; *Missouri Republican*, 12 Mar. 1823, ibid., p. 22; *Missouri Intelligencer*, 1 Apr. 1823, ibid.

CHAPTER 4. THE ARIKARA WAR

1. *Missouri Republican* (Saint Louis), 15 Jan. 1823, in *The West of William H. Ashley: The International Struggle for the Fur Trade of the Missouri, the Rocky Mountains, and the Columbia, . . . 1822–1838*, ed. Dale L. Morgan (Denver, Colo.: Old West Publishing Co., 1964), p. 19.

2. Charles L. Camp, ed., *James Clyman, Frontiersman: The Adventures of a Trapper and Covered-Wagon Emigrant as Told in His Own Reminiscences and Diaries* (Portland, Ore.: Champoeg Press, 1960), pp. 5–7.

3. Ibid., p. 7. *See also* Thomas Hempstead to Joshua Pilcher, 12 Feb. 1823, in *The West*, ed. Morgan, p. 20; *Missouri Republican*, 12 Mar. 1823, ibid., p. 22; *Missouri Intelligencer* (Franklin), 1 Apr. 1823, ibid.

4. *St. Louis Enquirer*, reprinted in *Missouri Republican*, 19 Mar. 1823, in *The West*, ed. Morgan, p. 22. *See also Missouri Republican*, 12 Mar. 1823.

5. *Missouri Intelligencer*, 1 Apr. 1823.

6. Camp, ed., *James Clyman*, pp. 7–8.

7. Ibid., p. 8.

8. Ashley to *Missouri Republican*, 4 June 1823, in *The West*, ed. Morgan, p. 25.

9. Camp, ed., *James Clyman*, p. 8. Cedar Fort was also known as Fort Recovery.

10. Ibid., p. 9.

11. Ashley to *Missouri Republican*, 4 June 1823, pp. 25–26.

12. Ibid., p. 26. *See also* p. 233nn76–77; unknown member of Ashley's party to unknown recipient, 17 June 1823, printed in *National Intelligencer* (Washington, D.C.), 3 Sept. 1823, ibid., pp. 32–33; and Camp, ed., *James Clyman*, p. 9.

13. Camp, ed., *James Clyman*, p. 9.

14. Ashley to *Missouri Republican*, 4 June 1823, p. 26.

15. Ibid.

16. Camp, ed., *James Clyman*, p. 9.

17. Ashley to *Missouri Republican*, 4 June 1823, p. 26.

18. Camp, ed., *James Clyman*, pp. 9–10.

19. Unknown member of Ashley's party to unknown recipient, 17 June 1823.

20. Camp, ed., *James Clyman*, p. 12. *See also* Ashley to *Missouri Republican*, 4 June 1823, p. 26.

21. Camp, ed., *James Clyman*, p. 10.

22. Ashley to *Missouri Republican*, 4 June 1823, p. 26.

23. Camp, ed., *James Clyman*, pp. 10–11.

24. Ibid., pp. 11–12.

25. Ibid., p. 12.

26. Those killed included Aaron Stephens, John Matthews, John Collins, James McDaniel, Westley Piper, George Flager, Benjamin F. Sneed, James Penn, Jr., John Miller, John S. Gardner, Elliss Ogle, David Howard, and Reed Gibson. The wounded included Joseph Monsa, John Larrison, Abraham Ricketts, Robert Tucker, Joseph Thompson, Jacob Miller, Daniel McClain, August Dufren, Willis (a black man), James Davis, and Hugh Glass. Ashley made three casualty lists, each one using different spellings and, in some cases, different first names for the victims. *See* Ashley to Benjamin O'Fallon and the commanding officer at Council Bluffs, 4 June 1823, in *The West*, ed. Morgan, pp. 28–29; Ashley to *Missouri Republican*, 4 June 1823, ibid., p. 27; and Ashley to unknown recipient, 7 June 1823, printed in *Missouri Intelligencer*, 8 July 1823, ibid., pp. 30–31.

27. Glass to the parents of John S. Gardner, June 1823, ibid., p. 31. The original letter is in box 3536A, folder H75.14, State Archives Collection, South Dakota State Historical Society, Pierre.

28. *Brevet's South Dakota Historical Markers*, ed. N. Jane Hunt (Sioux Falls, S.Dak.: Brevet Press, 1974), p. 136. For accounts of Jedediah Smith's prayer, the monuments commemorating it, and the possibility that he was in command of the men on shore, *see* Dale L. Morgan, *Jedediah Smith and the Opening of the West* (Lincoln: University of Nebraska Press, 1964), pp. 52, 57, 381n23.

29. Ashley to unknown recipient, 7 June 1823.

30. Camp, ed., *James Clyman*, p. 12. *See also* Morgan, ed., *The West*, p. 235nn84–85.

31. Ashley to O'Fallon and the commanding officer at Council Bluffs, 4 June 1823.

32. Ashley to *Missouri Republican*, 4 June 1823, p. 27.

33. Ashley to unknown recipient, 7 June 1823.

34. Reported in Henry Atkinson to Edmund P. Gaines, 15 Aug. 1823, in *The West,* ed. Morgan, p. 240n137.

35. O'Fallon to William Clark, 24 June 1823, ibid., p. 37.

36. Quoted in Leavenworth to Atkinson, 20 Oct. 1823, in "Official Correspondence Pertaining to the Leavenworth Expedition of 1823 into South Dakota for the Conquest of the Ree Indians," ed. Doane Robinson, *South Dakota Historical Collections* 1 (1902): 204–5.

37. O'Fallon to Ashley, 20 June 1823, in *The West*, ed. Morgan, p. 36. *See also* p. 35; and Ashley to John O'Fallon, 19 July 1823, ibid., pp. 47–48.

38. O'Fallon to "Forty three men who deserted," 19 June 1823, ibid., pp. 34–35.

39. Morgan, ed., *The West*, p. 52; Leavenworth to Atkinson, 20 Oct. 1823, pp. 210–11.

40. Reported in O'Fallon to Clark, 3 July 1823, in *The West*, ed. Morgan, p. 44.

41. Leavenworth to O'Fallon, 21 July 1823, ibid., p. 52; Leavenworth to Atkinson, 20 Oct. 1823, pp. 210–11.

42. Ashley to John O'Fallon, 19 July 1823. The Bad River was known as the Teton River at that time.

43. Camp, ed., *James Clyman*, p. 13. Among Ashley's men, Hiram Allen and George C. Jackson served as lieutenants, Charles Cunningham and Edward Rose, as ensigns, one Fleming, as surgeon, Thomas Fitzpatrick, as quartermaster, and William Sublette, as sergeant major. Among the Missouri Fur Company men, Henry Vanderburgh was made captain, Angus McDonald, captain for the Indian contingent, Moses B. Carson, first lieutenant, and William Gordon, second lieutenant. Leavenworth to Atkinson, 20 Oct. 1823, p. 211.

44. Camp, ed., *James Clyman*, pp. 13–14.

45. Leavenworth to Atkinson, 20 Oct. 1823, pp. 215–16.

46. Ibid., pp. 217–18.

47. Ibid., p. 221. *See also* pp. 217–20.

48. Ibid., pp. 221–22.

49. Ibid., p. 222.

50. Ibid., pp. 222–23.

51. Reported ibid., p. 224.

52. Gale to Leavenworth, [11] Aug. 1823, quoted ibid., p. 226.

53. Reported ibid., pp. 227.

54. Ibid., pp. 227–28.

55. Ibid., p. 228.

56. Ibid., pp. 228–29.

57. Reported ibid., p. 229.

58. Ibid.

59. Ibid., pp. 230–31. *See also* p. 224.

60. Camp, ed., *James Clyman*, p. 14.

61. Leavenworth to "Chiefs and Warriors of the Ricaras nation of Indians," 14 Aug. 1823, in *The West*, ed. Morgan, p. 56.

62. Harrison Clifford Dale, *The Ashley-Smith Explorations and the Discovery of the Central Route to the Pacific, 1822–1829, with the Original Journals*, rev. ed. (Glendale, Calif.: Arthur H. Clark Co., 1941), p. 81.

63. Camp, ed., *James Clyman*, pp. 14–15.

64. Leavenworth to Atkinson, 20 Oct. 1823, p. 232.

65. Pilcher to Leavenworth, 26 Aug. 1823, printed in *Missouri Republican*, 15 Oct. 1823, in *The West*, ed. Morgan, pp. 57–58. For an examination of the war and the ensuing controversy, *see* William R. Nester, *The Arikara War: The First Plains Indian War, 1823* (Missoula, Mont.: Mountain Press Publishing Co., 2001).

66. Chittenden, *The American Fur Trade of the Far West: A History of the Pioneer Trading Posts . . . and of the Overland Commerce with Santa Fe*, 3 vols. (New York: Francis P. Harper, 1902), 2:601.

67. Robinson, "Official Correspondence," pp. 235–36n.

68. [Robinson], "The Aricaras Last Stand," *Wi-iyohi* 4 (1 Mar. 1951): [7].

69. Paul Wilhelm, Duke of Württemberg, "First Journey to North America in the Years 1822 to 1824," trans. William G. Bek, *South Dakota Historical Collections* 19 (1938): 404–5, 428.

70. "Journal of Truteau on the Missouri River, 1794–1795," in *Before Lewis and Clark: Documents Illustrating the History of the Missouri, 1785–1804*, ed. A. P. Nasatir, 2 vols. (Saint Louis, Mo.: Saint Louis Historical Documents Foundation, 1952), 1:296–97.

71. *Tabeau's Narrative of Loisel's Expedition to the Upper Missouri*, ed. Annie Heloise Abel, trans. Rose Abel Wright (Norman: University of Oklahoma Press, 1939), p. 135.

72. Gary E. Moulton, ed., *The Journals of the Lewis & Clark Expedition*, 13 vols. (Lincoln: University of Nebraska Press, 1983–2001), 3:161, 170, 173.

73. Ibid., 3:161.

74. "Journal of Truteau," p. 258.

75. Brackenridge, *Views of Louisiana; Together with a Journal of a Voyage Up the Missouri River, in 1811* (1814; repr., Chicago: Quadrangle Books, 1962), p. 258.

76. *Tabeau's Narrative*, pp. 148–49.

77. Roy W. Meyer, *The Village Indians of the Upper Missouri: The Mandans, Hidatsas, and Arikaras* (Lincoln: University of Nebraska Press, 1977), p. 75.

78. Ibid., pp. 7–8, 63–65.

79. Ibid., pp. 60–61.

80. Ibid., pp. 69–72.

81. *Tabeau's Narrative*, p. 190. *See also* Meyer, *Village Indians*, pp. 76–77.

82. Meyer, *Village Indians*, pp. 15–16; David J. Wishart, *The Fur Trade of the American West, 1807–1840: A Geographical Synthesis* (Lincoln: University of Nebraska Press, 1979), p. 51.

83. Meyer, *Village Indians*, chap. 2. Meyer calls this chapter "The Fatal Impact."

84. Ibid., p. 28; *Tabeau's Narrative*, pp. 122–24.

85. "Journal of Truteau," p. 296. Roy Meyer wrote that Truteau's comments about the Sioux's treatment of the Arikaras probably include "some exaggeration" (*Village Indians*, p. 28).

86. *Tabeau's Narrative*, p. 130.

87. Meyer, *Village Indians*, pp. 47–49; Camp, ed., *James Clyman*, p. 8.

88. *Chardon's Journal at Fort Clark, 1834–1839: Descriptive of Life on the Upper Missouri; . . . of the Ravages of the Small-Pox Epidemic of 1837*, ed. Annie Heloise Abel (Pierre, S.Dak.: Department of History, 1932), p. 105.

89. *The North American Journals of Prince Maximilian of Wied*, ed. Stephen S. Witte and Marsha V. Gallagher, trans. William J. Orr, Paul Schach, and Dieter Karch, 3 vols. (Norman: University of Oklahoma Press, 2008–2012), 2:177. *See also* 2:178–79.

90. Meyer, *Village Indians*, p. 54.

91. "Journal of Truteau," p. 297.

CHAPTER 5. LIFE OF A TRAPPER

1. Dale L. Morgan, *Jedediah Smith and the Opening of the West* (Lincoln: University of Nebraska Press, 1964), pp. 76–77, 79–80, 96–97, 385n3.

2. Charles L. Camp, ed., *James Clyman, Frontiersman: The Adventures of a Trapper and Covered-Wagon Emigrant as Told in His Own Reminiscences and Diaries* (Portland, Ore.: Champoeg Press, 1960), p. 15; Daniel T. Potts to Thomas Cochlen, 7 July 1824, in *The West of William H. Ashley: The International Struggle for the Fur Trade of the Missouri, the Rocky Mountains, and the Columbia, . . . 1822–1838*, ed. Dale L. Morgan (Denver, Colo.: Old West Publishing Co., 1964), p. 79. According to historian Louis J. Clements, Henry's party included Johnson Gardner, Daniel S. D. Moore, Moses ("Black") Harris, Milton Sublette, Hugh Glass, James Bridger, and six to nine others. Clements, "Andrew Henry," in *The Mountain Men and the Fur Trade of the Far West*, ed. LeRoy R. Hafen, 10 vols. (Glendale, Calif.: Arthur H. Clark Co., 1965–1972), 6:183.

3. Potts to Cochlen, 7 July 1824. The chronology of the Henry party's movements in the fall of 1823 is difficult to determine definitively. Moses ("Black") Harris said that Mandans attacked the party on 20 August, but that is impossible if Henry first went to Fort Kiowa with Ashley on 1 September. Dale Morgan believes that Harris mistook the month and that the attack actually occurred closer to 20 September. Morgan, ed., *The West*, p. 248n206.

4. Leavenworth to Macomb, 20 Dec. 1823, ibid., pp. 68–69.

5. Reported ibid.

6. Reported ibid.

7. Ibid.; Cooke, *Scenes and Adventures in the Army; or, Romance of Military Life* (1857; repr., New York: Arno Press, 1973), pp. 137–39; [Hall], "The Missouri Trapper," *Port Folio* 19 (Mar. 1825; collected ed., Philadelphia: Harrison Hall, 1825), p. 219; Edmund Flagg, "Adventures at the Head Waters of the Missouri," *Louisville Literary News-Letter* 1 (7 Sept. 1839): 326; Morgan, *Jedediah Smith*, p. 391n2; Morgan, ed., *The West*, 248n210. Fitzgerald ascended the Missouri River in 1825 as a member of the Atkinson-O'Fallon expedition and was mustered out of the service at Jefferson Barracks in Saint Louis on 19 April 1829. He was then a private in Company C of the Sixth Regiment and was described as a carpenter. Morgan, *Jedediah Smith*, p. 391n2.

8. Charles L. Camp, ed., *George C. Yount and His Chronicles of the West, Comprising Extracts from His "Memoirs" and from the Orange Clark "Narrative"* (Denver, Colo.: Old West Publishing Co., 1966), pp. 197–209; Leavenworth to Henry Atkinson, 20 Oct. 1823, in "Of-

ficial Correspondence Pertaining to the Leavenworth Expedition of 1823 into South Dakota for the Conquest of the Ree Indians," ed. Doane Robinson, *South Dakota Historical Collections* 1 (1902): 211.

9. Morgan, ed., *The West,* pp. 246–47n191; Bartholomew Berthold to Bernard Pratte, 14 Nov. 1823, ibid., p. 62; Richard T. Holliday to [William Clark], 16 Feb. 1824, ibid., p. 73; Leavenworth to Macomb, 20 Dec. 1823. At some point in their upriver journey, Citoleux's traders likely passed Harris's little party going down to Fort Atkinson. If Glass was indeed with Citoleux at the time, and the Fitzgerald who traveled with Harris was one of his deserters, then one wonders what circumstance kept the two men from meeting—or if one of the premises is false.

10. Berthold to Pratte, 14 Nov. 1823; Holliday to [Clark], 16 Feb. 1824; Leavenworth to Macomb, 20 Dec. 1823; Cooke, *Scenes and Adventures*, pp. 145–46; Myers, *Pirate, Pawnee, and Mountain Man: The Saga of Hugh Glass* (Boston: Little, Brown & Co., 1963), pp. 162–63.

11. *St. Louis Enquirer*, 7 June 1824, in *The West*, ed. Morgan, p. 76; Cooke, *Scenes and Adventures*, p. 150; [Hall], "The Missouri Trapper," p. 218; Camp, ed., *George C. Yount*, pp. 203–4.

12. *St. Louis Enquirer*, 7 June 1824.

13. O'Fallon to Clark, 9 July 1824, in *The West*, ed. Morgan, pp. 82–83.

14. Flagg, "Adventures," p. 326; Camp, ed., *George C. Yount*, p. 204; *St. Louis Enquirer*, 7 June 1824.

15. Camp, ed., *James Clyman*, p. 18.

16. Ibid., pp. 27–29. *See also* p. 25; and Morgan, *Jedediah Smith*, pp. 109–10.

17. Morgan, *Jedediah Smith*, pp. 91–93, 112–13.

18. Flagg, "Adventures," p. 326.

19. Quoted in F. F. Stephens, "Missouri and the Santa Fe Trade," *Missouri Historical Review* 11 (Apr.–July 1917): 292.

20. Eric Jay Dolin, *Fur, Fortune, and Empire: The Epic History of the Fur Trade in America* (New York: W. W. Norton & Co., 2010), p. 258. *See also* pp. 256–57, 259–60.

21. Ibid., pp. 260–64.

22. Willard, "Autobiography," sec. 2, p. [11], Rowland Willard-Elizabeth S. Willard Papers, 1822–1921, WA MSS S-2512, box 1, folder 1, Beinecke Library, Yale University, New Haven, Conn.

23. Ibid., pp. [11–13].

24. Ibid., p. [12]. Willard also mistakenly asserted that Indians clubbed Glass to death along the Colorado River a couple of years after he met him. Ibid., p. [14]. *See also* Ellsworth, *Washington Irving on the Prairie; or, A Narrative of a Tour of the Southwest in the Year 1832*, ed. Stanley T. Williams and Barbara D. Simison (New York: American Book Co., 1937), pp. 53–57.

25. Camp, ed., *George C. Yount*, p. 205.

26. Flagg, "Adventures," pp. 326–27.

27. Camp, ed., *George C. Yount*, pp. 205–6. Of course, the distance is exaggerated.

28. Flagg, "Adventures," p. 327.

29. Weber, *The Taos Trappers: The Fur Trade in the Far Southwest, 1540–1846* (Norman: University of Oklahoma Press, 1971), p. 110; Charles L. Camp, "George C. Yount," in *Mountain Men*, ed. Hafen, 10:414. Some historians, noting that Yount did not come to the Southwest until 1826 and believing his account of Glass to be a first-hand recollection, have concluded that Glass arrived in the region later than 1825. Weber, for example, suggested that Yount may have meant Pratte when he named Provost as Glass's employer because Provost had left the area before 1826.

30. *Osborne Russell's Journal of a Trapper*, ed. Aubrey L. Haines (Lincoln: University of Nebraska Press, 1965), p. 82.

31. T. D. Bonner, *The Life and Adventures of James P. Beckwourth, Mountaineer, Scout, and Pioneer, and Chief of the Crow Nation of Indians* (New York: Harper & Brothers, 1856), p. 107.

32. *Osborne Russell's Journal*, p. 45.

33. Ibid., p. 51.

34. Ibid., p. 60.

35. Camp, ed., *George C. Yount*, p. 205.

36. Chittenden, *The American Fur Trade of the Far West: A History of the Pioneer Trading Posts . . . and of the Overland Commerce with Santa Fe*, 3 vols. (New York: Francis P. Harper, 1902), 1:328.

37. Ibid., 1:329.

38. Ibid., 2:705.

39. *The North American Journals of Prince Maximilian of Wied,* ed. Stephen S. Witte and Marsha V. Gallagher, trans. William J. Orr, Paul Schach, and Dieter Karch, 3 vols. (Norman: University of Oklahoma Press, 2008–2012), 2:115, 127. *See also* Myers, *Pirate, Pawnee, and Mountain Man*, p. 219.

40. Maximilian, *North American Journals*, 2:127–28, 235. *See also* 1:xxxii, 3:7.

41. Ibid., 3:300–301.

42. Ibid., 3:301–2.

43. Flagg, "Adventures," p. 327. For information on Gardner, *see* Aubrey L. Haines, "Johnson Gardner," in *Mountain Men*, ed. Hafen, 2:157–59.

44. Bonner, *Life and Adventures*, pp. 255–56, 258. *See also* pp. 253–54; 257.

45. *Osborne Russell's Journal*, p. 123.

46. Astor to Chouteau, Aug. 1832, Chouteau Family Papers, 1752–1946, A0274, Missouri History Museum Archives, Saint Louis.

47. Harvey L. Carter, "William H. Ashley," in *Mountain Men*, ed. Hafen, 7:23–34. For a detailed biography, *see* Richard M. Clokey, *William H. Ashley: Enterprise and Politics in the Trans-Mississippi West* (Norman: University of Oklahoma Press, 1980). Clokey discusses Ashley's call to halt trapping in order to replenish the beaver population on pp. 199–200.

48. James E. B. Austin to Stephen Austin, 6 Sept. 1824, in *Annual Report of the American Historical Association for the Year 1919*, vol. 2, *The Austin Papers*, ed. Eugene C. Barker, 2 vols. (Washington, D.C.: Government Printing Office, 1924), 1:891.

49. Chittenden, *American Fur Trade*, 1:250; Louis J. Clements, "Andrew Henry," 6:173–84. *See also* Linda Harper White and Fred R. Gowans, "Traders to Trappers: Andrew Henry and the Rocky Mountain Fur Trade," *Montana the Magazine of Western History* 43 (Winter 1993): 58–65, (Summer 1993): 54–63.

50. Barbour, *Jedediah Smith: No Ordinary Mountain Man* (Norman: University of Oklahoma Press, 2009), p. 6. For biographical information, *see* Harvey L. Carter, "Jedediah Smith," in *Mountain Men*, ed. Hafen, 8:331–48.

51. Willis Blenkinsop, "Edward Rose," in *Mountain Men*, ed. Hafen, 9:335–45.

52. Gerald C. Bagley, "Daniel T. Potts," ibid., 3:249–62.

53. Charles L. Camp, "James Clyman," ibid., 1:233–52.

54. Cornelius M. Ismert, "James Bridger," ibid., 6:85–104.

55. Fehrman, "The Mountain Men — A Statistical View," ibid., 10:10, 14.

56. Ibid., 10:9–15; Goetzmann, "The Mountain Man as Jacksonian Man," *American Quarterly* 15 (Autumn 1963): 409; Walker, "The Mountain Man Journal: Its Significance in a Literary History of the Fur Trade," *Western Historical Quarterly* 5 (July 1974): 307–18.

57. William H. Goetzmann, *Exploration and Empire: The Explorer and the Scientist in the Winning of the American West* (New York: Alfred A. Knopf, 1966), p. 106.

58. Myers, *Pirate, Pawnee, and Mountain Man*, pp. 228–29.

59. Coleman, *Here Lies Hugh Glass: A Mountain Man, a Bear, and the Rise of the American Nation* (New York: Hill & Wang, 2012), p. 19.

60. Goetzmann, *Exploration and Empire*, p. 107.

61. Hofstadter, *The American Political Tradition and the Men Who Made It* (New York: Alfred A. Knopf, 1948), pp. 55–56, 58.

62. Goetzmann, *Exploration and Empire*, p. 107. For one exchange in the battle over the character of the mountain man, *see* Goetzmann, "The Mountain Man as Jacksonian Man," which opened the argument. Harvey L. Carter and Marcia C. Spencer critiqued Goetzmann's conclusions in "Stereotypes of the Mountain Man," *Western Historical Quarterly* 6 (Jan. 1975): 17–32. Goetzmann responded in "A Note on 'Stereotypes of the Mountain Man,'" *Western Historical Quarterly* 6 (July 1975): 295–300, and Carter returned barbs in "A Reply," ibid., pp. 301–2.

63. Walker, "Mountain Man Journal," p. 317.

CHAPTER 6. CREATING A WESTERN LEGEND

1. Young, "The Hugh Glass Monument," in *Homestead Years, 1908–1968*, ed. Mrs. Lloyd I. Sudlow (Bison, S.Dak.: *Bison Courier*, 1968), p. 171.

2. Ibid., pp. 171–76.

3. House, "The Wail of a Coyote," ibid., p. 176.

4. Young, "The Hugh Glass Monument," p. 171.

5. Ibid., pp. 171–72.

6. Ibid., pp. 172–73.

7. Neihardt, *The Song of Hugh Glass* (New York: Macmillan Co., 1915), p. 16.

8. Young, "Hugh Glass Monument," p. 173.

9. Fred Jennewein, quoted in "Old Timers Sponsor Hugh Glass Memorial at Bison," in *Homestead Years*, ed. Sudlow, p. 175.

10. "John G. Neihardt, Noted Poet, Dedication Speaker—At Bison in 1939," ibid., p. 174.

11. Neihardt, *A Cycle of the West* (New York: Macmillan Co., 1949), p. v.

12. Neihardt, *Song of Hugh Glass*, p. viii.

13. Neihardt, *Cycle of the West*, pp. v-vi.

14. Ibid., p. x. *See also* Lucile F. Aly, *John G. Neihardt*, Boise State University Western Writers Series (Boise, Idaho: Boise State University, 1976), p. 13.

15. Neihardt, *Song of Hugh Glass*, p. viii. *See also* Neihardt, *The River and I* (New York: G. P. Putnam's Sons, 1910).

16. Neihardt, *The Splendid Wayfaring: The Story of the Exploits and Adventures of Jedediah Smith and His Comrades* . . . (New York: Macmillan Co., 1920).

17. Neihardt, *Song of Hugh Glass*, p. vii.

18. Neihardt, *Cycle of the West*, p. vi.

19. Neihardt, *The River and I*, p. 23. *See also* Julius T. House, *John G. Neihardt: Man and Poet* (Wayne, Nebr.: F. H. Jones & Son, 1920), pp. 7–9.

20. Aly, *John G. Neihardt*, p. 14.

21. Ferris, *Life in the Rocky Mountains: A Diary of Wanderings on the Sources of the Rivers Missouri, Columbia, and Colorado, 1830–1835*, 2d ed., ed. LeRoy R. Hafen (Denver, Colo.: Old West Publishing Co., 1983), pp. 392–93.

22. Stanley T. Williams and Barbara D. Simison, "Introduction," in Ellsworth, *Washington Irving on the Prairie; or, A Narrative of a Tour of the Southwest in the Year 1832*, ed. Williams and Simison (New York: American Book Co., 1937), p. 5.

23. Ellsworth, *Washington Irving on the Prairie*, pp. 53–54.

24. Ibid., pp. 55–57.

25. [Sage], *Scenes in the Rocky Mountains, and in Oregon, California, New Mexico, Texas, and the Grand Prairies; or, Notes by the Way* . . . (Philadelphia: Carey & Hart, 1846), p. 117. For a biography of Sage, *see* John A. Spalding, comp., *Illustrated Popular Biography of Connecticut* (Hartford, Conn.: Case, Lockwood, & Brainard Co., 1891), pp. 107–8.

26. [Sage], *Scenes in the Rocky Mountains*, pp. 117–18.

27. Ibid., p. 118. Although Sage visited Taos, he did not mention meeting Glass there, and he probably gained his information sec-

ondhand from other trappers who may have recalled Glass living there in earlier times. Another possibility, as some writers have concluded, is that an imposter pretending to be Glass lived in Taos and regaled visitors with his tales. *See* Aubrey L. Haines, "Hugh Glass," in *The Mountain Men and the Fur Trade of the Far West*, ed. LeRoy R. Hafen, 10 vols. (Glendale, Calif.: Arthur H. Clark Co., 1965–1972), 6:170–71.

28. Haynes and Haynes, eds. *The Grizzly Bear: Portraits from Life* (Norman: University of Oklahoma Press, 1966), p. 50.

29. Ruxton, *Ruxton of the Rockies*, comp. Clyde Porter and Mae Reed Porter, ed. LeRoy R. Hafen (Norman: University of Oklahoma Press, 1950), p. 253.

30. Ibid., p. 254.

31. Ibid.

32. Ibid., p. 255.

33. Edgeley W. Todd, "James Hall and the Hugh Glass Legend," *American Quarterly* 7 (Winter 1955): 367; Cattermole, *Famous Frontiersmen, Pioneers and Scouts; the Vanguards of American Civilization* (Chicago: Coburn & Newman Publishing Co., 1883); Triplett, *Conquering the Wilderness; or, New Pictorial History of the Life and Times of the Pioneer Heroes and Heroines of America* (Minneapolis, Minn.: Northwestern Publishing Co., 1888), pp. 428–29.

34. Chittenden, *The American Fur Trade of the Far West: A History of the Pioneer Trading Posts . . . and of the Overland Commerce with Santa Fe*, 3 vols. (New York: Francis P. Harper, 1902), 2:698.

35. Ibid., 2:698.

36. Van Osdel, *Historic Landmarks: Being a History of Early Explorers and Fur-Traders, with a Narrative of Their Adventures in the Wilds of the Great Northwest Territory* (n.p., [1915]), p. 135. *See also* pp. 132–34; and Robinson, *History of South Dakota*, 2 vols. ([Logansport, Ind.]: B. F. Bowen & Co., 1904), 1:108–9.

37. Putney, *In the South Dakota Country*, 2 vols. (Mitchell, S.Dak.: Educator Supply Co., 1922), 1:87.

38. *Back-Trailing on the Old Frontiers*, illus. Charles M. Russell (Great Falls, Mont.: Cheely-Raban Syndicate, 1922), p. 8.

39. Vanderpol and McCain, *Stories for Young Dakotans: The Stories of the Men and Women Who Changed the Lonely Prairie into the South Dakota of Today*, 2d ed. (Sioux Falls, S.Dak.: Will A. Beach Printing Co., 1942), p. 84.

40. Garst, *When the West Was Young* (Douglas, Wyo.: Enterprise Publishing Co., 1942), p. 97. *See also* pp. 98–109; Putney, *In the South Dakota Country*, 1:88–91; and Vanderpol and McCain, *Stories for Young Dakotans*, pp. 82–83.

41. Barker, *Our State: A History for the Sixth Grade* (Mitchell, S.Dak.: Educator Supply Co., 1937), pp. 60–62.

42. Schell, *South Dakota: Its Beginnings and Growth* (New York: American Book Co., 1960), pp. 59–60.

43. *See* Johnson, *South Dakota: A Republic of Friends*, [rev. ed.] (Pierre, S.Dak.: Capital Supply Co., 1919), pp. 49–50; and Neihardt, *The Song of Hugh Glass*, with notes by House (New York: Macmillan Co., 1919).

44. Workers of the South Dakota Writers' Project, comps., *Both Sides of the River* (Sioux Falls, S.Dak.: Midwest Press & Supply Co., 1942), p. 39. *See also* pp. 35–38.

45. Federal Writers' Project, Works Progress Administration, State of South Dakota, comp., *A South Dakota Guide* (1938; repr., Pierre: South Dakota State Historical Society Press, 2005), p. 211.

46. Neihardt, *Splendid Wayfaring*, p. 138, quoted ibid.

47. Manfred, "The Making of *Lord Grizzly*," *South Dakota History* 15 (Fall 1985): 201. *See also* Manfred, *Lord Grizzly* (1954; repr., University of Nebraska Press, 1983), p. xv.

48. Manfred, "Making of *Lord Grizzly*," p. 201.

49. Quoted in *Book Review Digest: Fiftieth Annual Cumulation, March 1954 to February 1955 Inclusive*, ed. Mertice M. James and Dorothy Brown (New York: H. W. Wilson Co., 1955), p. 586.

50. Quoted ibid.

51. Manfred, "Making of *Lord Grizzly*," pp. 210–11. *See also* John R. Milton, "Foreword," in Manfred, *Lord Grizzly*, p. v.

52. Manfred, "Making of *Lord Grizzly*," pp. 201–2, 207.

53. Ibid., pp. 202–3.

54. Ibid., pp. 203–4.

55. Reported ibid., p. 206. *See also* pp. 202–5.

56. Milton, "Foreword," pp. xi–xii.

57. Manfred, *Lord Grizzly*, p. xv.

58. Manfred, "Making of *Lord Grizzly*," p. 215.

59. *Conversations with Frederick Manfred*, moderated John R. Milton (Salt Lake City: University of Utah Press, 1974), p. 117. Manfred also admitted to mistakenly placing George Yount with Glass

in 1823; actually, Yount only met Glass in the Southwest a few years later.

60. Manfred, *Lord Grizzly*, pp. 1, 8, 13, 16–17, 47–48, 50.

61. Ibid., pp. 51–57, 77–81, 83–84, 86.

62. Ibid., pp. 106–7, 133–34, 222.

63. Coleman, *Here Lies Hugh Glass: A Mountain Man, a Bear, and the Rise of the American Nation* (New York: Hill & Wang, 2012), pp. 199–200.

64. Myers, *Pirate, Pawnee, and Mountain Man: The Saga of Hugh Glass* (Boston: Little, Brown & Co., 1963), pp. 3, 228–29.

65. Ibid., p. 4.

66. Kirkel, "Hugh Glass: Fighting Firebrand of the Frontier," *Gunsmoke* 1 (Aug. 1951): 25, 31.

67. Moyers, *Famous Heroes of the Old West* (New York: Grosset & Dunlap, 1957), p. 14.

68. Lambert, "The Hugh Glass Story" (n.p.: Dakota Music Co., 1966), p. 2. *See also* "Hugh Glass Meets the Bear," *Internet Movie Database*, imdb.com.

69. Chrisman, "He Lived for Revenge," *Saga* 7 (Jan. 1954): 70.

70. Covington, "Alone and Left to Die!" *True West* 10 (Sept.–Oct. 1962): 70.

71. Young, "Hugh Glass' Empty Revenge," *Real West* 7 (May 1964): 14, 52. Four years later, the magazine published another article on Glass by Norman B. Wiltsey, who suggested that, during his crawl, Glass repeatedly considered giving up. Each time, however, he reminded himself, "a *man* don't quit!" Wiltsey, "A Man Don't Quit," *Real West* 11 (June 1968): 36.

72. Lewis, "Hugh Glass—Mountain Man," *Great West* 3 (Feb. 1969): 38, 43.

73. Milton, *South Dakota: A Bicentennial History* (New York: W. W. Norton & Co., 1977), pp. 17–18. *See also* pp. 19–23.

74. Crist, "This Week's Movies," *TV Guide* 23 (5 Apr. 1975): A-10. *See also Man in the Wilderness* (1971; DVD release, Burbank, Calif.: Warner Bros. Entertainment, 2008); *Pressbook* for *Man in the Wilderness* (n.p.: Warner Bros., 1971); and Coleman, *Here Lies Hugh Glass*, pp. 200–201.

75. Coleman, *Here Lies Hugh Glass*, pp. ix, 209–10.

76. *See*, for example, ibid., p. 4.

77. Ibid., p. 213.

78. Ellison, "Hugh Glass: The Survivor," *South Dakota Magazine* 3 (June–July 1987): 20.

79. Peterson, "Hugh Glass' Crawl into Legend," *Wild West* 13 (June 2000): 78.

80. Bradley, *Hugh Glass* (Calistoga, Calif.: Monarch, 1995), p. 117.

81. McMurtry, *The Wandering Hill*, The Berrybender Narratives (New York: Simon & Schuster, 2003), pp. 1–2, 5, 15. *See also* Punke, *The Revenant* (New York: Carroll & Graf, 2002), pp. 12–14.

82. McClung, *Hugh Glass, Mountain Man* (New York: Morrow Junior Books, 1990), pp. vii, x.

83. Glass, *Mountain Men: True Grit and Tall Tales* (New York: Random House Children's Books, 2001), p. [16].

84. La Due, *Crawl into the Night: A Story about Hugh Glass* (Mud Butte, S.Dak.: Joy in the Morning Publishing Co., 2008), p. 57.

85. Carl W. Hart, *Amazing Stories from History: Intermediate Level* (Ann Arbor: University of Michigan Press, 2009), p. ix. *See also* chap. 6.

86. "Welcome, Frontiersmen," *American Frontiersman*, "Premier Issue," [2012]: 4.

87. Spencer, "Wildest & the Toughest: Hugh Glass—John Colter—John Johnston," ibid., p. 26. *See also* Edward E. Leslie, *Desperate Journeys, Abandoned Souls: True Stories of Castaways and Other Survivors* (Boston: Houghton Mifflin Co., 1988), chap. 17. For a discussion of survival literature in the tradition of Glass, *see* Coleman, *Here Lies Hugh Glass*, pp. 213–17.

88. Pictured in Will G. Robinson, "Hugh Glass," *Wi-iyohi* 20 (1 July 1966): 1. *See also* Young, "Hugh Glass Monument," p. 173.

89. "Lemmon Commemorates Journey of Hugh Glass," *Mitchell* (S.Dak.) *Daily Republic*, 12 July 1973.

90. Young, "Hugh Glass Monument," p. 173. *See also* "Lemmon Commemorates Journey of Hugh Glass."

91. Soraya Nadia McDonald, "Won't You People Please Just Give Leonardo DiCaprio an Oscar Already?" *Washington Post*, reprinted in *Mitchell Daily Republic*, 1 Oct. 2015. *See also* Lauren Donovan, "Historic Rendezvous," *Bismarck* (N.Dak.) *Tribune*, 11 June 2015, bismarcktribune.com.

92. Quoted in Donovan, "Historic Rendezvous."

93. Ibid.

94. Ibid.

95. Quoted in Michael Zimny, "Lemmon-Based Artist John Lopez to Unveil New Monument to Hugh Glass," *Arts & Culture*, South Dakota Public Broadcasting, 29 Mar. 2015, sdpb.org.

96. Quoted in Donovan, "Historic Rendezvous."

97. Ibid. *See also John Lopez Sculpture: Grand River Series* (n.p.: John Lopez Studio, 2014).

98. Kella Rodiek, "Mitchell Artist Spends June in Residence at Crazy Horse Memorial," *Mitchell Daily Republic*, 5 July 2015, mitchellrepublic.com.

CHAPTER 7. AND WHAT ABOUT THE BEAR?

1. Frank Dufresne, *No Room for Bears* (New York: Holt, Rinehart & Winston, 1965), p. 111. *See also* Paul Schullery, "The Grizzly Today," in Harold McCracken, *The Beast That Walks Like Man: The Story of the Grizzly Bear* (1955; repr., Lanham, Md.: Roberts Rinehart, 2003), pp. 9–16; William H. Over and Edward P. Churchill, *Mammals of South Dakota* (Vermillion: Museum and Department of Zoology, University of South Dakota, 1941), pp. 10–11; "Grizzly Bear," *National Geographic*, animals.nationalgeographic.com; and "Grizzly Bear," National Wildlife Federation, nwf.org. One writer claims that a few bears still roamed South Dakota's Badlands region after 1900. [Richard Cropp], "Bears!" *Wi-iyohi* 18 (1 Dec. 1964): 7.

2. McCracken, *Beast That Walks Like Man*, pp. 105–6.

3. Ibid., pp. 121–22.

4. Brackenridge, *Views of Louisiana; Together with a Journal of a Voyage up the Missouri River, in 1811* (1814; repr., Chicago: Quadrangle Books, 1962), pp. 55–56.

5. Paul Schullery, *Lewis and Clark among the Grizzlies: Legend and Legacy in the American West* (Guilford, Conn.: Falcon, 2002), p. 50.

6. William H. Wright, *The Grizzly Bear: The Narrative of a Hunter-Naturalist* (1909; repr., Lincoln: University of Nebraska Press, 1977), pp. 13–14; Schullery, *Lewis and Clark among the Grizzlies*, p. 53; [Ord], "Zoology of North America," in Guthrie, *A New Geographical, Historical, and Commercial Grammar*, 2 vols., 2d. American ed. (Philadelphia: Johnson & Warner, 1815), 2:291, 299–300. McCracken discussed George Ord's description of the grizzly bear in *The Beast That Walks Like Man*, pp. 285–90.

7. Gary E. Moulton, ed., *The Journals of the Lewis & Clark Expedition*, 13 vols. (Lincoln: University of Nebraska Press, 1983–2001), 7:256. *See also* Wright, *Grizzly Bear*, p. 22.

8. Schullery, *Lewis and Clark among the Grizzlies*, p. 54.

9. Ibid., pp. 54, 57. McCracken included a checklist based on Merriam's grizzly bear classification in *The Beast That Walks Like Man*, pp. 291–304.

10. Schullery, *Lewis and Clark among the Grizzlies*, p. 26.

11. Jefferson to Lewis, 20 June 1803, in *Letters of the Lewis and Clark Expedition, with Related Documents, 1783–1854*, ed. Donald Jackson (Urbana: University of Illinois Press, 1962), p. 63.

12. Moulton, ed., *Journals*, 2:142.

13. Schullery, *Lewis and Clark among the Grizzlies*, p. 12.

14. Moulton, ed., *Journals*, 3:186, 188. *See also* 3:148.

15. Ibid., 9:128.

16. Ibid., 4:31.

17. Ibid.

18. Ibid., 4:48, 84–85.

19. Ibid., 4:113, 118. *See also* Schullery, *Lewis and Clark among the Grizzlies*, pp. 12–13.

20. Moulton, ed., *Journals*, 4:141.

21. Ibid.

22. Ibid., 4:151.

23. Ibid., 4:242.

24. Ibid., 4:256.

25. Ibid., 4:292–93. *See also* John Bakeless, *Lewis & Clark, Partners in Discovery* (New York: William Morrow & Co., 1947), p. 191.

26. Schullery, *Lewis and Clark among the Grizzlies*, pp. 85–94.

27. Moulton, ed., *Journals*, 4:336, 338.

28. Schullery, *Lewis and Clark among the Grizzlies*, p. 100.

29. Godman, "The Philadelphia Bear Cubs," in *The Grizzly Bear: Portraits from Life*, ed. Bessie Doak Haynes and Edgar Haynes (Norman: University of Oklahoma Press, 1966), p. 19.

30. Wright, *Grizzly Bear*, pp. 229–30.

31. Over and Churchill, *Mammals*, p. 10.

32. *The Journals of Zebulon Montgomery Pike, with Letters and Related Documents*, ed. Donald Jackson, 2 vols. (Norman: University of Oklahoma Press, 1966), 2:293. *See also* 2:276, 278–79, 283–84, 292, 294.

33. McCracken, *Beast That Walks Like Man*, p. 122.

34. *Kit Carson's Autobiography*, ed. Milo Milton Quaife (Chicago: R. R. Donnelley & Sons Co., 1935), pp. 37–39.

35. J. W. Buel, *Heroes of the Plains; or, Lives and Wonderful Adventures of Wild Bill, Buffalo Bill, Kit Carson . . .* (1881; repr., New York: N. D. Thompson & Co., 1882), pp. 36–38. Although cinnamon bears are actually part of the black bear species, in Buel's time they were popularly believed to be close relatives of the grizzly bear, and Buel clearly intended to evoke a bear with the grizzly's size and supposed ferocity.

36. Over and Churchill, *Mammals*, p. 10.

37. Roosevelt, *Hunting Trips on the Prairie and in the Mountains* (1885, as *Hunting Trips of a Ranchman*; repr., New York: G. P. Putnam's Sons, 1900), p. 225. *See also* Roosevelt, *Hunting the Grisly, and Other Sketches: An Account of the Big Game of the United States and its Chase with Horse, Hound, and Rifle* (1893, as *The Wilderness Hunter*; repr., New York: G. P. Putnam's Sons, 1903).

38. Wright, *Grizzly Bear*, pp. 230–31.

39. Schullery, *Lewis and Clark among the Grizzlies*, p. 67.

40. Ibid., pp. 67–69.

41. Roosevelt, *Hunting Trips*, p. 197–98.

42. Ibid., p. 200. *See also* p. 198. Paul Schullery noted the unlikelihood of grizzly bears learning new behavior from being shot but suggested that there may have been some "selective culling" as more aggressive bears were killed and shier ones avoided confrontation and survived. Schullery, *Lewis and Clark among the Grizzlies*, p. 119.

43. Parkman, *The Oregon Trail: Sketches of Prairie and Rocky-Mountain Life*, illus. ed. (1892; repr., Boston: Little, Brown, & Co., 1904), p. viii.

44. Schullery, *Lewis and Clark among the Grizzlies*, p. 97.

45. Wright, *Grizzly Bear*, p. 93.

46. Schullery, *Lewis and Clark among the Grizzlies*, pp. 97–98. *See also* Fred R. Gowans, *Mountain Man & Grizzly* (Orem, Utah: Mountain Grizzly Publications, 1986).

47. *Osborne Russell's Journal of a Trapper*, ed. Aubrey L. Haines (Lincoln: University of Nebraska Press, 1965), pp. 47, 84.

48. Wright, *Grizzly Bear*, pp. 256, 258–59.

49. Wright, *Grizzly Bear*, p. 262.

50. J. Knox Jones, Jr., et al., *Mammals of the Northern Great Plains* (Lincoln: University of Nebraska Press, 1983), pp. 267–68.

51. Ibid., p. 268.

52. Ibid., p. 267.

53. Schullery, *Lewis and Clark among the Grizzlies*, p. 63.

54. Ibid., p. 116. *See also* pp. 12, 115, 213n3; Burroughs, ed., *The Natural History of the Lewis and Clark Expedition* (East Lansing: Michigan State University Press, 1995), p. 282; Walcheck, "Wapiti: The Ubiquitous American Elk Was a Staple in Both the Diet and the Journals of Lewis and Clark," *We Proceeded On* 26 (Aug. 2000): 31; and Walcheck, "Pronghorns, as Documented by the 1804–06 Lewis and Clark Expedition," *We Proceeded On* 24 (Aug. 1998): 8–9.

55. George Armstrong Custer to Elizabeth Bacon Custer, 15 Aug. 1874, Marguerite Merington Papers, New York Public Library, New York, N.Y.

56. Grinnell, "Zoological Report," in William Ludlow, *Report of a Reconnaissance of the Black Hills of Dakota, Made in the Summer of 1874* (Washington, D.C.: Government Printing Office, 1875), p. 81. *See also* Robert M. Utley, *Cavalier in Buckskin: George Armstrong Custer and the Western Military Frontier* (Norman: University of Oklahoma Press, 1988), p. 137.

57. Grinnell, "Zoological Report," p. 81.

58. Roosevelt, *Hunting Trips*, pp. 197, 210–11, 215, 223–24.

59. McCracken, *Beast That Walks Like Man*, p. 172.

60. Mills, *The Grizzly: Our Greatest Wild Animal* (Boston: Houghton Mifflin Co., 1919), p. 275.

61. McCracken, *Beast That Walks Like Man*, pp. 105, 162–63, 170. Of course, grizzly bears were not the only creatures being killed in large numbers. The story of the destruction of the buffalo herds has often been told. Indeed, it was common behavior for European Americans to shoot whatever walked, ran, or flew. Botanist John Bradbury, who traveled up the Missouri in 1811, was typical of western travelers. While walking in the woods along the river, he found some passenger pigeons. They were, he said, in "prodigious flocks," and when landing, covered "an area of several acres in extent, and are so close to each other that the ground can scarcely be seen." He quickly returned to camp to exchange his rifle for a "fowling-piece,"

and within a few hours, shot "271," then "desisted." Not surprisingly, there are no passenger pigeons today. Bradbury, *Travels in the Interior of America, in the Years 1809, 1810, and 1811* . . . (London: Sherwood, Neely, & Jones, 1817), p. 44.

62. Schullery, *Lewis and Clark among the Grizzlies*, pp. 71–72.

63. David Rockwell, *Giving Voice to Bear: North American Indian Rituals, Myths, and Images of the Bear* (Niwot, Colo.: Roberts Rinehart, 1991), p. 5.

64. Douglas R. Parks, *Myths and Traditions of the Arikara Indians* (Lincoln: University of Nebraska Press, 1996), chaps 7, 47.

65. Rockwell, *Giving Voice to Bear*, pp. 1–7.

66. Schullery, *Lewis and Clark among the Grizzlies*, p. 72.

67. Edmund Morris, *Theodore Rex* (New York: Random House, 2001), pp. 172–74. *See also* pp. 626–27.

68. Schullery, *Lewis and Clark among the Grizzlies*, p. 73.

69. *Man in the Wilderness* (1971; DVD release, Burbank, Calif.: Warner Bros. Entertainment, 2008). *See also* Nick Jans, *The Grizzly Maze: Timothy Treadwell's Fatal Obsession with Alaskan Bears* (New York: Plume, 2006), pp. 203–5.

70. Schullery, *Lewis and Clark among the Grizzlies*, p. 73.

71. Jans, *Grizzly Maze*, pp. xii, 136.

72. Craighead, Sumner, and Mitchell, *The Grizzly Bears of Yellowstone: Their Ecology in the Yellowstone Ecosystem, 1959–1992* (Washington, D.C.: Island Press, 1995), pp. 491–92.

73. Quoted in John K. Hutchens, *One Man's Montana: An Informal Portrait of a State* (Philadelphia: J. B. Lippincott Co., 1964), pp. 207–8.

CONCLUSION

1. *The Personal Narrative of James O. Pattie*, intro. by William H. Goetzmann (1831; repr., Lincoln: University of Nebraska Press, 1984), p. 29. *See also* ibid., pp. 28, 36.

2. Goetzmann, "Introduction," in *Personal Narrative of James O. Pattie*, p. ix.

3. Victor, *The River of the West: Life and Adventure in the Rocky Mountains and Oregon* . . . (Hartford, Conn.: Columbian Book Co., 1870), p. 50.

4. Steckmesser, *The Western Hero in History and Legend* (Norman: University of Oklahoma Press, 1965), pp. 245, 247. *See also* p. 9.

5. Milton, "Foreword," in Manfred, *Lord Grizzly* (1954; repr. Lincoln: University of Nebraska Press, 1983), pp. vii-ix.

6. Alter, *James Bridger, Trapper, Frontiersman, Scout and Guide: A Historical Narrative* (1925; repr., Columbus, Ohio: Long's College Book Co., 1951), p. 29.

7. Honig, *James Bridger: Pathfinder of the West* (Kansas City, Mo.: Brown-White-Lowell, 1951), p. 13.

8. Vestal, *Jim Bridger, Mountain Man: A Biography* (Lincoln: University of Nebraska Press, 1970), pp. 55, 310n2. *See also* Alter, *James Bridger*, pp. 20, 533; and Chrisman, "He Lived for Revenge," *Saga* 7 (Jan. 1954): 70.

9. [Hall], "The Missouri Trapper," *Port Folio* 19 (Mar. 1825; collected ed., Philadelphia: Harrison Hall, 1825), p. 216.

10. Doane Robinson's handwritten poem is on the front endpaper of the copy of *The Song of Hugh Glass* that Neihardt inscribed to him. It is located in the McGovern Library, Dakota Wesleyan University, Mitchell, S.Dak.

11. Steckmesser, *Western Hero*, p. 250.

12. Dale L. Morgan, *Jedediah Smith and the Opening of the West* (Lincoln: University of Nebraska Press, 1964), p. 391n2; Cornelius M. Ismert, "James Bridger," in *The Mountain Men and the Fur Trade of the Far West*, ed. LeRoy R. Hafen, 10 vols. (Glendale, Calif.: Arthur H. Clark Co., 1965-1972), 6:85-104.

13. Steckmesser, *Western Hero*, pp. 249, 255. *See also* pp. 244-45.

14. Ibid., pp. 242-43, 247.

15. Ibid., pp. 246-47, 249.

16. Wishart, "Fur Trade Lore," in *Encyclopedia of the Great Plains*, ed. Wishart (Lincoln: University of Nebraska Press, 2004), p. 302.

17. Billington, "The Frontier and I," *Western Historical Quarterly* 1 (Jan. 1970): 18.

18. Billington, *Westward Expansion: A History of the American Frontier*, 2d. ed. (New York: Macmillan Co., 1960); Schell, *History of South Dakota*, 4th ed., rev. John E. Miller (Pierre: South Dakota State Historical Society Press, 2004); Wishart, *The Fur Trade of the American West, 1807-1840: A Geographical Synthesis* (Lincoln: University of Nebraska Press, 1979); White, *"It's Your Misfortune and None of My Own": A New History of the American West* (Norman: University of Oklahoma Press, 1991).

19. Blevins, *Give Your Heart to the Hawks: A Tribute to the Mountain Men* (Los Angeles: Nash, 1973), pp. xiii-xiv.

20. Schullery, "Introduction," in Laycock, *The Mountain Men* (1988; repr., New York: Lyons, 1996), p. ix.

21. Wishart, "Fur Trade Lore," pp. 301–2; Berry, *A Majority of Scoundrels: An Informal History of the Rocky Mountain Fur Company* (New York: Harper & Bros., 1961), pp. 49–57; Laycock, *Mountain Men*, pp. 132–38.

22. Lalire, "Glass and the Grizzly Story," *Wild West* 13 (June 2000): 6.

23. Goetzmann, "Introduction," pp. viii-ix.

Bibliography

ARCHIVAL COLLECTIONS

Chouteau Family Papers, 1752–1946, A0274. Missouri History Museum Archives, Saint Louis.

Letters Received by the Office of Indian Affairs, 1824–81. National Archives Microcopy No. 234.

Marguerite Merington Papers. New York Public Library, New York, N.Y.

Rowland Willard-Elizabeth S. Willard Papers, 1822–1921, WA MSS S-2512. Beinecke Library, Yale University, New Haven, Conn.

State Archives Collection. South Dakota State Historical Society, Pierre.

BOOKS AND FILMS

Alter, J. Cecil. *James Bridger, Trapper, Frontiersman, Scout and Guide: A Historical Narrative*. 1925; repr., Columbus, Ohio: Long's College Book Co., 1951.

Aly, Lucile F. *John G. Neihardt*. Boise State University Western Writers Series. Boise, Idaho: Boise State University, 1976.

Bagley, Jerry. *Daniel Trotter Potts, Rocky Mountain Explorer, Chronicler of the Fur Trade and the First Known Man in Yellowstone Park*. Rigby, Idaho: Old Faithful Eye-Witness Publishing, 2000.

Bakeless, John. *Lewis & Clark, Partners in Discovery*. New York: William Morrow & Co., 1947.

Barbour, Barton H. *Jedediah Smith: No Ordinary Mountain Man*. Norman: University of Oklahoma Press, 2009.

Barker, Eugene C., ed. *Annual Report of the American Historical Association for the Year 1919*. Vol. 2. *The Austin Papers*. 2 vols. Washington, D.C.: Government Printing Office, 1924–1928.

Barker, Matilda Tarleton. *Our State: A History for the Sixth Grade*. Mitchell, S.Dak.: Educator Supply Co., 1937.

Berry, Don. *A Majority of Scoundrels: An Informal History of the Rocky Mountain Fur Company*. New York: Harper & Bros., 1961.

Billington, Ray Allen. *Westward Expansion: A History of the American Frontier*. 2d ed. New York: Macmillan Co., 1960.

Blair, Walter and Franklin J. Meine. *Half Horse, Half Alligator: The Growth of the Mike Fink Legend*. Chicago: University of Chicago Press, 1956.

Blevins, Winfred. *Give Your Heart to the Hawks: A Tribute to the Mountain Men*. Los Angeles: Nash, 1973.

Bonner, T. D. *The Life and Adventures of James P. Beckwourth, Mountaineer, Scout, and Pioneer, and Chief of the Crow Nation of Indians*. New York: Harper & Brothers, 1856.

Brackenridge, Henry Marie. *Views of Louisiana; Together with a Journal of a Voyage Up the Missouri River, in 1811*. 1814; repr., Chicago: Quadrangle Books, 1962.

Bradbury, John. *Travels in the Interior of America, in the Years 1809, 1810, and 1811; Including a Description of Upper Louisiana . . . .* London: Sherwood, Neely, & Jones, 1817.

Bradley, Bruce. *Hugh Glass*. Calistoga, Calif.: Monarch, 1995.

Buel, J. W. *Heroes of the Plains; or, Lives and Wonderful Adventures of Wild Bill, Buffalo Bill, Kit Carson . . . .* 1881; repr., New York: N. D. Thompson & Co., 1882.

Burroughs, Raymond Darwin, ed. *The Natural History of the Lewis and Clark Expedition*. East Lansing: Michigan State University Press, 1995.

Camp, Charles L., ed. *George C. Yount and His Chronicles of the West, Comprising Extracts from His "Memoirs" and from the Orange Clark "Narrative."* Denver, Colo.: Old West Publishing Co., 1966.

————, ed. *James Clyman, Frontiersman: The Adventures of a Trapper and Covered-Wagon Emigrant as Told in His Own Reminiscences and Diaries*. Portland, Ore.: Champoeg Press, 1960.

Carson, [Christopher]. *Kit Carson's Autobiography*. Ed. and with an intro. by Milo Milton Quaife. Chicago: R. R. Donnelley & Sons Co., 1935.

Catlin, George. *Letters and Notes on the Manners, Customs, and Condition of the North American Indians*. 2 vols. 1841; repr., Minneapolis, Minn.: Ross & Haines, 1965.

Cattermole, E. G. *Famous Frontiersmen, Pioneers and Scouts; the Vanguards of American Civilization*. Chicago: Coburn & Newman Publishing Co., 1883.

Chardon, Francis. *Chardon's Journal at Fort Clark, 1834–1839: Descriptive of Life on the Upper Missouri; of a Fur Trader's Experiences among the Mandans, Gros Ventres, and Their Neighbors; of the Ravages of the Small-Pox Epidemic of 1837*. Ed. Annie Heloise Abel. Pierre, S.Dak.: Department of History, 1932.

Cheely-Raban Syndicate. *Back-Trailing on the Old Frontiers*. Illus. Charles M. Russell. Great Falls, Mont.: Cheely-Raban Syndicate, 1922.

Chittenden, Hiram Martin. *The American Fur Trade of the Far West: A History of the Pioneer Trading Posts and Early Fur Companies of the Missouri Valley and Rocky Mountains and of the Overland Commerce with Santa Fe*. 3 vols. New York: Francis P. Harper, 1902.

Clokey, Richard M. *William H. Ashley: Enterprise and Politics in the Trans-Mississippi West*. Norman: University of Oklahoma Press, 1980.

Coffin, Tristram Potter and Hennig Cohen, eds. *The Parade of Heroes: Legendary Figures in American Lore*. Garden City, N.Y.: Anchor Press/Doubleday, 1978.

Coleman, Jon T. *Here Lies Hugh Glass: A Mountain Man, a Bear, and the Rise of the American Nation*. New York: Hill & Wang, 2012.

Cooke, Philip St. George. *Scenes and Adventures in the Army; or, Romance of Military Life*. 1857; repr., New York: Arno Press, 1973.

Craighead, John J., Jay S. Sumner, and John A. Mitchell. *The Grizzly Bears of Yellowstone: Their Ecology in the Yellowstone Ecosystem, 1959–1992*. Washington, D.C.: Island Press, 1995.

Dale, Harrison Clifford. *The Ashley-Smith Explorations and the Discovery of a Central Route to the Pacific, 1822–1829, with the Original Journals*. Rev. ed. Glendale, Calif.: Arthur H. Clark Co., 1941.

Denig, Edwin Thompson. *Five Indian Tribes of the Upper Missouri: Sioux, Arickaras, Assiniboines, Crees, Crows*. Ed. John C. Ewers. Norman: University of Oklahoma Press, 1961.

Dolin, Eric Jay. *Fur, Fortune, and Empire: The Epic History of the Fur Trade in America*. New York: W. W. Norton & Co., 2010.

Dufresne, Frank. *No Room for Bears*. New York: Holt, Rinehart & Winston, 1965.

Ellsworth, Henry Leavitt. *Washington Irving on the Prairie; or, A Narrative of a Tour of the Southwest in the Year 1832*. Ed.

Stanley T. Williams and Barbara D. Simison. New York: American Book Co., 1937.

Federal Writers' Project, Works Progress Administration, State of South Dakota, comp. *A South Dakota Guide*. 1938; repr., Pierre: South Dakota State Historical Society Press, 2005.

Ferris, Warren Angus. *Life in the Rocky Mountains: A Diary of Wanderings on the Sources of the Rivers Missouri, Columbia, and Colorado, 1830–1835*. 2d ed. Ed. LeRoy R. Hafen. Denver, Colo.: Old West Publishing Co., 1983.

Flanagan, John T. *James Hall, Literary Pioneer of the Ohio Valley*. Minneapolis: University of Minnesota Press, 1941.

Frost, Donald McKay. *Notes on General Ashley, The Overland Trail, and South Pass*. Barre, Mass.: *Barre Gazette*, 1960.

Garst, Shannon. *When the West Was Young*. Douglas, Wyo.: Enterprise Publishing Co., 1942.

Glass, Andrew. *Mountain Men: True Grit and Tall Tales*. New York: Random House Children's Books, 2001.

Goetzmann, William H. *Exploration and Empire: The Explorer and the Scientist in the Winning of the American West*. New York: Alfred A. Knopf, 1966.

Gowans, Fred R. *Mountain Man & Grizzly*. Orem, Utah: Mountain Grizzly Publications, 1986.

———. *Rocky Mountain Rendezvous: A History of the Fur Trade Rendezvous, 1825–1840*. Provo, Utah: Brigham Young University Publications, 1976.

Guthrie, William. *A New Geographical, Historical, and Commercial Grammar*. 2 vols. 2d. American ed. Philadelphia: Johnson & Warner, 1815.

Hafen, LeRoy R., ed. *The Mountain Men and the Fur Trade of the Far West*. 10 vols. Glendale, Calif.: Arthur H. Clark Co., 1965–1972.

Hall, James. *Letters from the West; Containing Sketches of Scenery, Manners, and Customs; and Anecdotes Connected with the First Settlements of the Western Sections of the United States*. 1828; repr., Gainesville, Fla.: Scholars' Facsimiles & Reprints, 1967.

Hart, Carl W. *Amazing Stories from History: Intermediate Level*. Ann Arbor: University of Michigan Press, 2009.

Haynes, Bessie Doak and Edgar Haynes, eds. *The Grizzly Bear: Portraits From Life*. Norman: University of Oklahoma Press, 1966.

Hofstadter, Richard. *The American Political Tradition and the Men Who Made It*. New York: Alfred A. Knopf, 1948.

Honig, Louis O. *James Bridger: Pathfinder of the West*. Kansas City, Mo.: Brown-White-Lowell, 1951.

House, Julius T. *John G. Neihardt: Man and Poet*. Wayne, Nebr.: F. H. Jones & Son, 1920.

Hunt, N. Jane, ed. *Brevet's South Dakota Historical Markers*. Sioux Falls, S.Dak.: Brevet Press, 1974.

Hutchens, John K. *One Man's Montana: An Informal Portrait of a State*. Philadelphia: J. B. Lippincott Co., 1964.

Hyde, George E. *Pawnee Indians*. [Denver, Colo.]: University of Denver Press, 1951.

Irving, Washington. *Astoria; or, Anecdotes of an Enterprise beyond the Rocky Mountains*. Ed. Edgeley W. Todd. 1836; repr., Norman: University of Oklahoma Press, 1964.

Jackson, Donald, ed. *Letters of the Lewis and Clark Expedition, with Related Documents, 1783–1854*. Urbana: University of Illinois Press, 1962.

James, Mertice M. and Dorothy Brown, eds. *Book Review Digest: Fiftieth Annual Cumulation, March 1954 to February 1955 Inclusive*. New York: H. W. Wilson Co., 1955.

Jans, Nick. *The Grizzly Maze: Timothy Treadwell's Fatal Obsession with Alaskan Bears*. New York: Plume, 2006.

John Lopez Sculpture: Grand River Series. N.p.: John Lopez Studio, 2014.

Johnson, Allen and Dumas Malone, eds. *Dictionary of American Biography*. 20 vols. New York: Charles Scribner's Sons, 1928–1937.

Johnson, Willis E. *South Dakota: A Republic of Friends*. [Rev. ed.] Pierre, S.Dak.: Capital Supply Co., 1919.

Jones, J. Knox, Jr., David M. Armstrong, Robert S. Hoffman, and Clyde Jones. *Mammals of the Northern Great Plains*. Lincoln: University of Nebraska Press, 1983.

Kauffman, Henry J. *The Pennsylvania-Kentucky Rifle*. New York: Bonanza, 1960.

La Due, Margie. *Crawl into the Night: A Story about Hugh Glass*. Mud Butte, S.Dak.: Joy in the Morning Publishing Co., 2008.

Lamar, Howard R., ed. *The Reader's Encyclopedia of the American West*. New York: Thomas Y. Crowell Co., 1977.

Larpenteur, Charles. *Forty Years a Fur Trader on the Upper Missouri: The Personal Narrative of Charles Larpenteur, 1833–1872.* Ed. Elliott Coues. 2 vols. 1898; repr., Minneapolis, Minn.: Ross & Haines, 1962.

Laycock, George. *The Mountain Men.* Intro. by Paul Schullery. 1988; repr., New York: Lyons, 1996.

Leslie, Edward E. *Desperate Journeys, Abandoned Souls: True Stories of Castaways and Other Survivors.* Boston: Houghton Mifflin Co., 1988.

Ludlow, William. *Report of a Reconnaissance of the Black Hills of Dakota, Made in the Summer of 1874.* Washington, D.C.: Government Printing Office, 1875.

McClung, Robert M. *Hugh Glass, Mountain Man.* New York: Morrow Junior Books, 1990.

McCracken, Harold. *The Beast That Walks Like Man: The Story of the Grizzly Bear.* With an essay by Paul Schullery. 1955; repr., Lanham, Md.: Roberts Rinehart, 2003.

McMurtry, Larry. *The Wandering Hill.* The Berrybender Narratives. New York: Simon & Schuster, 2003.

[Manfred, Frederick]. *Conversations with Frederick Manfred.* Moderated John R. Milton. Salt Lake City: University of Utah Press, 1974.

————. *Lord Grizzly.* Foreword by John R. Milton. 1954; repr. Lincoln: University of Nebraska Press, 1983.

Man in the Wilderness. 1971; DVD release, Burbank, Calif.: Warner Bros. Entertainment, 2008.

Maximilian, Prince of Wied. *The North American Journals of Prince Maximilian of Wied.* Ed. Stephen S. Witte and Marsha V. Gallagher. Trans. William J. Orr, Paul Schach, and Dieter Karch. 3 vols. Norman: University of Oklahoma Press, 2008–2010.

Meyer, Roy W. *The Village Indians of the Upper Missouri: The Mandans, Hidatsas, and Arikaras.* Lincoln: University of Nebraska Press, 1977.

Mills, Enos A. *The Grizzly: Our Greatest Wild Animal.* Boston: Houghton Mifflin Co., 1919.

Milton, John. *South Dakota: A Bicentennial History.* New York: W. W. Norton & Co., 1977.

Morgan, Dale L. *Jedediah Smith and the Opening of the West.* Lincoln: University of Nebraska Press, 1964.

———, ed. *The West of William H. Ashley: The international Struggle for the Fur Trade of the Missouri, the Rocky Mountains, and the Columbia . . . 1822–1838*. Denver, Colo.: Old West Publishing Co., 1964.

Morris, Edmund. *Theodore Rex*. New York: Random House, 2001.

Moulton, Gary E., ed. *The Journals of the Lewis & Clark Expedition*. 13 Vols. Lincoln: University of Nebraska Press, 1983–2001.

Moyers, William. *Famous Heroes of the Old West*. New York: Grosset & Dunlap, 1957.

Myers, John Myers. *Pirate, Pawnee, and Mountain Man: The Saga of Hugh Glass*. Boston: Little, Brown & Co., 1963.

Nasatir, A. P., ed. *Before Lewis and Clark: Documents Illustrating the History of the Missouri, 1785–1804*. 2 vols. St. Louis, Mo.: St. Louis Historical Documents Foundation, 1952.

Neihardt, John G. *A Cycle of the West*. New York: Macmillan Co., 1949.

———. *The River and I*. New York: G. P. Putnam's Sons, 1910.

———. *The Song of Hugh Glass*. New York: Macmillan Co., 1915.

———. *The Song of Hugh Glass*. Notes by Julius T. House. New York: Macmillan Co., 1919.

———. *The Splendid Wayfaring: The Story of the Exploits and Adventures of Jedediah Smith and His Comrades . . . .* New York: Macmillan Co., 1920.

Nester, William R. *The Arikara War: The First Plains Indian War, 1823*. Missoula, Mont.: Mountain Press Publishing Co., 2001.

Oglesby, Richard Edward. *Manuel Lisa and the Opening of the Missouri Fur Trade*. Norman: University of Oklahoma Press, 1963.

Over, William H. and Edward P. Churchill. *Mammals of South Dakota*. Vermillion: Museum and Department of Zoology, University of South Dakota, 1941.

Parkman, Francis. *The Oregon Trail: Sketches of Prairie and Rocky-Mountain Life*. Illus. ed. 1892; repr., Boston: Little, Brown, & Co., 1904.

Parks, Douglas R. *Myths and Traditions of the Arikara Indians*. Lincoln: University of Nebraska Press, 1996.

Pattie, James O. *The Personal Narrative of James O. Pattie*. Intro. by William H. Goetzmann. 1831; repr., Lincoln: University of Nebraska Press, 1984.

Paxton, John A. *St. Louis Directory and Register, Containing the Names, Professions, and Residence of All the Heads of Families and Persons in Business* .... St. Louis, Mo.: n.p., 1821.

Pike, Zebulon Montgomery. *The Journals of Zebulon Montgomery Pike, with Letters and Related Documents.* Ed. Donald Jackson. 2 vols. Norman: University of Oklahoma Press, 1966.

Pressbook for *Man in the Wilderness.* N.p.: Warner Bros., 1971.

Punke, Michael. *The Revenant.* New York: Carroll & Graf, 2002.

Putney, Effie Florence. *In the South Dakota Country.* 2 vols. Mitchell, S.Dak.: Educator Supply Co., 1922.

Randall, Randolph C. *James Hall: Spokesman of the New West.* [Columbus]: Ohio State University Press, 1964.

Robinson, Doane. *History of South Dakota.* 2 vols. [Logansport, Ind.]: B. F. Bowen & Co., 1904.

Rockwell, David. *Giving Voice to Bear: North American Indian Rituals, Myths, and Images of the Bear.* Niwot, Colo.: Roberts Rinehart, 1991.

Ronda, James P. *Astoria & Empire.* Lincoln: University of Nebraska Press, 1990.

Roosevelt, Theodore. *Hunting the Grisly, and Other Sketches: An Account of the Big Game of the United States and its Chase with Horse, Hound, and Rifle.* 1893, as *The Wilderness Hunter*; repr., New York: G. P. Putnam's Sons, 1903.

———. *Hunting Trips on the Prairie and in the Mountains.* 1885, as *Hunting Trips of a Ranchman*; repr., New York: G. P. Putnam's Sons, 1900.

Russell, Osborne. *Osborne Russell's Journal of a Trapper.* Ed. Aubrey L. Haines. Lincoln: University of Nebraska Press, 1965.

Ruxton, George Frederick. *Life in the Far West.* Ed. LeRoy R. Hafen. 1849; repr., Norman: University of Oklahoma Press, 1951.

———. *Ruxton of the Rockies.* Comp. Clyde Porter and Mae Reed Porter. Ed. LeRoy R. Hafen. Norman: University of Oklahoma Press, 1950.

[Sage, Rufus B.] *Scenes in the Rocky Mountains, and in Oregon, California, New Mexico, Texas, and the Grand Prairies; or, Notes by the Way* .... Philadelphia: Carey & Hart, 1846.

Schell, Herbert S. *History of South Dakota.* 4th ed. Rev. John E. Miller. Pierre: South Dakota State Historical Society Press, 2004.

———. *South Dakota: Its Beginnings and Growth.* New York: American Book Co., 1960.

Schullery, Paul. *Lewis and Clark among the Grizzlies: Legend and Legacy in the American West.* Guilford, Conn.: Falcon, 2002.

Smurr, J. W. and K. Ross Toole, eds. *Historical Essays on Montana and the Northwest.* Helena: Western Press, Historical Society of Montana, 1957.

Spalding, John A., comp. *Illustrated Popular Biography of Connecticut.* Hartford, Conn.: Case, Lockwood, & Brainard Co., 1891.

Steckmesser, Kent Ladd. *The Western Hero in History and Legend.* Norman: University of Oklahoma Press, 1965.

Stevens, Walter B. *Centennial History of Missouri (The Center State): One Hundred Years in the Union, 1820–1921.* St. Louis, Mo.: S. J. Clarke Publishing Co., 1921.

Sudlow, Mrs. Lloyd. I., ed. *Homestead Years, 1908–1968.* Bison, S.Dak.: *Bison Courier*, 1968.

Sullivan, Maurice S. *The Travels of Jedediah Smith: A Documentary Outline, Including the Journal of the Great American Pathfinder.* Lincoln: University of Nebraska Press, 1992.

Sunder, John E. *Joshua Pilcher: Fur Trader and Indian Agent.* Norman: University of Oklahoma Press, 1968.

Tabeau, Pierre-Antoine. *Tabeau's Narrative of Loisel's Expedition to the Upper Missouri.* Ed. Annie Heloise Abel. Trans. Rose Abel Wright. Norman: University of Oklahoma Press, 1939.

Triplett, Frank. *Conquering the Wilderness; or, New Pictorial History of the Life and Times of the Pioneer Heroes and Heroines of America.* Minneapolis, Minn.: Northwestern Publishing Co., 1888.

Utley, Robert M. *Cavalier in Buckskin: George Armstrong Custer and the Western Military Frontier.* Norman: University of Oklahoma Press, 1988.

———. *A Life Wild and Perilous: Mountain Men and the Paths to the Pacific.* New York: Henry Holt & Co., 1997.

Vanderpol, Jeannette A. and Lynn Paley McCain. *Stories for Young Dakotans: The Stories of the Men and Women Who Changed the Lonely Prairie into the South Dakota of Today.* 2d ed. Sioux Falls, S.Dak.: Will A. Beach Printing Co., 1942.

Van Osdel, A. L. *Historic Landmarks: Being a History of Early Explorers and Fur-Traders, with a Narrative of Their Adventures in the Wilds of the Great Northwest Territory*. N.p., [1915].

Vestal, Stanley. *Jim Bridger, Mountain Man: A Biography*. Lincoln: University of Nebraska Press, 1970.

Victor, Frances Fuller. *The River of the West: Life and Adventure in the Rocky Mountains and Oregon . . . .* Hartford, Conn.: Columbia Book Co, 1870.

Weber, David J. *The Taos Trappers: The Fur Trade in the Far Southwest, 1540–1846*. Norman: University of Oklahoma Press, 1971.

White, Richard. *"It's Your Misfortune and None of My Own": A New History of the American West*. Norman: University of Oklahoma Press, 1991.

Wishart, David J., ed. *Encyclopedia of the Great Plains*. Lincoln: University of Nebraska Press, 2004.

——. *The Fur Trade of the American West, 1807–1840: A Geographical Synthesis*. Lincoln: University of Nebraska Press, 1979.

Workers of the South Dakota Writers' Project, comps. *Both Sides of the River*. Sioux Falls, S.Dak.: Midwest Press & Supply Co., 1942.

Wright, William H. *The Grizzly Bear: The Narrative of a Hunter-Naturalist*. 1909; repr., Lincoln: University of Nebraska Press, 1977.

Writers' Program, Work Projects Administration. *Missouri: A Guide to the "Show Me" State*. American Guide Series. New York: Duell, Sloan & Pearce, 1941.

ARTICLES, THESES, AND SHEET MUSIC

Baird, Don. "Hugh Glass, Fugitive Gunsmith." *Muzzle Blasts* 24 (June 1963): 7–8, 16, 38.

Beardsley, J. L. "The Hunter Who Died Twice." *Pioneer West* 6 (Feb. 1972): 19–23, 63–64.

Billington, Ray Allen. "The Frontier and I." *Western Historical Quarterly* 1 (Jan. 1970): 4–20.

Carter, Harvey L. "A Reply." *Western Historical Quarterly* 6 (July 1975): 301–2.

———— and Marcia C. Spencer. "Stereotypes of the Mountain Man." *Western Historical Quarterly* 6 (Jan. 1975): 17–32.

Chrisman, J. Eugene. "He Lived for Revenge." *Saga* 7 (Jan. 1954): 42–43, 70–71.

Covington, E. Gorton. "Alone and Left to Die!" *True West* 10 (Sept.–Oct. 1962): 46–47, 70, 72.

Crist, Judith. "This Week's Movies." *TV Guide* 23 (5 Apr. 1975): A-10.

[Cropp, Richard]. "Bears!" *Wi-iyohi* 18 (1 Dec. 1964): 1–7.

Donovan, Lauren. "Historic Rendezvous." *Bismarck* (N.Dak.) *Tribune*, 11 June 2015, bismarcktribune.com.

Ellison, Douglas W. "Hugh Glass: The Survivor." *South Dakota Magazine* 3 (June–July 1987): 20–21, 23.

Flagg, Edmund. "Adventures at the Head Waters of the Missouri." *Louisville Literary News-Letter* 1 (7 Sept. 1839): 326–27.

Goetzmann, William H. "The Mountain Man as Jacksonian Man." *American Quarterly* 15 (Autumn 1963): 402–415.

————. "A Note on 'Stereotypes of the Mountain Man.'" *Western Historical Quarterly* 6 (July 1975): 295–300.

"Grizzly Bear." *National Geographic*, animals.nationalgeographic. com.

"Grizzly Bear." National Wildlife Federation, nwf.org.

[Hall, James.] "The Missouri Trapper." *Port Folio* 19 (Mar. 1825; collected ed., Philadelphia: Harrison Hall, 1825), pp. 214–19.

"Hugh Glass Meets the Bear." *Internet Movie Database*, imdb.com.

Kirkel, Stephen. "Hugh Glass: Fighting Firebrand of the Frontier." *Gunsmoke* 1 (Aug. 1951): 25–31.

Lalire, Gregory. "Glass and the Grizzly Story." *Wild West* 13 (June 2000): 6.

Lambert, Harold B. "The Hugh Glass Story." N.p.: Dakota Music Co., 1966.

"Lemmon Commemorates Journey of Hugh Glass." *Mitchell* (S.Dak.) *Daily Republic*, 12 July 1973.

Lewis, Emily H. "Hugh Glass—Mountain Man." *Great West* 3 (Feb. 1969): 38–43, 58–61.

McDonald, Soraya Nadia. "Won't You People Please Just Give Leonardo DiCaprio an Oscar Already?" *Washington Post*, reprinted in *Mitchell* (S.Dak.) *Daily Republic*, 1 Oct. 2015.

Manfred, Frederick Feikema. "The Making of *Lord Grizzly*." *South Dakota History* 15 (Fall 1985): 200–216.

Paul Wilhelm, Duke of Württemberg. "First Journey to North America in the Years 1822 to 1824." Trans. William G. Bek. *South Dakota Historical Collections* 19 (1938): 7–462.

Peterson, Nancy M. "Hugh Glass' Crawl into Legend." *Wild West* 13 (June 2000): 28–32, 77–78.

Randall, Randolph C. "Authors of the *Port Folio* Revealed by the Hall Files." *American Literature* 11 (Jan. 1940): 379–416.

Robinson, Doane, ed. "Official Correspondence Pertaining to the Leavenworth Expedition of 1825 into South Dakota for the Conquest of the Ree Indians." *South Dakota Historical Collections* 1 (1902): 179–256.

[Robinson, Will G.] "The Aricaras Last Stand." *Wi-iyohi* 4 (1 Mar. 1951): [1–8].

———. "Hugh Glass." *Wi-iyohi* 20 (1 July 1966): 1–6.

Rodiek, Kella. "Mitchell Artist Spends June in Residence at Crazy Horse Memorial." *Mitchell* (S.Dak.) *Daily Republic*, 5 July 2015, mitchellrepublic.com.

"Six Pence Reward." *Pittsburgh Gazette*, 23 Apr. 1795.

Spencer, Jim. "Wildest & the Toughest: Hugh Glass—John Colter—John Johnson." *American Frontiersman*, "Premier Issue" [2012]: 26–29.

Stephens, F. F. "Missouri and the Santa Fe Trade." *Missouri Historical Review* 11 (Oct. 1916–July 1917): 289–312.

Todd, Edgeley W. "James Hall and the Hugh Glass Legend." *American Quarterly* 7 (Winter 1955): 362–370.

Walcheck, Ken. "Pronghorns, as Documented by the 1804–06 Lewis and Clark Expedition." *We Proceeded On* 24 (Aug. 1998): 4–9.

———. "Wapiti: The Ubiquitous American Elk Was a Staple in Both the Diet and the Journals of Lewis and Clark." *We Proceeded On* 26 (Aug. 2000): 26–32.

Walker, Don D. "The Mountain Man Journal: Its Significance in a Literary History of the Fur Trade." *Western Historical Quarterly* 5 (July 1974): 307–318.

Watkins, Albert, ed. "Notes of the Early History of the Nebraska Country." *Publications of the Nebraska State Historical Society* 20 (1922): 1–379.

White, Elaine Matthiesen. "The Hugh Glass Legend and Its Literary Treatment." Master's thesis, University of Idaho, 1968.

White, Linda Harper and Fred R. Gowans. "Traders to Trappers: Andrew Henry and the Rocky Mountain Fur Trade." *Montana the Magazine of Western History* 43 (Winter 1993): 58–65, (Summer 1993): 54–63.

Wiltsey, Norman B. "A Man Don't Quit." *Real West* 11 (June 1968): 35–37.

Young, Bob. "Hugh Glass' Empty Revenge." *Real West* 7 (May 1964): 14–16, 49–52.

Zimny, Michael. "Lemmon-Based Artist John Lopez to Unveil New Monument to Hugh Glass." *Arts & Culture*, South Dakota Public Broadcasting, 29 Mar. 2015, sdpb.org.

Index